Studying Islam in Practice

This book presents Islam as a lived religion through observation and discussion of how Muslims from a variety of countries, traditions and views practise their religion. It conveys the experiences of researchers from different disciplinary backgrounds and demonstrates the dynamic and heterogeneous world of Islam. The fascinating case studies range from Turkey, Egypt, Morocco and Lebanon to the UK, USA, Australia and Indonesia, and cover topics such as music, art, education, law, gender and sexuality. Together they will help students understand how research into religious practice is carried out, and what issues and challenges arise.

Gabriele Marranci is Director of the Study of Contemporary Muslim Lives research hub based in the Department of Anthropology at Macquarie University, Australia. He is also Honorary Associate Professor at Cardiff University's Centre for the Study of Islam in the UK. His books include *The Anthropology of Islam* (2008) and *Faith, Ideology and Fear: Muslim Identities Within and Beyond Prisons* (2009).

Also available:

Studying Buddhism in Practice
John S. Harding

Studying Hinduism in Practice
Hillary P. Rodrigues

Studying Islam in Practice

Edited by
Gabriele Marranci

Routledge
Taylor & Francis Group

LONDON AND NEW YORK

First published in 2014
by Routledge
2 Park Square, Milton Park, Abingdon, Oxon OX14 4RN

and by Routledge
711 Third Avenue, New York, NY 10017

Routledge is an imprint of the Taylor & Francis Group, an informa business

British Library Cataloguing in Publication Data
A catalogue record for this book is available from the British Library

Library of Congress Cataloging-in-Publication Data
Studying Islam in practice / [edited by] Gabriele Marranci.
pages cm. -- (Studying religions in practice)
1. Islam--21st century. 2. Islamic sociology.
3. Islam--Customs and practices. I. Marranci, Gabriele.
BP161.3.S78 2014
297--dc23
2013031220

ISBN: 978-0-415-64397-9 (hbk)
ISBN: 978-0-415-64398-6 (pbk)
ISBN: 978-1-315-85095-5 (ebk)

Typeset in Bembo
by Taylor & Francis Books

Printed and bound in the United States of America by
Edwards Brothers Malloy

Contents

List of illustrations

Series Preface: Studying Religions in Practice

General Editor: Hillary P. Rodrigues

The intent of this series is to assemble an assortment of texts that primarily instruct by addressing two aspects of human activity. One aspect is the practice of religion, and the other is how such practice is studied. Although these books may be profitably consulted on their own, they are ideal supplements to a comprehensive introductory textbook on each of the traditions in question. This is because introductory texts are rarely able to attend adequately to the range of activities that are integral features of most religious traditions. However, religious practice is a vast field of study, and each anthology in this series makes no claim to providing a complete picture of either the religion it addresses or its rich assortment of practices. Instead, the objective in this series is to provide the reader with vignettes of religious practices within particular traditions, as viewed through the experiences of scholars engaged in the study of these religions. As such, the series offers readers a window onto both the 'doings of religion', and the scholarly study of those doings.

As scholars who study religion in its varied dimensions, and as instructors who teach about religion, we routinely scout for resources to enhance our students' learning experience. We wish to teach them about various religions, but also to teach them about the scholarly endeavour of studying religion. Introductory textbooks, however comprehensive they might be in providing necessary factual and foundational information, are typically unable to convey the richness of religious life as experienced by practitioners. By necessity, introductory textbooks tend to favour history, intellectual developments, and teachings from written sources of and about the tradition. Even when they address religious practice, the tone in these textbooks is generally distant and explanatory, rather than descriptively engaging and evocative. Additionally, since the author's persona and presence are often excised from the accounts, these books do little to get across to students what scholars who engage in research actually do and experience. This series is designed to address some of these lacunae.

Each book in this series contains an assortment of pieces written specifically for the anthology in question by established scholars in their field. Other series that focus on practice tend to be collections of translations of religious texts about religious practices, or are anthologies of classic articles previously published in scholarly journals. Texts of the former type are actually still slanted to the textual tradition, while those of the latter type do not have novice students as their intended audience. The essays in the volumes of this series are purposely crafted differently from typical articles published in scholarly journals, chapters in edited academic volumes, or papers presented at scholarly conferences. They are even different in style from what one might find in textbooks and ethnographic anthropological literature, although recent writings from the latter category are probably closest in stylistic character. The writings in these collections derive from the memories, notes, photos, videos, and such, of scholars who were in the process of studying, and who still continue to study, some aspect of religious practice.

The sensibilities within, and tone of, these writings are partly derived from postmodern orientations, which indicate that, regardless of whether one is an insider or an outsider, one's understanding of reality is always partial. A pervasive and generally erroneous belief is that insiders to a tradition (i.e. adherents) know the *real* meaning of what is transpiring when they engage in religious activities. However, even for religious insiders, that is, believers and participants in a religious practice – such as a pilgrimage or rite of passage – the understanding of the phenomenon they are experiencing is always mediated by their own backgrounds, cultural familiarity, age, experience, degree of interest in their religion, and so on. They do not necessarily know 'the' meaning of what is going on, simply because they are insiders. Each insider's understanding is partial. Nevertheless, one effective way to learn about religious practice would be to read about these activities from the perspective of insiders. But the volumes in this series are not collected writings by religious insiders about their practices, however valuable and interesting such accounts might be. Rather, these are writings by persons engaged in the academic study of religion.

Those who embark on the scholarly study of religious phenomena are often outsiders (although not exclusively so), and place themselves in an unusual position. They often seek to understand as much as they can by engaging as deeply with the phenomenon studied (striving to become akin to insiders), but then also attempt to convey what they have understood to others (typically fellow outsiders). They may read the literature of the religion, study the ancient languages of its scriptural texts, learn local contemporary languages, travel to distant places, and live among the cultures where the religion is found and practised. In certain respects, this often makes them more informed than the unschooled insider. Anthropologists refer to the process of immersing oneself within a culture, while maintaining a scholarly stance, as participant observation. Although not all of the contributors to these anthologies utilize a robust anthropological field methodology, they all utilize the approach of participation, observation, and reporting back on what they have experienced, observed, and reflected upon.

The final category of reflection is particularly significant when distinguishing the insider's experience from that of the scholar. Religious practitioners need not report on their experiences to anyone. Their religious activities typically emerge within the framework of their cultures. Their lives are affected in particular ways during the course of their activities, and these effects influence and orchestrate the practitioners' subsequent thoughts and actions. These processes work to sustain and transform the cultural matrix of the practitioners. In contrast to this, scholars immerse themselves into the practitioners' religious culture and patterns of activity, seek to inform themselves about the traditions that they are studying, and strive to extricate themselves from those contexts to report back to their own milieu on what they have learned. Unlike the conventional scholarly formats in which they report their findings, which may include reading papers at academic conferences, publishing articles in peer-reviewed journals, writing book-length monographs, or contributing chapters to edited scholarly volumes, the contributions in these collections are perhaps unique in character. The authors are expected to reveal something about their process of engagement with the activities they study.

The discipline of religious studies is often misunderstood. Some people think it is religious education, others that it is akin to theology. Neither of those is true, for the study of religion is not conducted to inculcate others into a particular religious tradition, and it does not have the objective of developing the religious content of a particular religion. The study of religion takes religion in all of its manifestations, including religious education and theology, as its object of study. Scholars of religion attempt to understand, with a vigorous blend of objectivity and empathetic curiosity, all facets of the human religious response. The methodological tools for such study may be drawn from other disciplines such as anthropology, sociology, literary criticism, history, psychology, and so on, often selected because they are well suited to the religious phenomenon under consideration. As previously mentioned, since the focus of the contributions in these anthologies is on contemporary practices, the methods of participant observation central to the discipline of anthropology are highlighted here. This does not mean that all the scholars featured in these volumes are anthropologists, or even that their primary methodology is anthropological. However, the basis of their narratives is an anthropologically grounded experience of being scholars who are active participants in some phenomenon related to the practice of religion, which they are attempting to learn about, understand, and eventually convey to others.

Studying religious practice can be a messy and challenging process. One does not always know what to expect, where to go to best observe it, where to situate oneself during a rite, the degree to which one should participate in the practice, the amount of primary preparation needed, or the amount of descriptive content to provide when sharing the experience with others. One does not always understand aspects of what one has observed, what certain actions and activities might mean, and how other participants, particularly insiders, are experiencing the processes. One does not always have the best attitude, the most open-mindedness, optimal physical health, and other such attributes when actually engaged in the process of research. It may take many hours, days, weeks, years, and even decades of experiential immersion in a culture, and painstaking study of texts and other material, for scholars to deepen their understanding sufficiently to report on it. And even that is always regarded as a work in progress, a contribution that may be refined by the subsequent work of the same or other scholars. The contributions in these anthologies are written from the disposition that the scholarly study of religion is an ongoing process. It is also a process in which we invite the reader to participate by revealing aspects of the research process often concealed from view in most scholarly literature. Moreover, these contributions are not exclusively writ-ten by outsiders for outsiders. They are written by scholars, who, whether or not they belong to the religious tradition under study, assume a scholarly stance of engaged objectivity and empathetic distance with that religion as they engage in their research. Through their descriptive narrative vignettes, they invite the reader to share in their experiences, however briefly and partially, while they were engaged in some features of their research.

Almost anyone who has some experience with teaching about religion and cul-ture knows the efficacy of storytelling. Not only is it an ancient and well-tested technique through which religious beliefs are conveyed and culture trans-mitted, but the narrative is equally effective in eliciting and maintaining the attention of a student audience. The first-person story is one of the most engaging forms of the narrative. Tell a person what you did, saw, thought, and felt, and you are much more likely to garner their interest. Within that encounter there is the possibility for learning to occur.

The objective in these essays is primarily pedagogic. These are true stories of the experiences of real persons engaged in some of the activities of their dis-cipline. It is hoped that they convey to the reader not only some details of what the study of religion entails, but, as significantly, the rich textures of humanity's religious life. One might find within these narratives revelations that the author did not always use good judgement in certain instances, that they initially misunderstood what was transpiring, and so on. The honesty within the narrative portion of each contribution would likely be suspect if these stories did not contain features of surprise, puzzlement, or missteps. However, these narratives are not relatively superficial journalistic or travellers' accounts of adventures written to satisfy the reader's need for entertainment or to satiate some passing curiosity. Embedded within the narrative descriptions and in the discussions that follow the reader will also find remarkable details and useful information that derives from corollary facets of solid and rigorous scholarly work. It is hoped that the reader comes away with an enhanced appreciation and understanding of the religious tradition they are studying, as well as of the disciplines and methodologies through which it is studied.

Acknowledgements

I enjoyed editing *Studying Islam in Practice* and for this I deeply thank Professor Hillary Rodrigues who insisted that I contribute to his book series *Studying Religions in Practice*. I wish to thank Lesley Riddle, the former senior publisher in religion and anthropology at Routledge, for her support in the first steps of this work, as well as Katherine Ong for her patience and help during the final production of the book. *Studying Islam in Practice* developed during my move from Singapore to Sydney, Australia, where I accepted a new position, and during some difficult times that have affected my life. Yet it has always been rewarding to work with enthusiastic scholars who embraced the project with conviction. I am very grateful to all of them for the time they have devoted to this book and their patience with my requests. I wish to thank my department at Macquarie University, and in particular Dr Chris Houston and Dr Lisa Wynn for their support and for accepting my invitation to contribute at rather short notice. Finally, let me thank Siobhan Irving for her assistance with the manuscript, which has benefited greatly from her proofreading skills and suggestions.

Introduction

Studying Islam in practice

Gabriele Marranci

This book is not a traditional text book on Islam. Rather, it is suggested that you read this book together with a good introduction to Islam as a religion. This book focuses on contemporary aspects of Muslim lives and practices of Islam as researched and experienced by scholars. In other words, the aim is not to widen your knowledge in theory and analysis, but rather to share experiences with you: experiences of conducting research with Muslims. The authors of the following chapters are anthropologists, sociologists, and religious studies experts. Although among the authors are both Muslims and non–Muslims, the methodology and discussions that follow are exclusively social scientific.

Gregory Bateson has suggested, 'epistemology is always and inevitably personal. The point of the probe is always in the heart of the explorer: What is my answer to the question of the nature of knowing?' (1979: 98).[1] *Studying Islam in Practice* offers the reader a keyhole through which to observe the 'nature of knowing', which the contributors have experienced during their studies of different Muslim communities. Ethnographies, theories, and ideas inform academic articles, chapters, and books; the reader is always in contact with the final product: a synthesis. By contrast, the road towards such final product – the epistemological process, that alchemy of unexpected events, reactions and counter-reactions, silence and chaos, fear, joy, and worry – remains in the personal coffer of the scholar. What are the feelings, the impressions, and the experiences of those academics who write the clean, polished works we read? What does it mean to be 'in' the dynamic of research? It is a question that I, as a student, wondered about yet feared to ask.

Undergraduates as well as doctoral students may come to know some anecdotal stories about their supervisors' research, but in the majority of cases, the actual fieldwork experience, the day-to-day research, remains unshared. This is, in my experience, even more so when Islam is the focus of the research. Students are provided in many universities with methodology and research skills, but often these examples are abstracted from the actual 'experience' of fieldwork.

Academic, researcher, fieldworker, anthropologist, sociologist, religious study expert – but human? The humanity fades away, bleached by a respect of academic standards, word-count limitations, and a traditional shyness – the never named but always present effort to 'be scientific'. In *Studying Islam in Practice*, the shyness is reversed in the assertion of being human and the acknowledgement of emotions, frustrations, and controversial feelings. Indeed, working with humans and trying to 'answer to the question of the nature of knowing' means facing challenges both within oneself and in environments often marked by deep differences.

I still remember one of my first days of fieldwork conducted at the end of the 1990s. I was conducting a research on Rai music, an Algerian pop music popular among the Algerian second generations in Paris.[2] As part of my research, I needed to visit an Algerian music shop in a notorious French suburb known for social issues and high criminality. When I emerged from the underground station, I found myself in squalid, intimidating surroundings that were unlike anything I have ever before experienced in my native Florence. It was the first time I realized how the French government had transformed some *banlieues* into deposits of unwanted humanity and no-go areas. I did not reach the music shop. I turned and took the first train back to my city accommodation. Surely I realized what culture shock implies. It took more than a couple of days of preparation to start my research in such a neighbourhood again. As a young researcher my fear and disorientation that day left me wondering whether I would ever become a good fieldworker. Indeed, I could not know that I was not the first to experience such sense of disorientation, since the literature I had consulted never mentioned such events or reflections. Today research is conducted in different settings, from exotic countries to cyberspace. Each of these environments has its own challenges and rewards. Yet, after 9/11 and the so-called 'war on terror', studying Islam and Muslims present some global challenges: the mass media's continuous interest in Islam, general widespread misinformation, and the pernicious so-called Islamophobia. In *Studying Islam in Practice*, academics from different backgrounds show how they have conducted their research in such varied contexts. Indeed, in this book, the reader can encounter the experience of both male and female researchers at different stages of their careers and research. *Studying Islam in Practice* shows also how heterogeneous Islam is as a religion and how varied, if not deeply different, Muslim communities are.

The structure of each chapter provides the reader with a preamble, where the author describes the topic, a narrative, in which the research experience is illustrated, and a discussion, where the author develops some relevant points of the narrative. Despite the framework of each chapter, the authors have provided their own unique style, voice, and reflections of their research experience and how they have observed Islam in practice. The chapters end with some suggestions for further reading and a biographical note that helps the reader to know more about the author's interests and career.

The first chapter brings us to Morocco where we observe dynamics of gender, family, and the complex relationship between religion and social institutions, such as families. Yet we also observe the hospitality of Moroccans and how the research is assimilated within the cultural context. Curtis shares her experience of Ramadan, one of the main religious events in Islam, while researching a music festival. She became fascinated by the role women have within the family in organizing festivities and how such a role has an impact in keeping the Moroccan culture 'woven together'. The chapter helps the reader to follow the researcher's feelings while interacting with a different cultural context, one in which, often, her lifestyle does not make sense to her hosts. It is through the naiveté of simple everyday life that Curtis, as a researcher, penetrates the reality of Moroccan culture.

While Ramadan is a religious practice enmeshed in cultural traditions and norms, the next three chapters focus on Islam as a social regulator. In his chapter, Rosen, a student of Clifford Geertz who has conducted decades of research in Morocco, introduces us to the mysterious and complex world of juridical courts. Rosen reminds us how sharia is not a single abstract legal system but rather a 'rich array of factors that inform a legal system that holds meaning for nearly a quarter of all humankind'. Rosen shares his interactions with informants and the long observations of court cases, which helped him to understand realities that may contradict Western expectations about Muslims and, in this case, Moroccan society. This was the case when Rosen discovered that, not infrequently, Moroccan Jews preferred Muslim courts to their own Jewish legally recognized courts.

In another country, Egypt, another anthropologist, Wynn, observes another contradiction within the legal debate of what may be halal (permissible) or haram (forbidden) in Islam. In Egypt, as in many other Muslim countries, premarital sex is perceived as a serious sin and may affect a person's marriage prospects. Of course, while there is no mark of male virginity, female virginity can be traditionally tested by the presence or absence of 'virginal blood'. It is not surprising that new medical procedures, such as hymenoplasty, receive particular attention in Egyptian mass media. Wynn, in several years of field-work in Cairo and Alexandria, examines rulings in Islamic jurisprudence for and against hymenoplasty. Through her research, which she vividly presents (including a few potentially embarrassing moments, such as when she was asked to 'smell' a thirty year-old virginal blood-stained cloth by of one her female respondents), Wynn shows the contradictory rulings about hymenoplasty. She rightly suggests that this is evidence of the 'extent to which debate and independent reasoning thrive in contemporary Islam', contrary to stereotypes which present Islam as a religion frozen in a dark past.

Drennan, an Islamic studies scholar, offers us a window on the processes involving religious opinions in Islam, better known as fatwas. The word fatwa may likely remind the reader of Khomeini's infamous fatwa against Salman Rushdie, the author of *The Satanic Verses*. Many will be surprised to discover that Khomeini's death sentence edict against the writer was not a fatwa as Sunni Muslims understand the term. Drennan shows what fatwas are and how

Muslim communities – and especially Muslim communities in the 'West' – use fatwas in their daily lives to reduce the contradictions between conducting a Muslim life in a non-Muslim environment.

We then move to Turkey, where the anthropologists Delaney and Houston have conducted two different research projects. Delaney lived in a Turkish village from 1980 to 1982. As we can read in her narrative, she guides us through the village discourse of the hajj and the celebration of the connected Kurban Bayramı (Arabic: Eid al Adha), the feast of the sacrifice. Through the narration of her informants, Delaney is able to show how her friends and respondents experienced the pilgrimage. Delaney received a Fulbright Fellowship in 1984 to conduct research among Turks in Belgium. She witnessed another, this time secular, form of hajj: the migration from the Turkish villages to the European metropolis. Delaney discusses this different ritual, made no less than the religious one, of expected acts and hopes. Delaney's fieldwork in two different locations and within two different contexts allowed her to observe a hidden link that shows how Islam as a discourse may reach beyond the sacred. In his chapter, Houston guides us in a very personal journey though the complexity of politics and Islam in Turkey, looking at both the human and political dynamics through a phenomenological approach. He reveals to the reader the impossibility of dividing personal life from the research identity. Houston is surely able to open the coffer and share vivid images not only of fieldwork, but of how fieldwork changes the life of a fieldworker. Art, life, and experience become part of that 'question of the nature of knowing'.

From Turkey we move to California, where Blomfield, an anthropologist, introduces us to her fieldwork among Shi'a Muslim women. Her research is a personal journey through the life of these women and their Muslim identity within the secular context of the USA. Her narrative is vivid and we observe again how research cannot be isolated from personal experience, and from one's past and present, such as when she relates the story of being asked to help in washing the body of a deceased elderly woman. While she was doing so, her mind went to the image of her own mother and questions of whether one day her mother's body would be treated with the same deep respect and human contact, whether she would be able to wash it in a final physical embrace, or if a funeral parlour would take the responsibility, as often happens in Western societies. Emotions, sharing, and learning are clearly presented as part of research in this account.

While Blomfield describes her experiences of researching women, Nilan, in her chapter, presents the difficulties that researchers may face in different cultural and gender contexts. She conducted research with Indonesian Muslim men in both Australia and Indonesia. Her chapter is reflexive about the position of the researcher and she also emphasizes the importance of ethical research.

Balzani shares how she entered a fieldwork on Ahmadi Muslims in the UK nearly by chance, as often happens. We follow her difficulties in studying, in the aftermath of 9/11, a group discriminated against both as Muslims and as a minority living alongside an orthodox Muslim majority. The difficult life of Ahmadis in Pakistan, where they are often persecuted, followed the migration of Pakistanis to the UK. Balzani, after describing Ahmadi Muslims' religious traditions and practices, shows the intra-tensions that permeate within the wider Muslim communities, even in the West.

Still in the UK, Shannahan explores how gender and sexuality shape Muslim women's experience of mosques. Shannahan guides us through her research with interesting observations about the role of the researcher. For instance, she reveals how she had to bring her child with her during interviews and the consequent potentiality of the clash of roles – researcher versus parent. Shannahan concludes, in a different context but similarly to Nilan, that a researcher must be aware of how his or her subjectivity impacts upon and influences the research topic and his or her respondents.

Berg, in 'Where heaven meets earth: music and Islam in everyday life and encounters', transfers us from the UK to Lebanon and Palestine to guide us through the complex relationship between music and Islam and how religiously accepted music is produced. Among the accepted 'music' is that produced by Hamas in Palestine and Hezbollah in Lebanon inciting resistance and praising 'the martyrs'. Berg's narrative illustrates how the research progressed and how opinions about music tend to be divided. Berg shows the reader the several opinions and voices, which counter the stereotyping that has affected many Western discussions concerning Islam and music.

The next author, Jiwa, although relocating us in the West, this time in New York, still discusses a topic linked to arts and Islam. Jiwa presents here the development of a special event. On 19 January 2002, at the Cathedral of St John the Divine in New York City, the 'Reflections at a Time of Transformation: American Muslim artists reach out to New Yorkers in the aftermath of September 11' was presented. The exhibition was aimed at 'healing wounds', 'building interfaith and intercultural bridges', and offered an occasion to show the differences existing within the Muslim community. Jiwa provides a vivid account of the tensions and difficulties faced by the artists in this context. Jiwa explains that his work with Muslim artists attempts to free the limited representation of Muslims as a mere expression of theological beliefs and shows the complexity existing within Muslim communities and their aesthetic practices.

Food is not just for survival or palate pleasure: it may mark cultural and religious norms. Fischer, an anthropologist who provides an interesting multiple location fieldwork (London and Kuala Lumpur), guides the reader through his own exploration of halal (permitted food) practice among Malay Muslims in London. He spent a great deal of time in halal restaurants, in butchers, grocery stores, supermarkets, and hypermarkets selling halal products. As an anthropologist, we can see how Fischer progresses in his research observing and participating in the everyday life of his informants. We can appreciate, from his narrative, the relevance of paying attention to details observed while at the homes of his respondents and Malay friends. Again, the reader can appreciate how the final result of any research, a publication or report, is the result of dynamics of relationships that are much more complex than the final output often represents; in other words, the output of the research is nothing else than the tip of the iceberg.

Yet fieldwork is not the only methodology available as many others are used in social science, as sociologist Moosavi shows us. Moosavi shares his own reflections about studying a sensitive topic in the aftermath of 9/11: conversion to Islam. His research, based again in the UK, faced several challenges, such as being a male researcher hoping to interview some female converts who felt uncomfortable being alone with the interviewer. We have seen in previous chapters how context, gender, and religious ideas have an impact on how scholars conduct their research. In this case, Moosavi, as a Muslim himself, found the solution in allowing another person trusted by the interviewee to attend the interview. This brings him to reflect on the fact that conducting research with Muslims means that Islamic teachings, the political context, and the researcher's personality all play a role in the overall aspects of the research.

Research on contemporary Islam and Muslims is not limited to geographical locations and face-to-face interactions. Islam and Muslims have a high visibility within cyberspace. Bunt, a leading expert on cyber-Islam, recounts in his chapter the changes that this field of research has witnessed, including changes in technology, methodology, and analysis, but also the change in topics discussed by Muslims and about Muslims. The interest in Islam and Muslims in cyberspace has recently increased exponentially but with it also increases the risk for the researcher, as Bunt explains. Bunt shows how in the context of cyber-Jihad new cyber material became increasingly sophisticated; as Bunt states, 'the field is virtual, but has a real-world impact at many levels, with increasing implications for Muslims in local and global contexts'.

The final two chapters deal with another relevant aspect of Islam: education. Muslims do not have a single teaching system, but instead as in many aspects of Islam, environmental factors, history, and culture produce unique forms. Winkelmann discusses her experience of studying madrasas for girls in India. Again, as a female scholar she faced different challenges. One of the interesting aspects is that she was able to have access to a relevant madrasa for girls through the support of male members of the Tablighi Jamaat movement. One of the challenges Winkelmann faced involved dress code. Working in India, a country with a large Muslim population but Hindu in majority, each of her decisions, such as to cover her hair or not, caused a reaction on one or the other side of the communities. Another reality she had to face was the numerous clichés about 'foreign' women. In her vivid narration, she provides a clear example of how fieldwork may turn dangerous and how researchers should be careful. Her first-hand account of life within the madrasas and the lives of her young informants captivates the reader. Lukens-Bull, in the last chapter of the book, takes us to Indonesia. Not only does he offer a narrative of the complexity of Islamic education in Indonesia, but he also provides a very personal reflection on fieldwork and how difficult it can be when things go wrong – as in the case when he had to save his wife from a severe form of dehydration. Yet, he was also fully welcomed within the Indonesian Muslim society. In particular, he had to face the ethical dilemma of being a non-Muslim who, however, was perceived and accepted as Muslim. This self-reflection is one of the most valuable aspects of Lukens-Bull's chapter.

From Morocco to Turkey and passing through India, Pakistan, Lebanon, Palestine and Indonesia, the USA, the UK, and Malaysia, *Studying Islam in Practice* shows the experience of the researcher, from different disciplinary backgrounds, in what is the variegated, dynamic, and heterogeneous world of Islam, formed by hundreds of languages and dialects, traditions, and beliefs. This book is an introduction to such a world, one that common stereotypes often misrepresent as monolithic and frozen in time. It is the human, with his or her own unique personality, idiosyncrasies, defects, and merits that researchers, as humans, meet, interact with, and, in particular, learn from: the practice can be 'Islamic' yet the practitioner is always human.

Note on transliteration

The number of languages and dialects the book covers is far too hetero-geneous to allow me to provide any indication of how each of them should be read and pronounced. Hence, the authors of each chapter have adopted the most convenient and clear transliteration system used in their own field of research. To facilitate clarity, however, non-English words have been kept to a necessary minimum.

Notes

1 Bateson, G. (1979). *Mind and Nature: A Necessary Unity*. New York: Dutton.
2 An old article from my research can be found online at www.muspe.unibo.it/wwcat/period/ma/index/number5/marranci/marr_0.htm

Chapter 1

On fasting in Fes

Learning about food, family, and friendship during fieldwork in Morocco

Maria F. Curtis

Preamble

Fasting (*sawm*) is one of the five central pillars of the Islamic faith, along with accepting the oneness of Allah (*shahada*), performing the five required daily prayers (*salat*), making a pilgrimage to Mecca (hajj), and alms and charity (*zakat*). Ramadan is the month of fasting and the holiest month of the Islamic lunar calendar when Muslims fulfil one of the obligations of their faith. Ramadan is a sacred and joyful period, bringing quiet days of fasting from sun-up to sun-down when one tries to remain 'clean' in one's thoughts, speech, and action. Fasting is seen largely as a purification process, and one that restores human beings to a closer state of sinlessness. To not fast during Ramadan is amongst one of the major sins in Islam; and to curse, gossip, or treat another person badly while fasting may void one's fast. Fasting during Ramadan is to take part in solidarity across the Muslim world, when wealthier Muslims remember the poor and what it would feel like to walk in the shoes of a hungry and desperate person. Acts of charity (*sadaqa*) in the month of Ramadan are informal with people trying to share and invite guests with more frequency. Charity in the formal sense, *zakat*, is observed during Ramadan when individuals decide how much they can give in alms. Ramadan nights bring families and friends together around elaborate meals and special television programmes that provide entertainment. Ramadan is also an important time to consider broader cultural conceptualizations of gender within the context of family in Morocco.

Narrative

Despite hours of fasting and long spells of what appears to be virtual inactivity almost everywhere during the day, Ramadan nights become big celebrations where one not only eats, but eats extraordinarily well. It is always good to be a guest in Morocco, and it is especially good to be a guest during Ramadan. Hospitality is one of the central tenets of Islam and it manifests broadly in everyday cultural contexts. One is obligated to show others care and respect through acts of hospitality and charity, and it is believed that Allah rewards those who feed the hungry or those who are fasting. In Morocco everyone fasts and even those who do not show great religiosity during other times of the year observe the fast as well. Cultural expectations of fasting enforce this foundational pillar of faith across all strata of Moroccan society.

My research in Morocco since my first visit in 1997 has been focused on religion in everyday contemporary and urban settings. I have been particularly fascinated by women's responsibilities around organizing family festivities and how they appear to keep the whole of Moroccan culture woven together. In 2002 and 2003, I was in Fes, Morocco, conducting ethnographic fieldwork on the Fes Festival of World Sacred Music. I had lived with host families in the past and had known what it was like to experience Moroccan hospitality within a home setting, but I was less prepared to experience it this time as I was living with a roommate and volunteering in what seemed more like an office setting than 'the field'. While I had been adopted into families with whom I had lodged during my earlier stays in Morocco, I was adopted by nearly everyone I met in Fes, and increasingly so during Ramadan. The people I worked with worried that I was living alone in a cold old house in the older part of the city, the medina, away from the comfort of my own home and my husband who had stayed behind during my fieldwork stint. My narrative here focuses on Ramadan as a time devoted to asserting Islamic principles of family and community, and how my Moroccan friends and contacts sought to bring me into a recognizable family framework, a sort of makeshift fictive kinship, for my benefit and for theirs.

First, I should say a word about the Fes Festival of World Sacred Music. It began in 1994 as the result of increasingly negative media images concerning Muslims and Islam following the first Gulf War in Iraq. During the 1990s, when the USA launched its Desert Storm campaign against Sadam Hussein, this period marked a crucial turning point in American foreign policy. As a young person in college during the first Gulf War, for the first time in my life the media began increasingly and consistently to portray the Islamic world as eternally backward and 'other'. In 1994, a group of Sufi inspired, well-educated Moroccans wanted to turn the 'Desert Storm' metaphor on its head with a conference they called 'Desert Conference', and they invited participants to take part in discussions where people from the Abrahamic faiths (Judaism, Christianity, and Islam) meditated for a change on their similarities rather than their differences. Under the direction of Dr Faouzi Skali, a Moroccan cultural anthropologist and practicing Sufi, this small endeavour grew into a large international music festival of epic proportions. This festival garnered global attention and acclaim and inspired people to use the arts and music as forms of soft diplomacy to create similar festivals all around the world.

The great grandson of the Prophet Muhammad, Moulay Idris I, settled the city of Fes, considered the spiritual capital of Morocco, in 789 and today Fes welcomes in the world during the Fes Festival of World Sacred Music. This festival brings to life the core Islamic principles of *Ahl al-Kitab*, or people of the monotheistic traditions. The city abounds with spiritual musical performances in its concert and performance spaces, as well as in the gardens and shared public spaces of the city. I went to Fes to study this festival and how its underlying principles were an example of how progressive Islam reaches out to the rest of the world.

Unlike anthropologists that mostly observed objectively from afar in ethnographies of yesteryear, my presence at the Fes Festival led me to many opportunities to volunteer my time. The people working at the Fes Festival were simply too busy and understaffed to have a perfectly able-bodied person like myself sit around and observe them as they worked at a furious pace, bracing over a period of months to accommodate the thousands of people who would converge on the city for this once-in-a-lifetime yearly event. The annual festival was truly unique in that the line-up of speakers, artists, artwork, and musicians continued to change under new yearly themes and responded to significant current political events. My time in Fes that year marked the second war in Iraq in the wake of 9/11 and marked Morocco's first suicide bombing in Casablanca, which spurred a march of nearly one million people. The political tremors of what we would later come to call 'The Arab Spring' or 'The Arab Awakening' were felt the year I was in Morocco.

The festival organizers put me to work at any opportunity they could, and installed me in a small office, informing me that I was to be a translator. I would 'observe' as I had hoped and I would also do things to help out, like translate their entire festival programme from French to English. Because I was not really a translator, this job of translating took up much more of my time than I had anticipated and in the interim I managed to make some very good friends while in the office where I did learn a thing or two about Fes and Morocco. While I much appreciated the notion of 'applied' and 'engaged' anthropology and wanted very much to be useful, the tasks that I was given were not always easy for me to complete. In addition to translating French to English documents rather poorly, I also picked up VIPs from the Fes airport, accompanied our entrepreneurial Berber driver to transport said VIPs while they were in Fes, attended meetings of all sorts, got to know a steel magnolia cast of Fassia women who ran NGOs and organized trips to Mecca, and met a host of musicians, scholars, professors, World Bank execs, and activists of every shade and stripe. I also inadvertently became the subject of documentary films that I would never see. I met an Italian couple that was interested in the fact that I had accidentally rented a room that was really a former stable, and at times I tried interviewing international journalists who tried to interview me as I interviewed them. In other words, conducting fieldwork in this busy thoroughfare was a big adventure.

After surviving my first festival cycle in 2002, I was unlucky enough to be the only English-speaking person left who could help Moroccan vendors file their reimbursement forms for services they had already rendered for the World Bank-sponsored conference that was perhaps ironically named 'Giving a Soul to Globalization'. Amongst my favourite things I did while doing fieldwork was getting the chance to watch stage architects and sound crews set up performance sites in what were otherwise everyday places and watching the auditory and cultural transformations that would later take place when musicians arrived. This was particularly satisfying for me as a person with long-term interest in the cultural construction of ritual, and Fes was a wonderful place to observe people from different backgrounds, who rarely spoke the same language, come together to build twenty-first century public ritual sites. After the dust of the festival settled, the skeleton crew that made this sprawling festival happen stayed behind to get the whole thing started once again for the following year. It was not the experience I had expected to have, but then again, fieldwork is probably never what we expect it will be.

The office where I worked at the Fes Festival was essentially a part of what used to be a narrow corridor in an abandoned 'palace' where a wealthy family had lived in years past. Like many of the old families of Fes, the family who had owned the estate had simply moved to the larger urban areas of Rabat or Casablanca and over time, the site had no formal inhabitants. The French had tried to make Fes work as a colonial capital and had failed miserably. A temporary solution had been to give up on ever turning the honeycombed streets of the medina into a base for their colonial endeavours, so they simply relocated and built a very French looking town off in the distance now called "la ville nouvelle", or the new town. Now every town in Morocco has a ville nouvelle, and much anthropological ink has been spilled on the topic of the tremendous shift in Moroccan consciousness that occurred when Moroccans gradually abandoned their old towns in favour of something more 'modern'. The old medina of Fes is either terribly neglected or overly developed for tourists. Much of the medina, whose older portions date back to the middle ages, is currently inhabited by squatters who have taken up in houses whose owners no one can remember and an increasing number of expats hoping to turn Moroccan old world charm into a pretty penny by restoring old homes and opening bed and breakfast lodging for tourists.

Perhaps to save it from complete ruin and abandonment the palace where I worked became a Moroccan version of an NGO, called Fes Saiss, where free courses in reading, writing, and other practical life skills were offered to mostly women living nearby in the medina of Fes. Fes Saiss organized a wide variety of cultural and service events for the city, doing everything from hosting large group weddings for couples who could not afford the customary elaborate ceremonies, to organizing Andalusian music festivals, to collecting second-hand wheelchairs from Europe and dispensing them to the needy in Fes. Electrified with the potential of grassroots development made possible through micro finance projects, Fes Saiss also offered sewing and embroidery courses for women who wanted to launch their own home businesses selling traditional Moroccan hand-sewn clothing. Although Moroccans had rather easily left their medinas, they continued to purchase traditional clothing and cherish the notion of commissioning new pieces each year as styles change, so much so that this was a fundamental part of Ramadan. Although officially non-governmental, the organization's daily activities could quickly come to a halt if and when important government officials showed up for meetings, and Moroccan high tea would be the main event in the grand salon facing the pomegranate-lined central courtyard. This was after all a non-governmental organization (NGO) in a country that boasts one of the world's longest royal dynasties and what I came to think of not as a typical NGO, but a MONGO. I would sometimes be called in to meet visiting dignitaries in the elaborately decorated main salon of the palace complex. Our guests might have been dazzled by the antique furnishings and elaborate tile work and hand-carved plaster ceilings, but might have been reluctant to enter had they any idea that the roof above their heads was shouldering significant decay and verging towards foundational collapse. This is in some sense the essence of Fes, grand and evocative of an otherworldly precolonial elegance, yet nearly on the brink of disappearing due to extended periods of benign neglect.

The Fes Festival of World Sacred Music is ultimately a citywide weeklong music and arts festival that draws visitors from all around Morocco, Europe, and the USA, with musicians and speakers attending from all over the world. I had come to study competing notions of hospitality, traditional notions of Islamic hospitality alongside globalizing forces that ushered in the European and American notions of the hospitality industry and service-oriented models. It turned out that my being in Fes Saiss was the perfect place to experience Ramadan as both the Fes Festival itself and Fes Saiss were steeped in Islamic notions of hospitality, welcoming, and giving, and both reached out to the rest of the world through discourses of non-governmental development initiatives resting on older layers of Islamic authority as evidenced in the nearby Qarawiyyin University founded in 859.

My first clue that Ramadan had officially started the year I was in Fes was the sounds from my neighbours in the wee hours of the morning preparing to eat up before the *adhan*, or the call to prayer that sounds loudly five times daily from the four hundred or so mosque loudspeakers in the medina. They were up eating and drinking their *suhur*, the meal one eats during Ramadan prior to the morning call to prayer (*fajr*). Despite the very early hour, I could smell numerous dishes, soup, fresh bread, and *smen*, a cultured butter used on most breakfast breads. I knew I should get up because it would be impossible to eat at other times during the day. It was unusually cold that year and when my feet touched the cold tile floor, I simply retracted and crawled back under my stack of blankets. The lack of central heating along with my window that was prone to open on its own did make me feel like I was on a permanent camping trip. My room opened onto a courtyard, a riad-style home built around an interior garden and fountain, and to get to the bathroom or shower or to the kitchen I had to walk through a small grove of citrus trees. The house was truly beautiful and had been built as a place to host parties, yet despite its obvious charm it was often unbearably cold.

Later that morning, after I had summoned the courage to face the cold, I walked along virtually empty streets that would have normally been bustling with activity. The medina is famous for its never-ending stream of sounds, and it was a rather surreal experience to walk along the cobblestone path to my palace office corridor hearing only the tip-tap of my own feet. The street was eerily quiet and I felt at first as if I had been the last survivor in this town. I lived about ten minutes walking distance from Fes Saiss and routinely had breakfast on the way to work. Each morning I had grown accustomed to stopping off at a local bakery where I would order *qahwa mhersa* (broken coffee) and *hrsha*, a dense cornbread-like food made from semolina. I had grown so used to this food in the morning that I often wondered what I would eat when I returned to Texas as nothing I could think of seemed as fundamentally breakfast worthy as this. Even now, no coffee anywhere tastes as satisfying as *qahwa mhersa*, called 'broken coffee' because the dense milk would 'break' the sharpness of the strong Brazilian espresso.

On that first morning of Ramadan everything seemed to be closed or just barely starting to open. The bakery I had come to know and love as the place to catch up on Arabic music videos as I slurped my morning Joe had transformed into a literal mountain of *shabakiya*, syrupy sweet cookies eaten during Ramadan, and the customary pop music was replaced with Qur'anic recitation from an Egyptian television station. The *shabakiya* is the iconic reminder that Ramadan has arrived, a more daring cousin of the American funnel cake, with spices like cinnamon and gum Arabic kneaded into the dough, which is twisted into an attractive floral shape, then fried and dipped in honey and rolled around in sesame seeds and doused with a bit of orange blossom water. When Ramadan begins, you see *shabakiya* everywhere in quantities that suggest Moroccans fearlessly consume carbohydrates as if there is no fear of a diabetic future. After you get used to *shabakiya*, you tend to forget that in Morocco sweets can often come before the main meal; in fact, dessert can be the first of many long courses in a single meal. For an American like me who was cajoled into eating broccoli as a child to earn the right to have a dessert, *shabakiya* was a dream come true.

The owner of the café, who welcomed me each morning, cast me a sidelong glance and a solemn nod as if to say, 'It's Ramadan, please don't embarrass yourself by trying to eat here this morning'. I had heard stories about 'bad foreigners' who took to eating in McDonald's during Ramadan in the capital city of Rabat. I kept walking, nodding in return, regretting that I did not get up when I heard the neighbours eating next door. My stomach growled loudly as if in apparent protest as the bakery faded into the background.

I walked into the courtyard of Fes Saiss that morning and found only the daughter of the live-in guard and the stray cats she fed from her family's table scraps. She said to me 'Ramadan Mabrouk [Happy Ramadan], and what are you doing here?' Surprised a bit, I said that I had come to work like any other morning. She replied with more confidence than most six-year olds typically have, 'Well, don't you have Ramadan in your country? You should be asleep now, you know'. 'No, we don't exactly have Ramadan in my country like in Morocco because we have so many different religions, people celebrate differently'. My response prompted her to shake her head in disbelief. I had found that children were amongst the most useful teachers in Morocco; they had a knack for telling you when you were without a doubt in the cultural wrong and exactly how to return to a culturally perceived kind of normal. They could tell you what you were doing wrong without some of the sting you might feel from adults. Lesson learned, I thought, tomorrow I would eat around 4:00 a.m. in the morning, drink enough water to feel hydrated for the whole day, then go back to sleep like everyone else at *fajr*, and then sleep in. Then I would show up to work late, very late.

Not sure what else to do with myself, I slipped off into the cocoon of my little office space. I turned on the computer and my stomach growled again. More than food, I wondered with anxiety how I would manage my caffeine needs. Since coming to Morocco, I got used to drinking strong coffee and heavily minted green tea several times a day. I heard some voices in the courtyard and felt relief at not being alone amongst the hungry stray cats that prowled outside my office door. In came my closest work friend Btissam, cheerful as always. Indeed her name actually meant 'The one who smiles' and in the year I had known her she seemed to consistently live up to her name.

'My mom and I were a little worried about you this morning', she said with a bit of panic in her face. 'Oh, why is that?' I said. It turns out they were very bothered by the idea that I would be fasting all alone since fasting is largely done within the context of a family. 'You'll just come home with me everyday and eat, OK?' she said. 'You mean for thirty days I'll come to your house?' I responded with surprise. Btissam and her mother were amongst those overcome with sadness at my being separated from my husband during Ramadan; nothing could be worse than to be on your own during a month when you should be fasting with those you love. The very idea that I would get married and then a couple of months later go to do fieldwork by myself without my husband was really more than they could understand. At that time Btissam was in the process of planning her own engagement and wedding, and she so longed to get married quickly that my own choice of doing research away from my family confounded her at times. The whole thing seemed very esoteric to her, and she would ask me questions like 'Doesn't your husband worry for your safety? Are you not thinking of having children? Don't you worry what your husband will eat during Ramadan?' I tried to explain that my husband fully supported me and that I had planned my research project before I ever met my husband, that I was in a sense finishing my education which I had already been working on for a number of years. None of this really stacked up as it should for her, and her gentle worrying and disbelief did sometimes make me question myself as well. She was relieved to learn that my father-in-law called me weekly from Turkey and that I was in regular contact with all my family. My mother had sent me various care packages full of clothing and chocolates, which also confirmed that my family were concerned for me. The idea that I would spend a month eating at her house for Ramadan simply made sense for her; I was someone's wife, someone's daughter, someone's sister, and now she would be my adoptive family and that was that. I had felt this way on occasion about having lonely friends over for a Christmas dinner, and here I was again amazed at the utter athletic strength of Moroccan hospitality that made inviting a person over for thirty consecutive days just seem like the normal thing to do. Moroccans are all about family and, even in the most Western looking families, women did not leave their husbands' sides unless they were going to visit their mothers and fathers. These deeply held ideas about where married women should be never receded in the time that my Moroccan friends had known me, and the disbelief that I was voluntarily away from my husband to 'do research' came up again and again as evidence that American relationships must be rather flimsy. I was welcomed into Moroccan homes that year as my friends seemed to want to weave me into a family narrative that would make more sense. Btissam and her family were amongst the most concerned for my general welfare and they launched an all out assault on my presumed loneliness and vulnerability by inviting me as much as they could.

While I began the first day of Ramadan a bit hesitant at the idea of going home with Btissam every day, by the end of the day I was more than ready to join her. While my American head made me wonder if it was really OK to just show up many times as a guest at someone's home, my Moroccanized stomach and its growling became the alter ego that argued convincingly to 'just do it!' This was not the first time I had fasted, but the cold along with the hours spent at the computer seemed to make the day ten times longer than it really was. When I had fasted alongside my husband in Texas, life went on as normal and most others in the USA were not fasting which somehow seemed to make fasting more bearable. In the office in Fes, we would normally arrive around 9:00 a.m. having already eaten something. Essentially all day long people would circulate through the offices with piping hot Moroccan mint tea and the occasional surprise food that someone would bring in, followed by a two- to three-hour lunch break, topped off with more Moroccan tea, and whatever else might show up in terms of food. Sometimes Fes Saiss would serve food to people taking classes, leftovers from various functions would appear on the table in the workroom, or the family of the guard would bring things over. After leaving work, I would frequently be invited for teatime, or to a later dinner that might finish at 10:00 p.m. On the way home from work, I would pass several food stalls where I might pick up yet another snack, and then walk through the markets where I would pick up fresh ingredients for dinner. After dinner, I might have more tea or share another small snack of some kind with the family from whom I was renting. I had not been a serial eater in the USA, but with an abundance of food in so many forms all around me, I had 'gone native' and taken to eating and snacking most of the time I was awake in Morocco. For this reason, as Ramadan got underway that year in Fes, for the first few days I was unsure of what to do with myself since food had so abruptly departed my daily schedule. I had grown accustomed to eating essentially all day long, every day. I had been in Morocco long enough to forget that this was the Moroccan approach to food as it had also become my approach to food.

With no time dedicated to eating that day, I had somehow managed to get a lot of work done, so much so that I began to wonder how I ever got anything done at all with all the normal meals and snacks. That day as I tried to forget about being hungry, I suddenly became a very efficient translator, getting through several pages with enough time to ask the Arabic translator what he himself had been working on. My head hurt terribly and all I really wanted for *ftoor*, the fast breaking meal in the evening at sun-down, was a pot of tea or coffee. I looked around at those in the office who were chain smokers and began to feel much better about my own state of caffeine withdrawal and brain fog. By the end of the day my smoking friends looked tenser than I had ever seen them. Moroccans are not always known for their punctuality, but in that half hour before *ftoor* they certainly are aware of exactly how much time they have before they can break their fast. As the long-awaited hour approached, Btissam came in and scooped up my stuff saying, 'Mom called, the harira and shabakiya are waiting for us! Yallah n'mshiou! Let's go!'

We emerged from Fes Saiss to a hustle and bustle I had not seen in the morning. People looked both happy to be nearing the breaking of the fast and grumpy amongst the throngs of people who seemed to be moving slower than normal. It felt colder than usual, and my growling stomach had now finally fallen silent as if it had just given up. Normally Btissam and I would complete each other's sentences in whatever language came up first but that day we were quiet; what was left at the end of the first day of Ramadan was a steely determination to make it on the very next bus to get to a warm place to eat. As I had seen in the morning, *shabakiya* were everywhere in large circular piles that seemed to defy all laws of physics. I had wanted to buy something to take to my friend's home to offer her family when Btissam's thin hand pulled the back of my coat up on to the bus like a mother cat scooping up a lost kitten. 'No, today you are my guest'. Living up to her name once again, she smiled and her lips were dry and cracking from fasting. I handed her my ChapStick and others in the bus looked at me as if I were crazy. She pushed my hand down gently and said quietly 'I can't use ChapStick today, it would break my fast'. I started to ask why as it is not food, but her look told me this was not the moment to be an anthropologist. I chose not to tell her at that moment that I had been using it all day, both out of utter boredom and to ease my dry mouth, but her stifled laugh told me she knew that already. It was yet another time when being the anthropologist felt much like growing up again in a new culture; I felt a bit more childlike than a thirty-year-old could really bear.

We got off the bus and walked up the stairs to her apartment in the *ville nouvelle*. Indeed, the *harira* and *shabakiya* were ready for us along with a pitcher of water and a sparkling pair of glasses alongside a bowl of luscious dates. Btissam always dressed to the nines and one might have been misled by her flair for fashion, yet underneath her carefully accessorized ensembles was an intensely pious and modest young woman. She told me that she wanted to pray before eating, that is was best to be *muwadiyah*, or in a state of cleanliness after having taken ritual ablutions, when one breaks their fast. My stomach growled again and Btissam's mother showed me to the dining room while Btissam performed her prayer.

As I waited for her, the *harira* seemed to me the most perfect food in the world. My senses were heightened from fasting, and I could smell every ingredient in this soup and felt I could taste it just from the wafting steam that rose to my face. I could already taste the cilantro, celery leaves, tomatoes, garlic, lentils, chick peas, tomatoes, cumin, salt, onions, thin noodles, and of course the lamb. I came to Morocco five years earlier as a rather evangelical vegetarian. I had eventually given up because it just made no sense to be a vegetarian in Morocco where people generally ate so many vegetables anyway. When it was a big holiday, everyone ate meat and it was offensive to turn it down, so I had eventually just started eating it myself. When I previously lived with a family in Tangier, I experienced Eid al-Kbir, where everyone re-enacts the Old Testament story of Abraham who shows his willingness to sacrifice his son as an act of devotion to God, who then intervenes and calls for the sacrifice of a ram instead. After taking care of a ram for a couple of weeks that we kept in the family basement storage area, the family slaughtered it and feasted off it for days where there seemed to be nothing else on the menu other than meat. As my host family jubilantly offered me the roasted ear of the ram with couscous, or smoked ram brain and scrambled eggs for breakfast, simple grilled meat on kebab again seemed attractive to me if it meant leaving these other delicacies for the more thrill-seeking members of the family. This marked the official end of my time as a vegetarian. Before going to Morocco, I had never imagined the strong cultural connections between food and culture, and especially never imagined that I would one day trade in my vegetarian badge for an omnivorous one. At that particular moment during Ramadan in Fes, this former vegetarian fantasized about the lamb meat in the *harira*, so much so that I could almost not hear what people were saying around me.

Btissam arrived at the table with her white prayer scarf still loosely draped around her face. My carnivorous fantasies were a stark contrast to her composure and patience as she sat down gracefully to eat. Muslims say that during Ramadan our demons are chained down and cannot bother us, that we are able to reach higher levels of patience, *sabr*, without the meddling and interference of these creatures that lead us away from the straight path to Allah. I wished that I might also look as radiant as she did at that moment, but I was simply too hungry to smile any more. 'Yallah bsmillah', her mother pronounced, 'In the name of Allah', and she passed around dates and water for us to break our fasts with. After a couple of dates and glasses of water, I started to come to my senses a bit. Ever the ready teacher, Btissam's mother explained to me that I had just completed a day of fasting, that Allah would accept my fasting as a very important form of worship. My fasting was a re-enactment of what the first communities of Muslims would perform in the heat of the desert. She reminded us that even though we felt so hungry that our fasts were easier because it was not hot in Fes at that time. She told stories from Btissam's childhood of when the lunar month of Ramadan fell in the summer months and the fasting periods were much longer. 'Alhamdulillah', praise be to Allah, 'this will be an easy year to fast', she said, 'only twelve or so hours of fasting'. 'Ma fih wallo, nothing to it at all', she said. She must have read from my expression that it indeed seemed like a long time, and she cupped her hand on mine as if to encourage me.

Btissam's younger brother and sister joined us and both helped with bring-ing the many dishes to the table, one by one. I felt uncomfortable with the display of generosity, as I knew that Btissam was the sole breadwinner for her family. I imagined ways that I might try to bring food or buy ingredients. After the *harira*, I was more or less already full, yet obligingly I continued to eat as my Moroccan hosts insisted 'kuli, kuli', 'eat, eat!'

During a break between dishes, we watched some television shows, named *Lalla Fatima*, a show about an upper middle-class family living in Casablanca. It was developed specifically for Ramadan, and was truly very funny. The maid, Ayesha, was our favourite character, and she seemed to evoke a sort of rural Berber version of the *I Love Lucy Show*. At the end of the show, we watched as the television family came together to celebrate the love of a caring family, complete with children, a functional marriage, jobs and prom-ising marriage prospects, conspicuous consumption, a supportive extended family, and of course gorgeous traditional Moroccan clothing all around. The infectious spirit of the middle aged, sophisticated, and accomplished wife and mother, Lalla Fatima, the main character of the show, seemed to represent all that the modern Moroccan woman could and should be. She had it all, financial comfort, a lovely home, a stable family, and enough money to invite others and take care of those less fortunate. This list of 'must haves' seemed so much longer than the stereotypical list American women carry around inside their heads. I looked at Btissam and realized her inviting me was much more than simply taking care of me, it was her way of forgetting the disappointment she felt from her own father whose absence that night felt so large, and the pain of not living in a picture-perfect modern Moroccan family, but there is rarely if ever a television-perfect family anywhere. Ramadan is about monitoring close relationships, and as she worried about me being on my own, I also worried about her and her family and wondered how she managed to take care of everyone, always smiling.

Discussion

I spent many evenings that year with Btissam's family, and when I felt I needed to give my stomach a break and simply sleep more during Ramadan, Btissam's mother would show up at my door with *shabakiya* and *harira*. One day Btissam surprised me in the office with an elaborate Ramadan take-home meal that her mother had prepared. 'Tonight is the 27th night of Ramadan, Laylat al-Qadr, the night of power. Our good deeds are multiplied exponentially today, so be sure to pray for everyone you love and say your *tarawih*, the extra prayers. Allah will answer all your prayers tonight. Please pray for me, OK?' Knowing her as I did, I knew to pray for her family, and to pray for the future family that she would someday have. As Ramadan came to a close, we selected some new clothing and we went to the mosque of al-Qarawiyyin to pray that our fasts that year had been accepted. We wore our new *jalabas* and visited family and friends eating cookies and pastries at every stop. As quickly as food had exited our lives, it had now come back.

Btissam continued to be the person who watched over me while I did fieldwork, the person who took care of me when I got sick, the person I confided in during my bouts of homesickness, the person who took me to the sacred parts of the medina to say prayers before my long flight back home to the United States. She continues to send me encouraging notes and provide pure friendship over Facebook where we witness our children growing up across our computer screens. During Ramadan she still sends me gifts in the form of electronic cards and posts Ramadan congratulations to my Facebook timeline. Having completed Ramadan together made us more like family than friends, and I now understand the longing to be with her again for *iftar* is a gift, a lesson about tending to relationships for the long term and the privilege of living in the present with friends with whom we share a special bond. Ramadan shaves down beneath the many layers of the everyday that make us lose sight of those things that are not important to our spiritual development, forcing us to remember through the stillness of fasting those things that are truly most fundamental.

Anthropologists have long written about the role of ritual in the lives of human beings across the planet and about the cohesive properties that ritual imparts as it obliges individuals and communities to celebrate, mourn, and acknowledge rites of passage. During my time spent in Morocco doing fieldwork, I experienced Ramadan several times. In addition to the fascinating community cohesion it brings, one also notes during Ramadan strained relationships, isolation, and social pressure to feast and fast on a grand scale even when funds and resources are limited. Ramadan and other large-scale public rituals bring people together but also shine a spotlight on the fissures and discontinuities that we would rather ignore. My own position, as an American woman on her own during Ramadan, taught me much about gender expectations in Morocco. Ramadan at its centre is a celebration of traditional Muslim notions of family. What happens when families meet ideals, and cannot meet these ideals during Ramadan, tells us a great deal about Moroccan society in general. Rituals are cultural texts that tell the stories of our lives and punctuate the everyday.

Today I grow Moroccan mint in my garden that I found from an online organic nursery in North Carolina, and I have planted citrus trees in my Houston backyard that remind me of Fes, that city whose beauty and grace haunts me even still. I now regale my children with improvised Moroccan tea parties with the mint that takes over the garden the way Moroccan hospitality took over my own frame of reference. Homesickness while in the field is generally short-lived, but homesickness for the field is harder, because we can never really go back to that moment when we first discovered another culture, nor when we first discovered new parts of ourselves that we never knew existed.

Readings

For a discussion of the feminine side of Ramadan, see Marjo Buitelaar's *Feasting and Fasting in Morocco: Women's Participation in Ramadan* (Providence, RI: Berg, 1993), or about Moroccan women more generally, see Deborah Kapchan's *Gender on the Market: Moroccan Women and the Revoicing of Tradition* (Philadelphia: University of Pennsylvania Press, 1996). Carole Counihan's edited collection *The Anthropology of Food and Body: Gender Meaning and Power* (New York: Routledge, 1999) explores culturally determined gender–power relations though food, and Rami Zurayk's *Food, Farming, and Freedom: Sowing the Arab Spring* (Charlottesville, VA: Just World Books, 2012) looks at the political economy of food production.

Author

Maria F. Curtis lives in Houston, Texas, and teaches Anthropology and Cross Cultural Studies at the University of Houston-Clear Lake. She has conducted research in several cities in Morocco, in Turkey, and amongst American Muslims in the USA. She has written on diverse topics such as Islamic law and the ways in which American Muslim immigrant women counter Islamopho-bia through acts of generosity and festivals. She continues to be interested in the ways that renewed piety and Islamic religious beliefs come to life through ritual, music, new media, and public events. Additionally, Dr Curtis has focused her research on the many ways that contemporary Muslims challenge post-9/11 stereotypes and engage their communities to create spaces of larger public multifaith dialogue.

Chapter 2

Studying the Muslim family law courts in Morocco

Lawrence Rosen

Preamble

For Westerners Islamic law (sharia) may seem a subject of arcane knowledge or potential threat. Neither properly reflects the truth. Islamic family law, as actually practiced, is deeply entwined with the cultures in which it is embedded, whether it is in the Arabic-speaking world, the populous portions of South and Southeast Asia, or in the countries to which many Muslims have migrated. Seen up close, in the proceedings of the courts and in the assumptions about people and relationships that Islamic judges draw upon, one has the opportunity to understand much of Muslim life and society. Working from my own studies of such courts in North Africa and the writings of scholars who have spent innumerable hours observing actual disputes one can see the rich array of factors that inform a legal system that holds meaning for nearly a quarter of all humankind.

Narrative

Seated one morning in the mid–1960s in Bel Haj's café in the small city of Sefrou, Morocco, I glanced across the street and was struck by an idea. For months I had been working on various aspects of social organization among the people of the city as well as among several tribal groups living in the Middle Atlas Mountains just beyond the southern limit of the town. I had tried following various aspects of family life, including marriage and divorce, through life histories, genealogical renditions, and the occasional dispute. But as I looked at the small crowd gathered across the street I realized I had been missing an additional opportunity. For the people arrayed across from me were awaiting entrance to the bi-weekly sitting of one of the local courts, and it became immediately apparent that here was a domain in which people were not only seeking legal recourse to their various disputes but a venue through which I could see a host of cultural assumptions and relationships played out.

I knew a bit about the courts from my earlier work. I knew, for example, that the one across from the café dealt in civil and criminal matters, whereas the court adjacent to the mayor's office handled cases involving matters of personal status (marriage, divorce, filiation, inheritance) as well as those property cases based on documents drawn up by the notaries of that court. I knew, too, that the Code of Personal Status adopted in 1956 – a code that was to be amended several times over the course of my work – had more or less embraced the traditional Maliki school of Islamic law that had governed decisions before and during the French Protectorate (1912–56), but that there was a good deal of discretion, custom, and procedure that also went into any judicial mix. What I needed now was to gain access to the records and proceedings of that court.

Research permission is the bane of most anthropologists' field experience. I did have a general letter of permission from the Ministry of the Interior introducing me to local personnel and requesting their help with my work, but something more specific was undoubtedly going to be needed to facilitate a study of the courts. What I needed, I thought, was the name of someone in the Ministry of Justice and some entry to that person. So during my next trip to the capital I went to see the head of the national library, a man who had been very helpful previously and from whom I thought I might get access to the right official. Our tactic was pure Morocco: we found the librarian on the ground floor of the ministry, who suggested we ask someone in records a flight up, who thought an assistant just one floor higher might know whose name we needed on such a letter, who gave us the contact we needed on the top floor and even set up an appointment. When I met him, the official – who was himself to go on to a distinguished ministerial career of his own – could not have been more gracious, and in short order I had the desired letter, properly enclosed in an unsealed blue envelop of the sort used for governmental communications and addressed to the chief judge of the circuit in Sefrou.

Upon my return to Sefrou I dressed in a coat and tie and presented myself to the very large Berber guard at the entrance to the judge's office. He seemed deeply skeptical when I told him I had a letter for the judge from the ministry, but after having me wait a moment while he went inside he returned to ask me for the letter. When he came back he was all obsequious courtier. I was ushered into the judge's presence where I was greeted with a look of utter astonishment. Unable to read the letter's classical Arabic I had shown it to one of my language teachers, who also served as the court's expert on land. He told me it was not just an order that the court assist me generally but also directed the court to open all of its financial records to me – something I had not requested and certainly had no intention of pursuing, as I hastily assured the chief judge. This man later became a very dear friend; his son-in-law even came for his doctorate to our university. A graduate of the Qarawiyyin, the ancient mosque-university of Fes, he was highly experienced, scrupulously honest, and genuinely interested in education and comparative law. Some years later, during a visit to America, he asked me to arrange interviews with some of the administrators at our university, and upon returning home he wrote an article showing how a modern university could be privately funded and thus remain independent of the central government, as his own university in Fes had once been. That first day when I visited his office he immediately conducted me down to the court of personal status, introduced me to the judge (or *qadi*) of that court, and encouraged me to feel free to talk with him at any time.

And so it began. From the outset I realized that I would have to pursue my study, though, on three fronts simultaneously. Because I could not read the Arabic of the court records and because in those days most of the records were still handwritten rather than typed, I needed help in deciphering them. One of my other language teachers for the year I had been doing fieldwork was a wonderful grammar school teacher, a holder of the equivalent of a master's degree in Islamic law from that same Qarawiyyin University in Fes, and a deeply religious man of very modern orientation. Together, we set ourselves up in the clerk's office to sample and read cases. This had several advantages. Not only could we get the clerks' help with some of the records – which ranged in clarity from prized examples of high calligraphy to the nearly inde-cipherable – but we could watch how the clerks advised people who came into their office to commence a lawsuit. The result was greater insight into what went into and what was left out of petitions and judgments, as well as a better sense of how the clerks shaped lawsuits and assessed different judges' approaches to their decision-making.

The second leg of my work involved sitting in on the court sessions. The *qadi*, a small man with a bright red fez permanently affixed to his head and a soft gravelly voice, was not always easy to understand. Nor were the partici-pants who shouted, gesticulated, cried, or mumbled, always with one or another regional accent. A uniformed aide was also present, and as in any Moroccan office his role was that of conceptual translator to the official in charge, keeper of order among those petitioning for help, and devil's advocate for any proposi-tion he thought ought to be considered. The *qadi*, realizing I was having to deal with a lot of information and strange utterances, kindly placed me on a bench perpendicular to his desk where I could face everyone addressing the court and where the *qadi* could lean over occasionally to explain what was happening and allow me to listen in to the conversations on the side with his aide and occasional lawyer. It also meant that, just as people frequently addressed the aide rather than the judge, I on occasion also became the focus of an impassioned plea from a participant who was prepared to seek help wherever such parties thought they could find it. The *qadi* had no trouble with my taking notes or even recording sessions, though I chose not to do the latter.

The final leg of my work involved following litigants out of court. Having by now lived in the area for some time and speaking good colloquial North African Arabic I knew a wide range of people. Thus, when I encountered cases involving individuals or families I knew in other contexts, I was able to go to people related to or living close by the litigants – and sometimes to the parties themselves – and find out a lot more about the disputes than could be gleaned from the record or the proceedings alone. Ultimately, it was the combination of all three facets that came together as I began to learn about specific cases.

For example, in one of the first cases I encountered, Mohamed brought suit against his wife Itu claiming that she had left their home in violation of an earlier court order. He had even sent intermediaries to get her to return, but she refused. Itu, however, claimed that it was her husband who threw her out and that she had returned previously only for him to beat her. She also filed suit requesting a new place of residence, prior support, and the return of some of the household furnishings. The judge asked if the home had enough furnishings to be livable and if her relation with her husband had been consistently bad: she answered no to the first question and yes to the second. The *qadi* also noted that the couple's marriage certificate showed they were married three years before the case began, that the husband had paid a bridewealth sum of about US$70, and that the court experts had determined what the proper level of support should be for a rural woman like Itu.

In court, Mohamed said he would not move to a new residence because his wife is always trying to cause trouble, that the furnishings she was claiming were not very valuable, and that while it was her duty to do so it was he who actually supplied the bedding for the marriage. He cannot pay the support, he said, because he is poor, and asked why he should have to since it is she who is at fault for deserting him. Itu, however, said her husband is not poor and demanded that he take an oath in support of that claim. She even produced a notarized document in which witnesses testified that she did indeed return to her husband previously but left three days later after the beating, a claim to which she told the court she was also prepared to swear a holy oath. The judge asked if Mohamed had any proof that his wife did not return to him; he answered no. The *qadi* then noted that whereas the wife had the right to request a new place of dwelling, that the husband admitted to having her things and had not paid support, and the wife had provided proof of having once returned, therefore a new dwelling must be found; Mohamed must pay the back support and return the objects that belong to her, but Itu must return to live with her husband. Mohamed later appealed the *qadi*'s decision, but the higher court upheld the judgment without further comment.

The case thus contained a host of revealing features. In Islam it is the payment of a sum of money or goods from the husband or his family to the wife or her marital guardian (usually her father) that makes the marriage, rather than some ceremony. Indeed, it is by garnering such a bridewealth payment that a man demonstrates that he is someone who has a network of supporters, the key feature (rather than some rite of passage) that defines manhood in this society. Theirs is a world in which one must form relations of debt to show that one has been able to negotiate the world of kinship and allies, and is thus a person so deeply enmeshed in ties to others that one's actions become more predictable and reliable. Forging such bonds with others also shows that a man is conforming to the expectations of Islam and common sense by becoming a person whose knowledgeable actions have real-world consequences. Because marriage is essentially a contract, various conditions are read into it by the law while other provisions may be added by agreement between the parties. Thus, support and provision of a proper home are legally required of the husband, though recent changes in the law provide that wives – who may now be better educated than their husbands and regularly employed – may be equally responsible for these costs. While a husband could, in the past, divorce his wife arbitrarily – even without her knowing about it until it was an accomplished fact – recent changes in the law require that a husband register a divorce at the court, where the judge may impose certain costs on him. Yet the law also reads in, often as a matter of local custom, certain rights for the wife. Therefore, Itu's demand for a new place of residence 'among righteous people' is really a protection for her: in case of difficulties with her husband she will need reliable witnesses, who are not related to either party, to support her claims. Moreover, a legal fiction also works in her favor, for the marriage contract invariably lists the bridewealth payment but is typically silent about the goods (called 'the furnishings of the household') that should be purchased for the wife to bring into the union. In the event of divorce, however, virtually all 'furnishings' are thought to belong to the wife, even if they were acquired later in the marriage. So, one tactic commonly employed by the wife (and her mother) is to keep getting the husband to buy household items as a deterrent to the exercise of his arbitrary power of divorce or as insurance should he invoke that power.

Other clauses could have been added to the marriage contract by the parties. Itu, for example, could have bargained for a provision that requires her husband to issue a divorce either on her demand or under certain conditions. She could also have demanded that he not move her very far from her own relatives, or that he not take another wife without divorcing her first. Additionally, she may have accepted only part of the bridewealth initially, the remainder being due upon death of the husband, divorce, or on her demand, a condition that may have been included if the man is marrying up socially or her family suspects his motives and reputation. In ways both formal and subtle, then, I was beginning to see that women were not utterly without countervailing powers in this society. Indeed, watching the women in court, far from it being an exercise in observing male domination or utter deference to the judge, was (as some of the films noted below exhibit so graphically) to watch strong-willed individuals who often knew their legal rights and were prepared to argue strenuously for their recognition.

The case of Mohamed and Itu also showed how the Muslim judges tend to conduct their hearings. They usually began by determining exactly who is who in a case and the full range of their relationships. In addition, they often let the parties start challenging each other in order to see just how strongly they feel about the matter at hand. Whereas courts in Britain and the United States tend to restrict the issue before the court to a narrow question of what happened, Muslim judges commonly try to figure out what sorts of ties people have within their community. Judges told me that they wanted to know what people have done in the past as a way of helping to decide what the impact of their decision will be on the full array of individuals to whom the parties are attached. Moreover, judges indicate that they think of each case as virtually unique: Since no two people are the same and their situations constantly alter, the idea that similar cases should be decided similarly – so central to much of Western ideas of justice – seems to them an oxymoron. Moreover, whereas our court officials often think of themselves as extremely effective at determining facts (as, for example, through forensic and expert assessment), the Moroccan judges imagine that they are particularly adept at assessing persons. That is why, in Mohamed and Itu's case, the use of witnesses was so important. For what Itu could have done was to bring at least three, and preferably twelve, witnesses before one or two pairs of court notaries who would quiz the witnesses individually and then certify their testimony that Itu had indeed previously returned to her husband. In the past, individuals had to be certified as 'reliable witnesses', that is, as persons whose network of ties would tend to lead them not to lie lest they lose their credibility as partners in various enterprises and relationships. The document that Itu received from the notaries was highly persuasive to the court. Had Mohamed produced a similar document, as happens in a number of cases, the court would have asked which group was most likely to know the truth or to have sufficient distance from the litigant as to appear more believable.

Discussion

Certain general features thus began to command my attention as a result of learning about cases like those of Mohamed and Itu. Students of Islamic law usually emphasize the classical texts, particularly those from one of the four main schools of law that, having developed in the early centuries of Islam, are predominant in different Muslim countries. And while judges may indeed refer to passages in these texts on occasion, particularly in colonial and post-colonial times they have been mainly bound by codified laws. In the Moroccan case, the Code of Personal Status adopted shortly after independence in 1956 was somewhat liberalized a generation later and still further in 2004, a few years after the enthronement of the present King Muhammad VI. The revised code significantly enhanced the ability of women to obtain divorces and some portion of the marital property. But key to Islamic legal practice is not simply what is in the texts or the codes but the procedures and the broader cultural assumptions that both enable and contain judicial discretion. So, as we have already seen, had the court felt that it was truly at an impasse in determining crucial facts – such as whether Itu did or did not own certain furnishings – a decisive oath, taken at the mosque on a Friday, could be offered to whichever party the court felt was most likely to know the truth. Alternatively, in a case like that of Mohamed's claimed poverty or the proper level of support for Itu, the court could turn to experts attached to it for guidance.

Moreover, the court employs certain assumptions about people that are widely shared in the culture. For example, most people believe that men and women are fundamentally different, but that anyone who develops his or her reasoning powers, and thus exercised greater control over one's natural passions, may transcend the disposition of their gender. Justice, then, is thought to lie in treating people appropriately to their category, without denying the possibility of having personal characteristics that do not simply fit into one mold alone. Thus, one sees cases in which, notwithstanding the code requirement that custody of a child go in certain instances to the father, the court will award custody to the mother because she is more educated or has a more stable income. Indeed, in recent years the courts have quite independently developed a concept of the best interests of the child, just as they have begun, in recent decades, to rely more on notions of probability given that people move around so much that it is less easy than it once was to know a person's background, connections, and reliability.

Scholars sometimes distinguish between 'formal' and 'informal' mechanisms of social control – proceedings that involve an institution that specializes in such matters versus the multiplicity of ways in which parties and the surrounding community may offer alternative resolutions to or bring pressures to bear on the dispute at hand. Therefore, for example, it was common, as in the case of Mohamed and Itu, for the husband to make use of intermediaries in an attempt to get his wife to return to him. One recent study shows that in a survey of Moroccan litigants 84 percent had first tried to use go-betweens – usually family members, but occasionally neighbors – to help settle their dispute. In other instances one may go to the descendant of a local saint, to a respected elder, or even to a judge or notary outside of the court in an attempt to have the problem mediated. Even the role of gossip and potential scandal – particularly if it might affect others' relationships – might prove effective in resolving a dispute.

Working in the court also made it quite apparent that the judge's willingness to consider a very wide range of factors was consistent with the belief that a case is often about something more than the issue with which the judge has been presented. I was able to see in a number of cases, for example, that a marital dispute was connected to a fight involving other family members over property or inheritance, or that a claim to marital support was as much a dispute among the descendants of a saint over the income from gifts brought to the ancestor's shrine. This was just one of many places, then, in which the discretion of the judge to consider these other issues is crucial. And since most people told me that the decision in any legal case is not necessarily the end of the dispute I was not surprised to learn that many subsequent suits and non-legal encounters continued well after what might seem to have been a final judicial decision. Indeed, as many judges told me, their goal was not so much to resolve the dispute as to put people back into working relationships, where they might then be subject to various social constraints, rather than expect that the court's judgment would finally settle all of the issues.

Not everything that happens in court, then, can be fully grasped by what one sees during the court sessions or read in the record of a case. That is why it is so valuable to follow up a number of cases out of court and to see Islamic law, in its fullest sense, as it is actually practiced every day. When, therefore, I encountered a case for the first time involving someone from a small rural settlement where I was doing more detailed studies I made a point of trying to determine what else besides the facts mentioned in court might have been involved.

In this case, Lahsen (60) claimed to have married Kanza (45) with a proper bridewealth payment. However, he said, she had consistently refused to have the marriage contract signed even though they had been living together as man and wife for some months before she ran away. Kanza's lawyer told the court that she does not even know who this man is. Lahsen, however, presented a document in which twelve witnesses, all close neighbors, went separately before two different sets of notaries to swear that the couple had indeed been married for seven months before she left. The judge accepted Lahsen's claim, recognized the witnessed document as equivalent to a marriage contract, and ordered Kanza to return to her husband. When I mentioned the case to friends from their settlement, however, matters appeared more complex than were visible from the court proceedings alone.

The plaintiff, I was told, was a rather shady character who used to be well off but had wasted his money and was now unemployed. He had married repeatedly for short periods of time, and soon after their marriage Kanza realized her mistake and left him. She tried, through relatives and even the local prosecutor, to get Lahsen to divorce her, but he would not. When the court ordered her to return to him she refused to do so and even allowed herself to be sent to jail for failure to obey the court's order. After that, people from the settlement went to Lahsen, told him this was all very shameful, that she was not a reliable person, and that he should divorce her. He finally agreed, provided that Kanza forgave him any support payments. Unlike another man from their village, who engaged in frequent marriages and then made his wives so miserable that they were willing to pay him to get out of the union, in this case it was a combination of social pressure and shame that finally resulted in the divorce.

Cases like these were not, however, the only ones that might come before the *qadi*. While matters of marriage, divorce, and inheritance predominate in those chambers of the unified legal system that are usually known as the *qadis'* courts, jurisdiction may lie with this court – and sometimes simultaneously with the civil/criminal court – in certain matters relating to property disputes. An elderly man named Hamed thus told me about the time he added a room on top of his house, one wall of which could have been used by his neighbor. When the neighbor refused to pay his share of the common wall Hamed should have gone to the *qadi*'s court, preferably with witnesses, and obtained a document certifying the neighbor's non-payment. But Hamed did not do so. Now, years later, when the neighbor started to add a room to his house that made use of the party wall Hamed had a choice. In the *qadi*'s court the presumption is that the person who now starts to use an existing wall must have paid his share unless a notarized document to the contrary is presented. But in the civil court, which at that time had overlapping jurisdiction on various property matters, the presumption was exactly reversed. There, the burden was on the person now trying to use the shared wall to prove that he had contributed to its construction. After so many years, however, the neighbor could produce no witnesses. So, by choosing his court Hamed was able to prevail.

While Hamed's party wall case was no doubt an unusual situation, analogous tactics are constantly being employed, whether within or beyond the formal courts. One might, for example, seek an advisory opinion from an Islamic law scholar to present as guidance to the *qadi*. I have seen records in which numerous brief opinions were presented by each side, always written on one side of a scrolled-up document. (People joke that if you offer the scholar enough money he will write on both sides of the document and make it as long as a grown man's arm!) What this also demonstrates is that, particularly in the past, but not without continuing implications, it is the reputation of a judge that is crucial, sometimes for being susceptible to the influence of a noted scholar, sometimes for knowing that he is less likely to be overturned now that the modern legal system allows for cases to be appealed. To this day one hears stories of judges who are wise or clever in ferreting out the truth from contentious and not always truthful litigants, and whose opinions have thereby earned them an admiring following. In the past, the Berbers – who had a highly developed system of their own customary law that they regarded as fully consistent with Islam – had yet another practice: one party could require a group of co-swearers drawn from the defendant's kin group or nearby settlements to take an oath in the latter's support. But because the plaintiff could choose the lead swearer – and would always choose someone who was not willing to risk his reputation to support a false defense – the plaintiff was able to pressure the defendant's own group of associates to make him settle the matter.

My experiences in the courts obviously taught me a great deal about the law. But studying the courts also led me to see linkages to the culture and society of Morocco as a whole. If, for example, women possessed powers that frankly contradicted my previous assumptions about Islamic legal practice, some of the cases I saw in the court records surprised me even further. I was astonished, for example, to learn that not infrequently Moroccan Jews would bring their cases to the Muslim court even though they had legally recognized courts of their own. Historically, I learned, this was common throughout the Middle East. Studies of the Ottoman records, for example, are rich in such cases, as are the records of Morocco itself. By the time I began fieldwork in Morocco the Jewish community had largely departed, but I did see a couple of instances – and found records of many more – in which a Jew would bring suit in the court of the *qadi* rather than going to his own Jewish law court. These cases usually involved business relationships, rather than any marital situations, but the ease with which these cases might be brought before the Muslim courts was a clear indication of the complex ties that had made Morocco a place where Jews and Muslims had workable and interlocking ties of both a personal and financial nature over the course of many years.

Learning about the formal and informal mechanisms available to women to deal with their marital situations also attuned me to look more widely at a number of other relationships and cultural concepts. Further reading in the history of Islamic law and conversations with colleagues working in other parts of the Muslim world, for example, indicated that local practice was crucial to both legal and religious issues. Indeed, it is a mistake to think of Islam as a single, invariant thing emanating in pure form from seventh-century Arabia and becoming increasingly less pure the farther out it has reached in the world. To the contrary, there is neither one pure form (notwithstanding the claims of certain denominational adherents) nor – more crucially – is the amalgamation with local custom seen as a dilution by those who give it local practice. Indeed, one of the reasons Islam could spread (and continue to spread) with such success is that there is very little required to be a Muslim – basically, just the profession of faith in one God and Muhammad as the last of His prophets. Local custom, then, is seen as Islamic, not as some falling away from its pristine form. One encounters such sayings as 'custom govern law' or 'a contractual stipulation may take precedence even over the sharia' almost everywhere. Whether it is Muslims in Sumatra and Malaysia who trace descent through the woman's line and thus practice inheritance that does not conform with the rules in the Qur'an, or Moroccans who (to the chagrin of Saudis and others) believe in the intercession of saints, the capacity of Islam to incorporate local beliefs without people losing any sense of their being Muslim is a crucial factor in understanding why Islam is what people do and think, not just what is in some scholarly text. This amalgamation of religious precept and localized practice is no less visible in the courts than in any other domain of Moroccan life.

As we have seen, judges make a number of their decisions about the facts of a case based on their perception of those before them. To inquire, as they often do at the outset, about a person's 'origins' (in Arabic, *asel*) is not only to ask about where one was raised but about those social sources of one's nurturance, the customs by which one engages others, the extent to which one has used study or attachment to knowledgeable others to develop one's reasoning abilities, and the way in which one characteristically goes about understanding the actions of another. In the past, there were even experts in physiognomy attached to some Moroccan courts. But they were not there to assess a person's character based on some physical feature: they were there to determine if someone was really from the place he said he was. So, if a man said he had a contract with another based on a handshake, but the experts said that the place he is from does not accord with the shape of his nose or the cast of his eyes, and that the people from whom he really stems make contracts with certain verbal statements, then he is not telling the truth and should not win the case. This may seem 'irrational' to a Westerner until one thinks about all the factors that go into a jury's appraisal of a person's credibility, from 'body language' or sweating to other forms of demeanor on the witness stand. And it sends a clear signal that one must remain embedded in one's alliances if one is to carry credulity in the world. In other words, just as one can be a Muslim and practice an amalgam of local customs not all of which match some people's concept of 'pure' Qur'anic doctrine, so, too, legal decision-making may incorporate any number of highly distinctive local ways of thinking about people, truth, and property – all of which are still thought of as Islamic.

And therein lies an important question that can easily be put the wrong way. For one can ask: how Islamic are these contemporary courts, with their codes and their uses of some modern science? But that puts the matter the wrong way if, as in other domains of life, what might seem a contradiction to those of one culture is not viewed as such by members of another. It would be a mistake, then, notwithstanding all the influences of European codes or appellate structures, to think that the participants regard their process as any less Islamic for inclusion of these other elements – any more than they regard wearing Western-style clothes, shopping in a mall, or using a watch to determine the time to break the fast as inherently illogical or antithetical to their religion. For Islam, whatever else is true about it, is very much a religion of worldly engagement: it lives in the marketplace and in the negotiation of one's web of obligations, not because people are constantly asking if their bargains strictly accord with Islam or whether their profession of honest dealing will threaten supernatural sanction, but because Islam teaches that God endowed humankind with reason so people might better their situation and those of their dependents. By demonstrating one's reliability in the world of human affairs one shows conformity to this divine plan; worldly involvement is thus a moral and a religious act. A court is not a mosque, but it is a place for the enactment of those assumptions about human nature and human relations that are at the center of Islam, and the application of law is, therefore, no less a form of Islamic practice than are prayer or fasting or pilgrimage.

If studying the Islamic courts required reading records, attending hearings, and following litigants out of court, fully grasping what I was seeing has, over the course of the years, involved learning more about legal systems comparatively. I had to learn a fair amount about traditional Islamic law as well as the contents of the current code. I had to read as widely as I could about courts in other Muslim countries, the works of classical Islamic legal theorists, and the background to more recent legislation. As an anthropologist I also had to become more familiar with the literature in the anthropology of law. In time, I realized that while a law degree was certainly not indispensable to my work in this area – any more than one needs a theology diploma to study religion or an economics diploma to study the marketplace – I could certainly use an understanding of some of the concepts lawyers had developed in various systems of law. Because I was interested in developing American socio-legal studies as a kind of second field site, I decided to return to law school following three years of postdoctoral work and only then began to write up my study of the court of the *qadi* of Sefrou. From that first moment, though, when I looked across the road to the people gathered at the entrance to the court – and throughout many years of interviews and encounters embracing virtually every domain of Moroccan life – seeing the ideas and relationships of everyday life brought out in the courts has been enormously helpful in my general understanding of Muslim societies and the role law plays as a window into a broader world of social and cultural life. For that reason, if for no other, I have never regretted having crossed the street.

Readings

The vast literature on Islamic law is broadly divisible into studies of the textual sources and those relating to the practice of law in the courts. A good introduction to the former, as well as to the broader context of Islam are Malise Ruthven, *Islam in the World*, 2nd edition (New York: Oxford University Press, 2000), and Reza Aslan, *No God but God: The Origins, Evolution, and Future of Islam*, updated edition (New York: Random House, 2011). More details about Islamic legal texts and schools will be found in Joseph Schacht, *An Introduction to Islamic Law* (Oxford: Clarendon Press, 1964), Wael Hallaq, *The Origins and Evolution of Islamic Law* (Cambridge: Cambridge University Press, 2004), and Muhammad Khalid Masud, Rudolph Peters, and David Stephan Powers (Eds), *Dispensing Justice in Islam: Qadis and Their Judgments* (Leiden, Netherlands: Brill, 2006). For a study of Islamic law during the Ottoman period, see Judith E. Tucker, *In the House of the Law: Gender and Islamic Law in Ottoman Syria and Palestine*, new edition (Berkeley: University of California Press, 2000). Contemporary Islamic law practice is described for a Southeast Asian nation in Michael E. Peletz, *Islamic Modern: Religious Courts and Cultural Politics in Malaysia* (Berkeley: University of California Press, 2002); for Morocco and Iran by Ziba Mir-Hosseini, *Marriage on Trial: A Study of Islamic Family Law*, revised edition (London: I. B. Tauris, 2001); for Zanzibar in Erin Stiles, *An Islamic Court in Context* (New York: Palgrave Macmillan, 2009); and for Kenya in Susan F. Hirsch, *Pronouncing and Persevering: Gender and the Discourses of Disputing in an African Islamic Court* (Chicago, IL:

University of Chicago Press, 1998). Several excellent films show the workings of modern Muslim courts: among them are *Justice at Agadez* (which follows a *qadi* in Niger), *Divorce Iranian Style* (filmed after the revolution of 1979), and the fictional but highly accurate Iranian film *The Separation*.

Author

Lawrence Rosen is W. N. Cromwell Professor of Anthropology at Princeton University and Adjunct Professor of Law at Columbia University. A recipient of his university's Distinguished Teaching Award, he was a visiting fellow at Oxford and Cambridge universities, a Guggenheim Fellow, and was named to the first group of MacArthur Award Fellows. His books include *The Anthropology of Justice* (Cambridge: Cambridge University Press, 1989), *The Justice of Islam* (Oxford: Oxford University Press, 2000), *The Culture of Islam* (Chicago, IL: University of Chicago Press, 2002), *Law as Culture* (Princeton, CA: Princeton University Press, 2006), and *The Varieties of Muslim Experience* (Chicago, IL: University of Chicago Press, 2008).

Chapter 3

Hymenoplasty and the relationship between doctors and muftis in Egypt

L. L. Wynn

Preamble

In Egypt, some women who have had premarital sex disguise their lack of hymen through a surgical procedure, called hymenoplasty, in order to appear to be virgins when they marry. The procedure is deeply frowned upon by Egyptian society, and most physicians believe that it is not only religiously banned (*harām*) but also illegal and unethical. Yet one of the country's highest religious authorities, the Grand Mufti of the House of Jurisprudence (which is responsible for making official fatwas, or interpretations of Islamic law), has ruled hymenoplasty permissible, and contrary to popular belief, there is no law against it, nor is it against any medical ethics code in Egypt. Based on participant observation and interviews conducted in Cairo and Alexandria over several years, this chapter examines rulings in Islamic jurisprudence for and against hymenoplasty, as well as the justifications offered by doctors who secretly perform the operation, to appreciate the complex cultural logic that assesses both women's motives for hiding their sexual activity as well as the patriarchal hierarchy within families that attempts to meddle in the relationship between women and God. The case of hymenoplasty reveals the complex relationship between popular opinion, Islamic jurisprudence, and medicine in Egypt.

Narrative

Sex and marriage

I met Sara just before the turn of the millennium, when I was in Egypt doing my PhD research. She worked in an antiques shop in the touristy *souq* of old Cairo. I was drawn to her from the minute I met her, I think because she had such a prickly personality. Nearly every Egyptian I met was outgoing, friendly, and helpful, yet for some reason, the person I most wanted to hang out with was the one who was uncommunicative, taciturn, and sardonic. Sara had a gift for evading my questions. Maybe I saw her as an anthropological challenge. If I could get Sara to talk, then I could conquer fieldwork – maybe even anthropology itself. Maybe I just saw her as a refreshing change from all the friendly, helpful people around me.

I soon learned that one way you could get Sara to talk was by asking her about her current boyfriend. Then she would lose her typically wary expression and a comically beatific smile would cross her lips and she would exclaim, 'My love!' Over the years as I got to know Sara, I came to realize that the one defining aspect of her life was that she was always in love. When I first met her, her beloved was a man named Ali. He was already married with children, but she hoped that he would marry her as his second wife. She loved him, and she desperately wanted a child. He swore his love for her and kept promising to marry her, but he always had some excuse for not doing so. Finances were too tight, he'd tell her. His wife would divorce him if he took a second wife, and he couldn't break up his family. They dated for several years before she concluded that he was never going to marry her and broke it off. She told me that, in retrospect, she realized she shouldn't have had sex with him. 'A man will never marry you if you have sex with him first.'

After Ali there was Sadaga, the Saudi tourist, then Hosni, the Egyptian air conditioner repairman who was unemployed all winter long, then Bandar, a married Omani businessman, and then Ramzy, a distant cousin from Alexandria. She fell in love with each man, but none of them wanted to marry her except the cousin, and that ended quickly in divorce. (She blamed her mother-in-law.)

In 2008, I was starting a new research project on hymenoplasty in Egypt, and I figured the only way I was going to find anyone to talk to me about such a sensitive topic was through old connections. Women have their hymens surgically reconstructed in order to appear to be virgins when they marry, and they don't exactly advertise that 'I tricked my husband with a fake hymen!' So the first thing I did when I arrived in Cairo was ring Sara. I hoped she'd have some ideas about how to approach my research topic and find people to talk to me about it.

I picked her up from work at nine in the evening and we took a taxi to Azhar gardens, a new park that had been built over a reclaimed garbage dump near the old citadel of Muhammad Ali. It had winding paths up hills and through thick shrubbery where lovers could walk in privacy, maybe even steal a kiss, and a series of fountains that children liked to splash in. It was as dusty as the rest of Cairo, with every tree leaf covered in fine, brown grit that blew in from the desert, but at least there was green under the dust.

We paid our entrance fee, which meant a scuffle to see who was going to pay for both of us. I pushed in front of Sara to try to cram bank notes through the hole in the cashier's window before Sara could pay, but Sara grabbed my arm and shoved me aside. The amused cashier sided with Sara, saying, 'You're a guest in our country', and pushed my money back at me. Then we walked the paths until we could find a bench where we could sit and speak. It took 20 minutes before we found one that wasn't already occupied by a young couple.

Sara, tired after a long day's work, slumped onto the bench and told me she was dating a married man named Hamdi. He worked in a craft workshop near Sara's shop. I listened as she waxed rhapsodic about how much they were in love. 'He says we're going to get married next Eid [feast day]. My love!' she declared happily. I couldn't say I was surprised. I knew she would be in love with someone. The only thing in question was how long her infatuation would last.

'Have you, um, slept with him?' Sara didn't act offended by my intrusive question. After a decade of friendship, she was used to my bluntness. She just tossed her head to the left and clicked her tongue in that peculiar Egyptian gesture that means 'no'.

'I haven't even kissed him, except for once, a year ago.' Now that surprised me. I raised my eyebrows sceptically.

'I'm serious, Lisa. I'm not so naive anymore. I've learned. No matter how hard a man tries to seduce you, and no matter what promises he makes, no man will marry you after he has had sex with you. Hamdi thinks I'm a virgin.'

I was confused. 'How can he think that? Doesn't he know you were married to your cousin?'

'Yeah, but we got divorced before the dukhla.' The dukhla was the last stage of a courtship, the final party that celebrates the wedding and culminates in the night of consummation.

'You didn't sleep with your cousin?' She heard the incredulity in my voice and laughed humourlessly.

'Imagine that', she said drily, 'The only man that I didn't sleep with is the one I married.'

On reflection, that wasn't as ironic as it seemed. As Sara herself had pointed out, many Egyptian men seek to verify the 'purity' of their bride before marriage. The only women they're likely to follow through on marrying are the ones that refuse to sleep with them, because they reason that if a woman is willing to sleep with one man, she's probably slept with another, or would do so down the line.

'So what happens when you marry Hamdi and he finds out that you're not a virgin?'

In a low voice, Sara said, 'There's an operation you can do. It's called "stitching the hymen." But you have to do it right before the wedding night.'

I could hardly believe my luck. Sara had just brought up the precise topic I wanted to investigate, and I hadn't even told her about my new research project. I asked her to tell me more, but she hardly knew more than I did about how the operation worked. 'You should talk to a doctor', she advised, then changed the subject.

What reproductive health technologies can teach us about religion

There's a stereotype that anthropologists like to plant ourselves in some Stone Age village and learn about the customs and manners of headhunters, or track down an 'untouched' indigenous tribe in a remote jungle and see what happens if we give them a Coke bottle. But plenty of anthropologists work in cities, studying factory workers or particle physicists or new medical technologies.

I'm in this latter group. New medical technologies are 'good to think with' (to paraphrase the late, great French anthropologist Claude Lévi-Strauss) because they tend to be sites for debate, and whenever you get people debating, it's an opportunity to witness culture in action. Opinions about hymenoplasty, as we will see, reveal Egyptian attitudes toward ideal and proscribed sexuality, gender role expectations, beliefs about how an individual relates to God, assumptions about the appropriate expression of sexuality for men and women, and expectations about the role of religious and medical experts in individuals' sexual and reproductive lives.

Studying new reproductive health technologies can also elucidate the relationship between medicine and religion – they show us, for example, whether religious verdicts determine what is taught or not taught in medical schools, and to what extent scientists or physicians influence the rulings of religious scholars. By examining how popular opinion, religious clerics, and medical authorities interact to shape interpretations of new medical technologies, this case study of hymenoplasty contributes to our understanding of the link between Islam, sexuality, and modernity.

'Two stitches below or the Chinese method?' Lay attitudes towards hymenoplasty

Each time I came back to Egypt to continue my research project, Hamdi was still promising to marry Sara 'next Eid' (there are two Eids, or feast days, every lunar year). But when I saw Sara in 2010 and asked her if she was still planning on having a hymenoplasty done, Sara told me she was thinking about using the 'Chinese method' instead. When I asked her what that meant, she quipped, "'Two stitches below, or the Chinese method?'" Spelling out the phrase for me in my notebook, she then explained that it was a line from a recent television drama.

Each year, Egypt launches a new crop of holiday serials (*musilsilat*) on television that run for the entire month of Ramadan. The most popular are eagerly followed every night and the contents rehashed, discussed, and debated the following day. They're a little like soap operas with a finite ending, but unlike most English-language soap operas, these serials embed commentary on a range of social issues within the drama of fictional everyday lives, and, as anthropologist Lila Abu-Lughod has described, they are widely read by both critical and popular audiences for cultural and political meaning. They are also widely broadcast throughout the Arab world.

In Ramadan of 2010, one of the most popular Egyptian holiday serials was based on a famous old movie about smugglers, hashish, religion, and honour. In one scene, a woman who has had premarital sex and wanted to disguise this from her future husband seeks hymen reconstruction surgery. When she goes to the doctor and asks for his help, the doctor replies, 'two stitches below, or the Chinese [method]?'

'Two stitches below' expresses the widely understood idea that a ruptured hymen can be reconstructed through a quick and minor surgical procedure (called hymenoplasty or hymenorrhaphy by doctors). The 'Chinese method' refers to a Chinese-made virginity-simulation kit that the Egyptian media reported in 2009 could be purchased online. Consisting of a gelatine-based capsule with fake blood inside, if inserted into the vagina before sexual intercourse, the combination of body heat and friction would open the capsule and produce the illusion of virginal bleeding. In response to the media coverage, in March 2010, Egyptian politicians called for a ban on imports of this product. A Muslim Brotherhood parliamentarian, Sheikh Sayed Askar, argued that its availability would make it easy for Egyptian women to get away with premarital intercourse and would thus encourage illicit sex (*zina*).

Public concern over hymenoplasty and its representation in the media is not new in Egypt. The 2010 debate over the 'Chinese method' reignited debates that had been circulating for more than a decade. For example, an August 1999 article in the Arabic-language Egyptian press described a case where a girl was raped by her father and went to Sayyed Tantawi, the head Sheikh of Al-Azhar. Amongst other reparations mandated for this gross violation of Islamic law, Sheikh Tantawi said that the girl's family must provide hymenoplasty to her and must keep the rape secret so that she could marry in the future without the stigma of her father's action being permanently attached to her and affecting her marital prospects.

In July 2000, *Al-Ahram Daily Post* published a reader letter to the editor from a Cairo resident who sought a declaration from the mufti clarifying that there was a difference between a young woman who had been raped and one who engaged in sex willingly. The reader argued that the first one should be allowed to have hymenoplasty but the second should not, as this would 'open a door from hell to give permission to every girl to do whatever she likes before marriage' and then use surgery to appear to be a virgin again. Then, in December 2000, *Al-Ahram Daily Post* published an editorial by a physician named Dr Assem Zahran, who argued that, 'the government helps women who commit sin and seek to deceive their husbands by obtaining hymenoplasty so they can marry as any honourable woman'.

These articles and letters express a fear that the surgical procedure will enable and perhaps even encourage women to abandon religious doctrine governing sexual morals and deceive men. As I soon found out, such anxieties about hymenoplasty were common amongst most of the Egyptians with whom I spoke.

In 2012 I travelled to the 'Ameriyya slums on the outskirts of Alexandria, three hours north of Cairo, where I hoped to interview some of Sara's friends and relatives about hymenoplasty for my research project. Sara and I took a taxi on the highway for about half an hour until we came to the edge of the slums. There we had to switch to a 'tok-tok', a three-wheeled hired conveyance that moves at top speeds of about 20 kilometres per hour but navigates better than a car could through the muddy ruts and abandoned construction rubble that is liberally strewn about on the unpaved slum streets.

We rode the tok-tok as far as it would take us, then walked another fifty metres past small boys playing soccer, ducks foraging through a pile of garbage, and deep, sucking mud generated by sewage runoff. Then we climbed slowly up five flights of crumbling steps to get to the apartment of Sara's aunt. Inside was bright, colourful, and tidy, in vivid contrast to the filth and disorder just beyond the threshold. The walls were painted orange and yellow and the cement floor was covered with reed mats. Sara's relatives encouraged me to make myself comfortable on a daybed in front of the television and brought me soda to drink, while Sara's young cousin showed me her pet tortoise that was hiding under the bed. She placed it on a side table for me to admire, where it promptly urinated. She shoved it back under the bed and went to fetch a towel to wipe up the mess while I told Sara's relatives about my research project.

I explained to Sara's aunt, uncle, and three cousins that I was interested in documenting general attitudes about hymenoplasty, medical procedures, and religion. I reassured them that I wasn't interested in finding women who had actually had the operation. (Of course I would have been thrilled if someone wanted to tell me about her personal experience with hymenoplasty, but I wasn't actively seeking such individuals, and particularly not in this context where it would have embarrassed Sara's relatives.) They were enthusiastic about the project and sent the young cousin out to ask neighbours and friends if they would like to come and talk to me.

I spent several days in the 'Ameriyya slums where I talked to more than twenty-five people about hymenoplasty, and the attitudes that people expressed closely followed those that I had read in the newspapers. Hymenoplasty was immoral, they argued. It enabled women to 'laugh at' (i.e. take advantage of) their husbands. Sometimes, though, women might see it as a solution when men had 'laughed at them' (i.e. taken advantage of them by promising marriage and seducing them but not following through). But there were better ways to deal with that than an operation, my informants argued. The woman should get her brothers to defend her honour and force the man to marry her.

'It's a simple matter', Hajj Ahmed, a fisherman, explained to me. He was a fishmonger in his sixties, lean and brown and wizened from years of exposure to the elements. 'You go to the police station and you say, "So-and-so seduced my daughter and now he has to marry her." Then the police will force him to marry her.' I was astonished. How, I asked, could the police possibly force a man to marry? It was not, I thought, within the scope of their disciplinary power. Yet everyone listening agreed with Hajj Ahmed that the police would not hesitate to force a man to marry, and soon I realized the implication they were politely skirting around: that if a man did not marry, the woman's relatives could claim that he had raped her and the police would charge and imprison him. Hajj Ahmed's wife reminded me that a man could marry at very little expense if the wife's family agreed to waive the bride price, and could divorce her even more easily. A shotgun wedding followed by a quick divorce was perhaps not an ideal solution for either party, but at least it kept the man free of criminal charges, and would allow the woman to marry again later with the dignified status of divorcee.

The only women who went for hymenoplasty, my Alexandrian informants suggested, were those 'immoral women from the city' who had too much money, too little morals, and who probably lacked male relatives who could protect their honour. Similarly, they declared that the doctors who performed the procedure were 'without morals', 'not loving our Lord', 'not on the right path', and 'only loving money'. They were probably, they noted ominously, the same doctors who performed illegal abortions.

Another theme that emerged in the conversations I had with residents of these Alexandrian slums was a horror of the contamination of a virgin's pure blood by the impure, false blood produced by hymenoplasty. The blood of a hymen torn on the marriage night had profound cultural meaning for these working-class Egyptians. 'It is beautiful and pure, like a dove', Sara's aunt told me. To illustrate this point, she went into her bedroom to fetch a white cloth that was carefully folded up and stored in a plastic bag. She unfolded it and showed me the scattered bloodstains on it. 'This is from my wedding night', she declared proudly. 'Thirty years ago! It's so beautiful!' She held it to her nose and inhaled deeply. 'So pure and clean! Do you want to smell it?' Grinning at the novelty of being invited to smell someone's hymeneal blood, and frankly curious, I took a cautious sniff. The cloth smelled like perfume.

'Lovely!' I said politely. The woman pressed the cloth to her nose once more, inhaled happily, and then carefully folded it and tucked it into her bra.

Back in Cairo, I told a middle-class friend about the wonderfully scented bloody sheet that I'd been invited to smell. Enjee laughed. 'Those peasants! You can be sure we [urban, educated, middle-class Egyptians] don't go waving around the blood from the wedding night for everyone to see. That's a tradition from the country.' When I protested that I hadn't been visiting a village in the country but rather a crowded urban slum, she said dismissively, 'But you can be sure that they're recently emigrated from the countryside to the city. They end up living in the slums, but they keep their village traditions. It's people like that who really need hymenoplasty because they have to produce blood for the whole village. For people of our class, this is something private between husband and wife, and not every man requires that his bride be a virgin.'

What struck me when I was comparing the comments I got from working-class and middle- to upper-class informants was the way each group defined itself by what it was not. Their self-identity was constructed in comparison with what some other social group was rumoured to do. While Sara's Alexandrian relatives claimed that it was only rich and immoral city women who availed themselves of hymenoplasty, Enjee argued that city women didn't need hymenoplasty, because they didn't have to display proof of virginity to a wider social group, but rather could negotiate it within the private husband–wife relationship.

In short, for both groups, hymenoplasty was something that some other group of women did.

Religious positions on hymenoplasty

Islam is a global religion and religious rulings circulate transnationally through national media (including Egyptian television programmes which are watched throughout the Arab world and a plethora of Egyptian newspapers representing every political party and orientation), regional media (such as Al-Jazeera News, headquartered in Qatar), and cyberspace (including Islamic websites and a number of 'fatwa banks', or searchable online databases containing all of the fatwas issued by a particular organization). All of these forms of media have taken up the debate over hymenoplasty.

But the challenge when studying Islam ethnographically is how to understand the relationship between transnational media and what Muslims actually do in their everyday lives. How influential are these media in determining Egyptian opinions about a new reproductive health technology? This can only be determined by examining the media coverage of the technology and then comparing it with opinions and actions on the ground.

Thomas Eich has written about Egyptian debates around hymenoplasty in a 2010 article called 'A tiny membrane defending "us" against "them": Arabic Internet debate about hymenorrhaphy in Sunni Islamic law'. According to Eich, media coverage of the topic spiked in February 2007 when a well-known Egyptian television personality and former dean of the Women's Islamic Law (shari'a) Faculty at Al-Azhar University, Su'ad Salih, declared that hymenoplasty should be allowed not only for survivors of rape but also for women who had had sexual intercourse consensually and then 'repented their mistake'. Controversy ensued, along with attacks on Salih's authority and ability to interpret Islamic law.

A week later, the Grand Mufti who heads up Al-Azhar's House of Jurisprudence (Dar al-Ifta), Ali Goma'a, backed up Salih's ruling, and said that hymenoplasty could be used as a tool for a woman to save her marriage. Goma'a's reasoning was that a woman who married without a hymen would be judged by her future husband, and that it was not the husband's place to pass judgement on his wife. Only God could know if she had fully repented after violating Islamic law, and a husband did not have the right to interfere in that private relationship between a woman and God.

Another Al-Azhar scholar went even further. When Sheikh Khaled El Gindy, a member of the Higher Council of Islamic Studies, was interviewed by the Egyptian newspaper, *The Daily Star*, in the wake of the controversial ruling by the Grand Mufti, he argued that hymenoplasty levelled the playing field for men and women, rectifying an inequality conferred by nature – namely, the fact that men had no hymeneal equivalent that society could use to judge their sexual purity. *The Daily Star* quoted El Gindy as stating that

> Islam never differentiates between men and women, so it is not rational for us to think that God has placed a sign to indicate the virginity of women without having a similar sign to indicate the virginity of men ... Any man who is concerned about his prospective wife's hymen should first provide a proof that he himself is virgin.

In short, while the Egypt media has published a number of arguments against hymenoplasty that express anxiety about what it will do to the morals of Egyptian women and the harm it will do to their future husbands, several religious authorities in Egypt have publicly embraced the technology as a tool to protect women. Yet these liberal rulings by high-ranking Al-Azhar clerics do not represent the only religious opinions on this technology. As noted, it was a Muslim Brotherhood parliamentarian who led the outcry against the so-called 'Chinese method' of disguising a woman's lack of virginity, and religious scholars elsewhere in the Muslim world have ruled against the Islamic permissibility of hymenoplasty.

For example, in 2002 the Saudi mufti Sheikh Muhammad Saleh Al-Munajjid issued a carefully considered opinion (fatwa) ruling against hymenoplasty, which is reproduced in a University of Malaysia online fatwa database. Al-Munajjid musters several distinct arguments against it, but the most widely repeated of his arguments are the following two: first, he asserts, hymenoplasty is a route to deceit, because its near-sole purpose is to deceive a future husband about his wife's premarital sexual activity. It is thus a technique for 'concealing sin'. Second, the surgery 'makes it easy for young women to commit *zina*' (adultery/unlawful sexual activity).

In contrast with the Egyptian Azharite scholars, Al-Munajjid prioritizes the right of a man to not be deceived by his future wife over the right of a woman to not be judged by her future husband for a lack of hymen, whether that hymen has been torn due to consensual or non-consensual sexual activity, and regardless of whether she has 'repented' of any consensual sexual activity. He dismisses the possibility that women will suffer enduring shame and stigma within marriage by disclosing their lack of virginity, arguing,

> As regards what they say about preventing the husband from thinking badly of the woman, this may be achieved by informing him of the situation before marriage. If he accepts it, this is fine, otherwise Allah will compensate her with someone better.

Even if her hymen has been torn as a result of rape, Al-Munajjid argues that

> One of the principles of sharia is that harm cannot be removed by another harm. … [therefore] it is not permissible for a girl to remove harm from herself by having the hymen repaired and thus causing harm to a would-be husband.

The existence of contradictory rulings on the religious permissibility of hymenoplasty highlights the extent to which debate and independent reasoning thrive in contemporary Islam. A transnational religion without a central hierarchy, there are multiple schools of jurisprudence, and even in countries that have state-sponsored religious institutions like Egypt's Al-Azhar University that hold an official monopoly on issuing *fatawa* (plural of fatwa, a non-binding ruling of Islamic jurisprudence), we can see that conflicting rulings on a single issue coexist and circulate widely both in media coverage and in cyberspace. Individual Muslims make their own decisions about which interpretations of Islam to follow when there are contradictory rulings. They base these decisions on their own knowledge and interpretations of Islamic jurisprudence and on their confidence in a particular cleric.

But when we put these rulings of Islamic jurisprudence in dialogue with my ethnographic findings, we also see that formal rulings from leading Muslim scholars do not necessarily influence laypeople. The vast majority of Egyptian men and women whom I interviewed in both Cairo and Alexandria, regardless of gender or occupation or social class, expressed the belief that hymenoplasty was haram (i.e. religiously forbidden in Islam). When I told them about the multiple fatawa from Al-Azhar condoning the operation, most acted politely sceptical, while a few baldly told me that I was plainly mistaken. For example, when I told Ragab, a 19-year-old construction equipment repairman in the 'Ameriyya slums, about the Al-Azhar rulings, he scoffed and said, 'That's simply not true. No doctor who respects God would do it; it takes something away from God.' Amal, an upper middle-class journalist in her late forties living in Cairo, was slightly more circumspect in articulating her belief that I must not have my facts straight: 'I'm not a religious expert so I can't say completely', she told me, 'but generally it [hymenoplasty] is a kind of deception, and Islam disapproves of lying'. And without a doubt, she added, the operation was 'completely illegal'.

I soon realized that if I, a non-Muslim foreigner, wanted to make claims about Islamic jurisprudence when discussing this topic with my informants, I would have to carry around printouts of the original fatawa with me to show as proof.

Physician opinions on hymenoplasty

My informants' scepticism tells us a great deal about the relationship between religious authority and popular opinion in Egypt. Religious authorities may offer opinions – fatawa – about matters such as hymenoplasty, but that does not guarantee that most Egyptians will be aware of these opinions much less agree with them. Azharite clerics are often said to be in the pocket of the government, because the highest ranking amongst them are government appointees. Any fatwa that they offer on a political matter is often viewed with considerable scepticism as being dictated by the ruling party, and any fatwa that is at odds with popular opinion, even if not a political matter, is regarded with similar doubt.

Egyptian physicians who might be asked to perform this surgery find themselves caught uncomfortably in the middle, as I discovered when I interviewed several doctors.

The first one I interviewed was an old acquaintance, a retired professor of medicine from Al-Azhar University who, like Sara, I had met almost a decade earlier when I was doing my dissertation research. I made an appointment to meet Dr Garman at the hospital he owned. When I got to his office, he gestured for me to take a seat, rested his interlaced fingers atop a considerable pot belly, peered through his thick glasses and asked me, 'How are your belly dancer friends?'

Part of my PhD research on tourism had focused on belly dancers, who perform for both Arab and Western tourist audiences in hotel nightclubs and cruise ships, and I had originally met Dr Garman through one of these belly dancers when she was dating a friend of his. Belly dancers are greatly appreciated by Egyptians, who often pay them to perform at weddings and other happy events, but many Egyptians – including Dr Garman – also consider them to be women of loose morals and don't treat them with the same respect that they accord other 'respectable' women. Dr Garman apparently placed me in the same category as the dancers, because we had been chatting for only a couple of minutes when he said, 'So, you live in Sydney now? I'd love to see a picture of you in a bikini.' He leered at me from across his desk.

If I was surprised, it was because of the non sequitur, not the leer. During my dissertation research I had put up with all kinds of inappropriate remarks from men I was interviewing. But it never went further than talk, and long ago I had decided that mild sexual harassment was a small price to pay for gathering valuable ethnographic data. So I simply smiled blandly and got to the point of my visit. I explained that I was doing a research project on new reproductive health technologies in Egypt and was hoping I could interview him. He cheerfully agreed and so I asked him first about hymenoplasty.

'Let me be frank with you', he said, 'I do perform this surgery for women. I don't advertise the fact, and I don't tell people that I do it. I do it in my outpatient clinic, not here in the hospital. More privacy. I don't even tell other doctors that I do this surgery. But I do it because it saves women's lives.'

'What do you mean, it saves women's lives?' I wondered if he was referring to so-called honour killings, where male relatives murdered women who had disgraced the family name by having sex outside of marriage. They were rare, but whenever they did happen they were heavily covered in the media. Egyptian intellectuals, whether religious or secular, saw them as the manifestation of a kind of social sickness, the extreme end of a spectrum of cultural obsession with female purity.

I soon understood, however, that Dr Garman was speaking metaphorically, not literally. 'A woman who gets married and she's not a virgin, she has to live with that shame for the rest of her life, and her husband will never treat her the same if he knows it. It doesn't matter if she has repented before God. It doesn't matter if she was raped. He'll always be suspicious, always look down on her a little bit. And if I can fix that for her, do this surgery so that he doesn't doubt her, I can improve her entire life.

'Don't get me wrong', he continued, 'I won't do it for just anyone. The woman who wants this surgery has to demonstrate that she has repented.' I asked him why he cared if she had repented. Wasn't that a matter between the woman and God? 'I have to know that she's not going to make this mistake again', he argued. 'I don't want to do this surgery and then she goes out and sleeps with another guy she's not married to, and she destroys my work.'

Dr Garman suggested that I interview another gynaecologist friend of his who, he said, also performed hymenoplasty. But when I met this next doctor and asked about the surgery, he looked displeased. 'It's unethical', he told me flatly. When I told him about the Al-Azhar fatawa, he said, 'Any procedure which is not accepted by the Egyptian public cannot be religiously condoned.' He refused to admit that he performed it.

Afterward, reflecting on this second interview, I wondered: was Dr Garman mistaken in thinking that his friend performed this procedure? Or did he actually perform hymenoplasty but, because of the social stigma surrounding the technology, he didn't want to admit it to a strange anthropologist? I thought that the latter was more likely, considering the low view of doctors who offered hymenoplasty taken by my informants and the fact that the doctor himself mentioned that it was 'not accepted by the Egyptian public'. Most laypeople considered the procedure immoral, on a par with abortion, and condemned the doctors who performed it as irreligious and mercenary. It was thus not surprising that doctors would be reluctant to admit to performing hymenoplasty.

Discussion

Reproductive health technologies are mediated by medicine, religious orthodoxy, and popular opinion. Medical anthropologists such as Marcia Inhorn and Sherene Hamdy have studied new medical technologies in Egypt and found that the relationship between medical and religious authorities in Egypt is an intimate one. Medical authorities are influenced by the opinions of religious experts in deciding what procedures they will perform and teach. Conversely, religious authorities rely on medical experts to educate them about what is entailed in medical procedures so that they can make an informed ruling about their status in Islamic law.

In the case of hymenoplasty, however, we can see that the relationship between religious jurisprudists and physicians is also mediated by public opinion and cultural attitudes towards a medical procedure. Even though Azharite scholars, including the highest-ranking mufti, have stated clearly and unambiguously that doctors can and should perform the procedure when requested, most of the physicians that I interviewed described the procedure as either unethical or illegal, and very few admitted that they performed it. As a result, despite religious authorities' acceptance of the procedure, it is not taught in any Egyptian medical school, so the doctors who offer it must improvise, each developing his or her own technique.

In a context where hymenoplasty is popularly regarded as something sought by women of low morals and provided by doctors who get rich by trading in illicit medical procedures such as abortion, physicians have to grapple with the tension between what religious authorities and society consider morally acceptable.

The arguments in favour of hymenoplasty by El Gindy, Salih, and Grand Mufti Goma'a also grapple with cultural norms about acceptable sexual behaviour for men and women. The fatawa they have issued explicitly acknowledge the rather wide disparity between the equality of religion's expectation that both men and women will be equally chaste, and the unequal expectations of contemporary Egyptian society, which heavily penalizes women but not men for premarital sexual activity.

These Azharite rulings also acknowledge the cultural reality that women are often blamed for being raped and suffer enduring social stigma as a result. They appropriate hymenoplasty as a technique for safeguarding the survivors of rape from that stigma, by denying society the knowledge of the rape and providing privacy for the woman involved. In this sense, they aim to protect individuals, but in hiding rape, they risk perpetuating the cultural norms that keep rape secret and thus reinforce myths that rape is rare.

In short, the Azharite rulings take into account culture and the fact that it is not always in harmony with religious orthodoxy. They propose solutions that take advantage of medical technologies like hymenoplasty to protect women and regain the gender equality that religion demands and culture refuses.

In contrast, the rulings of Saudi mufti Al-Munajjid also acknowledge cultural norms that lead a man to reject a woman who lacks an intact hymen, regardless of her moral status before God. Better for the woman, Al-Munajjid argues, not to be married to a man who would judge her for this, particularly since there is always the risk that he might discover that which she seeks to keep hidden. Better for her to find a husband with whom she can be honest without fear of reprisal. This is a solution that aims to bring the realities of culture in line with the ideals of religion. It places broader social and cultural change above protection of individual victims. In itself, that is not necessarily a patriarchal or sexist – that is, gender unequal – position. Yet it clearly prioritizes protecting men from the harm of deceit over protecting women from the harm of social judgement. Moreover, in framing the problem of hymenoplasty in terms of the temptation it will offer to women – but not men – to commit *zina* (adultery), and consequently leaving women but not men to face social punishment as a result, Al-Munajjid's ruling perpetuates the cultural norms that enforce different standards of sexual behaviour for men and women.

In short, the religious rulings for and against hymenoplasty take different approaches to reconciling religious orthodoxy and the actual practice of Muslims. Caught between conflicting religious opinions and a disapproving general public, physicians who perform hymenoplasty do so in secret, just like the women who come to them for the procedure.

Readings

There are many online 'fatwa banks' where one can do keyword searches for fatwas on particular issues. Al-Azhar's Dar al-Ifta (House of Jurisprudence) offers a searchable online database in several languages available at www.dar-alifta.org.

The 2002 fatwa on hymenoplasty by the Saudi scholar Al-Munajjid mentioned in this chapter can be found on the Islamic Science University of Malaysia Fatwa Management System, available online at http://infad.usim.edu.my/modules.php?op=modload&name=News&file=article&sid=9497.

Thomas Eich's article, 'A tiny membrane defending "us" against "them"': Arabic internet debate about hymenorraphy in Sunni Islamic law' (*Culture, Health and Sexuality* 12, no. 7 (2010): 755–69) contains information about the historical sequence of fatwas and debate about hymenoplasty that occurred in Egypt in recent years.

For medical anthropology perspectives on the relationship between medical and religious authorities in Egypt, see Sherine Hamdy's *Our Bodies Belong to God: Organ Transplants, Islam, and the Struggle for Human Dignity in Egypt* (Berkeley: University of California Press, 2012) and the many books by Marcia Inhorn, such as *Local Babies, Global Science: Gender, Religion, and In Vitro Fertilisation in Egypt* (New York: Routledge, 2003).

Lila Abu-Lughod has written about Egyptian television serials in *Dramas of Nationhood: The Politics of Television in Egypt* (Chicago, IL: University of Chicago Press, 2008).

For perspectives on how belly dancers and, more generally, performing women are viewed in Egypt, see Karin van Nieuwkerk's '*A Trade Like Any Other': Female Singers and Dancers in Egypt* (Austin: University of Texas Press, 1995).

Author

L. L. Wynn (PhD) is Senior Lecturer in the Department of Anthropology at Macquarie University in Sydney. The research on which this chapter is based was funded by grants from Macquarie University and the Australian Research Council (Discovery Project 120103974). She is a National Teaching Fellow (2012–13), funded by the Australian government's Office of Learning and Teaching, and the recipient of a National Award for Teaching Excellence (2012). Lisa is the author of *Pyramids and Nightclubs: A Travel Ethnography of Arab and Western Imaginations of Egypt, from King Tut and a Colony of Atlantis to Rumors of Sex Orgies, Urban Legends about a Marauding Prince, and Blonde Belly Dancers* (Austin: University of Texas Press, 2007) and co-editor of *Emergency Contraception: The Story of a Reproductive Health Technology* (New York: Palgrave Macmillan, 2012).

Chapter 4

Studying fatwas

Global and local answers to religious questions

David Drennan

Preamble

One of the first areas that anyone interested in the study of Muslim societies and their intersections with the Islamic religious (textual) tradition will come across is the realm of Islamic law. Alongside the familiar realm of the court judge, the plaintiff, and defendant, and the various mundane yet detailed aspects of contract, business, family, inheritance, and criminal law, Islamic law also has a much more unique sphere, which I believe characterizes its unique relationship to Muslim societies. This is the realm of religious opinions, or fatwas. This chapter recounts a pivotal event that piqued my interest in this area, alongside discussing some of the fieldwork and engagement with fatwas that I have undertaken in order to plunge into the depths of this area more fully. It also aims to highlight the diverse ways Muslim communities – and especially Muslim communities in the 'West' – use fatwas within their daily lives.

Narrative

Not long after arriving in Sydney and settling into one of the major Muslim enclaves there, I was waiting to meet with an imam that I had come to know in order to become familiar with the local Muslim community on a more intimate level. We had arranged to meet after the *maghrib* (evening) prayer in one of the main mosques there, and I eagerly waited for the congregation to finish their devotions and disperse once the prayer service was complete. As is common in mosques everywhere, the imam was greeted after the prayer by scores of individual Muslims who had just prayed in the congregation with him. They wished him well, and asked regarding his health, family, and so on. Many asked him specific questions regarding their daily life or concerning current events. Living as a Muslim in the post-9/11 world apparently came with its own difficulties and stresses.

It was the last person in the congregation to greet the imam that caught my eye. He was shy, quiet, and although wearing a Muslim prayer cap on his head, was obviously a convert. I was too far away to hear what was being said, as his question was asked quietly, but I could clearly see the concerned look on the convert's face, and also the determination behind his eyes. The imam beckoned me over, introduced me to Daud, one of the newer members of his congregation, and invited us to accompany him to his office. Once inside, the imam explained that I am a researcher interested in Muslim minority communities and the unique problems facing them living as part of a wider, non-Muslim nation state, and Daud responded dryly that 'my situation is probably the perfect example for you to study'.

Daud had a particular problem in his personal life that, although by no means unique, up until that point was something I had never considered. He was a religiously observant convert to Islam in his mid/late twenties and, naturally, wanted to marry a practising Muslim woman, settle down, and eventually start a family. The problem was that this meant the vast majority of Muslim women in the wider community were of migrant heritage, or second-generation Australian-born Muslims of a different ethnicity. In Daud's case, he got to know a young Muslim woman of Arab descent through friends over the last few years and they were mutually interested in marrying and building a future life together. They had never spent time alone together (which they both understood was severely frowned upon religiously), but communicated electronically through emails and chat. The problem, however, was that the woman's family were unwilling to accept the fact that she wanted to marry a convert – let alone a non-Arab – and would not 'permit' her to do so. They even stated that they 'feared for her religion' if she were to marry him and were pressuring her to find someone else from the same heritage and background, so that everyone's life would be much easier.

Daud and his prospective partner were thus unsure of what to do next, felt oppressed because of the harsh treatment and felt as if a heavy burden had been placed on their shoulders. His partner felt conflicted because she truly felt that Daud would be good for her, but, at the same time, she did not want to disappoint her family. Both were worried about the entire situation and doubtful if the Islamic religious tradition itself even allowed their marriage in the first place. This was why Daud came to ask the imam for advice regarding where they stood, religiously, and what they could do to improve the situation.

The response by the imam and the way he dealt with the situation was illuminating. After making sure we were comfortable in his office and suitably refreshed with tea and snacks, he stated clearly and upfront that the marriage between two believing and practising adult Muslims was permitted, and further-more, that their piety and interest in the religion further indicated their suitability for each other. He explained somewhat practically that, if one partner was sometimes more religiously oriented than the other, over time this can cause problems between them. The imam stated that the husband and wife should be like 'garments' for each other and recited the Qur'anic verse in Arabic: 'they are garments for you, and you are garments for them' (Qur'an 2:187).

He explained that the Qur'anic use of the term 'garments' (*libas*, or clothes) meant that the husband and wife should support each other, 'beautify' each other through living their lives together harmoniously, and also hide and iron out each other's faults. This use of 'garments' in the verse is understood metaphorically, he explained, just as wearing appropriate clothing can make a person seem professional and smart, look more handsome, and also cover blemishes or scars on the body. The imam explained that the husband and wife, being garments for each other, play an important role in cementing the family structure, as marriage is a process of cooperation and negotiation between two individuals. He concluded by stating that one of the foundational aspects to this relationship relates to their religious understanding and practical religiosity.

In the case of Daud and his prospective wife, Daud explained that both were learning more about their religion together and that they already performed the obligatory daily prayers (*salat*), fasted the month of Ramadan (alongside some extra recommended days throughout the year), gave regular charity, and so on. He noted that his prospective wife took pride in the fact that she could help him learn how to read the Arabic alphabet and enjoyed listening to him discuss what he had been reading regarding the religion. Daud further explained that the father of his intended bride was not religiously observant, and that, as far as he knew, the family in general was not known for its religious practice or being from a scholarly lineage. He thus felt that objection to their marriage on 'religious' grounds, in this case, was misplaced and merely covered over a deeper issue.

After further probing and questioning, the imam concurred, and suggested that if their objection was merely due to prejudice, that this had no place in Islam and was not suitable grounds for a father to reject a prospective suitor for his daughter. He also stated clearly that nowhere in the Qur'an is there a prohibition for those born and raised in the Islamic faith to marry converts; it does, rather, list those expressly forbidden in marriage due to family and blood ties. He also noted that, at least in the Hanafi school of Islamic law – with which he was familiar and qualified in, and which most of the Arab world, Turkey, and South Asia had followed historically in terms of family law – an adult woman who was financially independent could contract her own marriage without parental or guardian consent. And this was especially true if her prospective husband was religiously educated, pious, and actively learning the religious intellectual tradition as Daud was.

Besides giving this more formal legal 'opinion' to Daud, the imam proceeded to discuss with him a number of strategies for attempting to win the family over and allow their marriage to progress without causing family strife. There was a lot of back and forth discussion between the two of them, and I noticed that Daud began to relax after the imam had given his clear opinion on the issue at the beginning. Daud's problem had moved from being religiously doubtful – in his eyes at least – to now being almost religiously sanctioned. The discussion had moved from the realm of religious permissibility to more practical means to help in the success of the endeavour. Suggestions made by the imam included seeking the support of empathetic family members, such as the woman's uncle (her father's brother), and other respected friends of the family, especially her father's friends. He also suggested speaking to another imam, who was respected by the particular family, and asking him to intercede on Daud's behalf. The imam also went the extra mile and told Daud that he would like to discuss the issue personally with his prospective wife if she would be willing to meet with him. This was because she was likely to be able to confirm Daud's take on her family's dynamics, and also provide more information so that the imam can advise them more fully.

Daud left the meeting feeling much more settled and less anxious about his decision to pursue the marriage; the relief was palpable on his face and in his body language. His demeanour immediately became relaxed once the imam clearly stated that he saw nothing religiously forbidden (haram) in their marriage, and brainstormed through various means to support and assist them in their endeavour. I found out around a year later that the couple had eventually married, and that the family had come to accept Daud after greater interaction with him and getting to know his character better. They did, in fact, consider him an excellent match for his wife, after all.

This was my first experience of seeing how Islamic law can function within a Muslim minority community in an informal and unregulated fashion, and the vital role played by the religious 'opinion' of imams and scholars, in order to negotiate a path for believing Muslims to navigate the multifaceted experiences they face in everyday life in a religiously beneficial way. Seeing how this particular imam responded, his manners, etiquette, and empathy towards Daud and his situation, alongside this direct interaction between him and a member of his community was something that felt truly empowering to me. It was no formal study of the law from dusty old books; even if the imam was merely relaying an established Islamic legal position (which in this particular case, he was), the personal method of engagement, and context, was unique. It piqued my interest and led me to turning my attention towards the study of these collected and published religious opinions, or fatwas, more formally in order for me to understand how they worked in their various contexts.

Afterwards, the imam explained to me that he viewed his role in the Muslim community as that of a mediator and facilitator: that his role was to help bring hearts (qulub) – by which he meant people's feelings about their daily life and relationship with each other – closer together, to tranquillity and peace. He reiterated to me that Islam as a religion poses no difficulty or hardship on people and Islamic law is a path of finding 'ease' (yusr) in whatever situation presents itself. He also informed me that, in his experience at least, it was increasingly difficult for the younger generation in the wider Sydney Muslim community to marry easily because of numerous social obstacles, many of which he felt were self-imposed rather than due to the Islamic religion.

Although this was his first case of having to deal with a Muslim convert, he quickly counted on his hand the number of times he had been approached in recent years with similar issues – whether both prospective partners were from different 'born' Muslim ethnicities, or even had the same ethnic heritage.

Discussion

Outside of the informal and personal fatwa-giving described in the narrative above, which generally leaves no trace for academic study unless you happen to be doing ethnography and participant observation at that time, fatwa collections exist both printed and online in almost every conceivable Muslim language. Ability in any of these languages, such as Arabic, Malay, Indonesian, Persian, Turkish, or Urdu, would be essential to engage in studying the genre of fatwa collections. Arabic would be particularly important if research is being undertaken on fatwas from the premodern period. Fatwas also exist in English and other European languages such as French, although as my research interest was regarding the Islamic intellectual tradition and the realm of qualified religious scholars (rather than lay preachers and Muslim televangelists who are active in European languages especially), I quickly realized that Arabic was a necessity. Being that part of my existing training was in Middle Eastern history, I worked on improving my Arabic language ability so that I could eventually read primary Arabic source texts. I combined my ongoing university studies with taking Arabic lessons privately within the local Muslim community, which, although taught using a different pedagogical method, was helpful in filling the gaps I had noticed in my language learning. In my case, that related mostly to issues of grammar and of course the technical vocabulary required to read Islamic 'legalese'. I feel that the local Muslim community is a resource that is often undervalued by researchers, and it was incredibly helpful for me.

I was lucky enough to be awarded research funding to travel to the Middle East as part of my PhD research. I used this to spend a sustained amount of time in Amman, Jordan, during 2011. Besides continuing formal study of Arabic intensively at an Arabic language institute there, I also spent time with a number of local Jordanian scholars who helped me learn how to navigate the Islamic legal genre of fatwa texts and related fields. This was not at all uncommon, and I frequently saw both Muslim and non-Muslim students of Arabic taking advantage of the opportunities available in studying Islamic law, Qur'anic exegesis, and other subjects with qualified Muslim religious scholars who were part of a continuing tradition of learning that stretched back generations.

At my teacher's insistence, and after my Arabic ability had been gauged to reach the required level, I began by looking at a modern fatwa compilation which he believed was an ideal starting point for my entrance into this genre. Rather than picking up the first volume of a multivolume medieval fatwa text, the text we settled on was a short collection of fatwas published by the internationally respected and popular Grand Mufti of Egypt, Ali Gomaa.

Being familiar with this through studying Islamic legal thought and history in a university setting definitely helped me quickly develop an ability to navigate this and other sources. Knowing that legal texts generally follow the structure of discussing ritual purity, prayer, and the other religious practices, before moving on to discuss family law and so on, was extremely helpful when I was looking up fatwas on a specific topic.

A surprising feature of this little fatwa collection for me was that within these 250 pages, Ali Gomaa managed to give over 1,500 fatwas in total – an absolutely incredible amount! Compared to premodern fatwa collections, this was very concise. A medieval North African collection, for example, contained approximately 6,000 fatwas and published in 13 volumes, with the last volume simply for indexing all of the contained material. In Ali Gomaa's case, this was achieved, I think, by him retaining the direct question and answer format, and by being extremely succinct in his responses. After engaging in study of the text for a while, I noticed that a little over one third of all the fatwas in it were related to religious practices (prayer, fasting, charity, and pilgrimage), with another third related to the sphere of social actions (especially family issues such as marriage, divorce, and inheritance). What surprised me the most, though, was that there were also around 300 fatwas, or around a fifth, devoted to areas such as creedal beliefs, the Qur'an and its exegesis, prophetic Hadith, legal theory, and Islamic history.

When I asked my teacher about this, he explained that fatwas are not simply law in the sense that we understand the term today, that is, simply legal rules relating to the permissibility or impermissibility of certain actions, but also have another aspect of being a type of guidance (*tarshid*) and religious cultivation (*tarbawiyya*) for the original questioner. In other words, beyond the more strictly legal level, fatwas explain and elucidate what the questioners need to know in order to function in society as religiously observant Muslims. He also noted that this is why the same mufti may answer the same question at two different times, and from two different people, giving two different answers based on their intentions and specific context.

This process of negotiation between the 'letter' and 'spirit' of the law, was something that I repeatedly came across when studying fatwas or through observing the interaction between everyday Muslims and imams within a Muslim community. The religious leaders, whether in Amman or in Sydney, and like the imam above, were expected by their congregation to immediately know the answer to whatever religious question they were asked. During my time observing them, and sometimes even asking my own questions, I witnessed the muftis recalling selections of Qur'anic verses entirely from memory, alongside a number of prophetic Hadiths and established rules from one or more Islamic legal schools. Only very rarely did I hear the mufti say 'I don't know', or 'Let me get back to you on that', and those were usually only on obscure or highly complex questions. They combined this knowledge of the Islamic textual tradition with insight into the dynamics of their particular

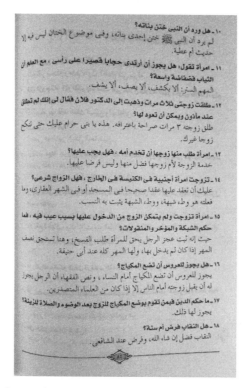

Figure 4.1 A sample page from Ali Gomaa's fatwa collection on personal status, marriage, and family law

context, in order to provide the most fruitful and beneficial solution to the questioner – in both a religious but also mundane sense. Oftentimes, the questions were merely the clarification of an existing point of doctrine or law, but in some cases, as with the opening narrative, the mufti and his fatwa became more deeply involved in the issue than expected.

Bearing in mind this importance of understanding the specific context when formulating fatwas, I then tried to relate this to my ongoing research: How is this contextualization and specificity of fatwas possible in the age of globalization? Considering that Muslim minority communities are spread around the world and the penetration and scope of the Internet is increasing globally, and thus a question can be asked to a mufti half a world away, how is this possible?

My experience with Muslim religious leaders had shown me that they tended towards interacting with their community at various levels, often working above and beyond the call of duty to help community members in difficult situations relating to marriage, divorce, inheritance, and so on. They

tended to know the dynamics of their local communities, the various prominent families and figures, plus how the dynamics of the community played out
regarding issues of interest. That way they could help negotiate a response to
the situation that was religiously sound, but also mediated or attempted to
mediate harmoniously between conflicted parties.

However, this is clearly not possible when dealing with a globalized Muslim
population, as there is no follow-up to issuing a fatwa. It is simply a considered
opinion on a point of religious law, and follow-up moves from the realm of
being a fatwa, to actual community engagement. This lack of follow-up is
especially apparent when Muslims are increasingly turning to the Internet and
other popular forms of media for religious knowledge, rather than religious
scholars themselves. When casually asking Muslims within the general age bracket
of late teens to early thirties where they took their religious knowledge from,
many responded that they looked to the Internet for religious answers and fatwas,
and they thought that their local imams and religious scholars were out of touch
with the social reality of their daily lives. This response was similar when I
asked the question in both Amman and Sydney, so it does not only relate to
Muslim minority communities.

Some of the people I asked replied that they enjoyed watching Islamic television
shows that included a 'phone in' component; the caller could phone the show
and ask for a fatwa. Others preferred using the Internet and visiting many of
the online fatwa websites in order to gain religious knowledge. Getting a
fatwa is now as easy as sending an email: you simply fill in your details as you
would any other Internet form, ask your question, and a few days later you
receive the response. Outside of that, fatwa websites contain 'fatwa banks', or
records of the ever-increasing number of existing fatwas. These are generally
divided according to the familiar subdivision structure of Islamic law and can
be perused even if not specifically searching for a fatwa, as many of my peers
regularly did. Others still preferred logging onto one of the many Islamic
discussion forums now found online – either more local or international in
scope and audience – in order to ask their question, discuss, and debate religious
matters. Although not strictly fatwa-giving, in the midst of the many epic
online arguments they engaged in, fatwas were often shared, debated, and
disagreed with, if not created by the debaters in question. All of these elements
provide fertile grounds for researching the interaction between Muslim communities – in this case online – and the Islamic textual tradition. In many cases,
rather than defer to contemporary Muslim religious scholars, the participants
in such discussions and debates were literally creating their own fatwas in
order to prove their points to other forum participants or website readers.

With the dynamism inherent in the Internet as discussed, how, then, do
Muslim religious scholars respond to this change of position and authority?
Many of them have likewise turned to the Internet in order to disseminate
their work, although, according to some of my participants, remain 'behind
the times'. Although fatwas remain a central part of their scholarly output and

Internet 'brand', they have also turned to using the likes of Facebook, Twitter, and YouTube in order to reach global audiences through lectures, tweets, photograph slideshows, and articles on a diverse range of topics. Many of these websites are also available for viewing in multiple languages. This, according to those younger Muslims that I asked, allowed them to feel more confident that the mufti was a competent religious scholar, and well respected globally for his religious knowledge. On top of that, seeing how the mufti speaks and acts through, for example, YouTube video lectures, increased their confidence and level of comfort in trusting the fatwas he also issued.

Going full circle from my initial opening narrative, then, my engagement in this dynamic area of fatwas and their relationship to Muslim communities opened up avenues of research and participation that I had never imagined when studying Islamic legal history and law in a university setting. The connection and interaction between the local scholar and the community was paramount in my decision to pursue my interest in fatwas for further research, although my ongoing work also highlighted that the younger generation of Muslims believed there was a disconnect between religious scholars and the issues they faced in their daily life. This went full circle through my expansion into the realm of Internet fatwas and debates, with Muslim Internet users, in a sense, becoming part of a new type of community construct – a cyber-community –

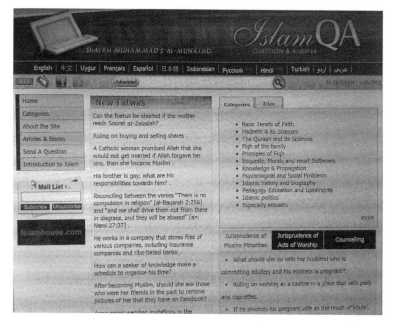

Figure 4.2 A screenshot of IslamQ&A: an online fatwa repository, published in multiple languages for a diverse Muslim audience

and using the various means at their disposal to assess the reliability and characteristics of online muftis through their use of language in articles and etiquette in online lectures.

Readings

There are a wealth of readings on the role of the mufti and fatwas in Muslim societies, past and present. They can loosely be divided into studies that focus on the textual content of fatwas and those that study the social and virtual environments in which they are found and published. Muhammad Khalid Masud, Brinkley Messick, and David S. Powers's (Eds), *Islamic Legal Interpretation: Muftis and Their Fatwas* (Cambridge, MA: Harvard University Press, 1996) remains the best starting point for a text-based introduction to the topic. Focusing on individual fatwas from the premodern and modern periods, it contextualizes them and discusses their relation to Islamic law and legal theory. Other important studies with a more anthropological focus include Brinkley Messick's *The Calligraphic State: Textual Domination and History in a Muslim Society* (Los Angeles: University of California Press, 1996). Although focusing on Yemen, Messick's study remains one of the most detailed and thorough regarding the place of the mufti in a Muslim society, and the transformation of that position brought about by modernization. Hussein Ali Agrama's writing on the anthropology of fatwas in Muslim societies is also important. See his 'Ethics, tradition, authority: toward an anthropology of the fatwa' (*American Ethnologist* 37, no. 1 (2010): 2–18). Also see his *Questioning Secularism: Islam, Sovereignty, and the Rule of Law in Modern Egypt* (Chicago: University of Chicago Press, 2012). In terms of the modern digital age, and the proliferation of fatwa sites and Islamic discussion groups, see Gary R. Bunt, *Islam in the Digital Age: E-Jihad, Online Fatwas and Cyber Islamic Environments* (London: Pluto Press, 2003). Also see his more recent *iMuslims: Rewiring the House of Islam* (Chapel Hill: The University of North Carolina Press, 2009). For an example of a modern fatwa collection in English, see Ali Gomaa, *Responding from the Tradition: One Hundred Contemporary Fatwas by the Grand Mufti of Egypt* (Louisville, KY: Fons Vitae, 2011). For a substantial introduction to the study of Muslims in Europe and North America, see Hisham A. Hellyer, *Muslims of Europe: The 'Other' Europeans* (Edinburgh: Edinburgh University Press, 2009), and Kathleen M. Moore, *The Unfamiliar Abode: Islamic Law in the United States and Britain* (Oxford: Oxford University Press, 2010).

Author

David Drennan is originally from the UK, and a PhD candidate at the University of Sydney, Australia. His research focuses on the legal methodology and fatwas of Shaykh Abdallah Bin Bayyah, an influential contemporary Muslim religious scholar and mufti who is widely known for his writings and focus on Muslim minority communities in Western societies. David was a recipient of the Australian government's Endeavour Research Fellowship Award in 2011, which saw him travel to Amman, Jordan, to undertake part of his ongoing research. Besides his academic work, David has been active in promoting interfaith dialogue and multicultural understanding within the diverse Sydney/Australian landscape.

Chapter 5

The hajj

Its meaning for Turkish Muslims

Carol L. Delaney

Preamble

This chapter discusses two different ethnographic projects. The first took place in a relatively remote mountain village in Turkey where I lived from August 1980 until July 1982. The second was conducted in 1984–5 among Turks living in Belgium. While the general focus of my research was the relation between religion and gender, particularly notions about procreation, this chapter concentrates on one of the major religious rituals – the hajj and its meanings.

Narrative

I first became aware of the notion of hajj in 1975 when, after having worked on an archaeological project in central Turkey, I traveled east to the village of Haran, near the Syrian border. Haran is believed to be the place where the biblical Abraham (Muslim Ibrahim) lived after his migration from Ur. I had long been interested in the story of Abraham and had a copy of a map of Haran drawn by T. E. Lawrence (Lawrence of Arabia) that indicated the well where, allegedly, Abraham's servant met Rebekah, the woman who would become the wife of Isaac. The villagers were very curious about the map, and when I insisted on being taken to the well, which was a bit outside the village, they commented that I was on a hajj (Turkish *hac* but pronounced the same as hajj). While my journey was a kind of pilgrimage, I could only think of it as an anti-hajj because of my critical interpretation of the Abraham story. Nevertheless, this incident remained with me and much later, as I will discuss below, made me think not only about the meaning of the hajj to Mecca among Turkish Muslims but also about what made it possible for them to attach the term to other journeys. If they could attach it to mine, then the hajj meant more than just the hajj to Mecca. Did the symbols and meanings of the hajj form a kind of archetype that structured other, but different, kinds of journeys undertaken by Turks and even by non-Muslims?

Although thrilled to be working on an archaeological project, I began to realize I was more interested in the people living in the village than in the ancient objects found there and decided to pursue a degree in cultural anthropology rather than in archaeology. Four years later, I returned to Turkey to conduct my dissertation research in a mountain village in the central part of the country (I would have preferred Haran, but that was not possible due to political tensions in the area at that time). At the time, the Turkish government had not given permits for foreigners to conduct research in villages because they assumed we would stir up trouble. But, by attaching myself to a rural medical team and visiting a number of villages, I was able first, to obtain permission from the headman of the village in which I wished to live. Then, with the support of a doctor, I was able to word my application in medical rather than religious terms so that it did not seem political and might even have been useful to the government.

The first night that I was finally established in my own mud-brick house in the village was the night of the military coup of September 12, 1980. For some time after the coup, Turks were not permitted to leave the country and thus could not go to Mecca on the hajj that year. However, despite that, I was able to witness the culminating and unifying ritual of the hajj, the Kurban Bayramı (Arabic: Eid al Adha), the Feast of the Sacrifice. This ritual commemorates the story when God (Allah) commanded Abraham to sacrifice his son, but at the last moment sent a sheep as substitute. Subsequently, at the Kurban, a sheep is usually, though not always, the animal that is sacrificed. Muslims everywhere perform the sacrifice at the same time whether they are at home or in Mecca.

Witnessing the sacrifice was very difficult for me. I had never seen an animal slaughtered. First the legs of the sheep were bound as Abraham's son had been bound, then the sacrificer soothed the animal by intoning a prayer and softly rubbing its neck. That did, of course, seem a more humane way of killing an animal than the method at a typical slaughterhouse. Still, it was not easy to watch the life being taken from the animal. Quickly, the sacrificer took a knife and slit its throat. The sheep did not die immediately but shook and moaned and there was a lot of blood. It made me very sad. While this was going on, one of the little boys who was watching told me that because God had provided a ram for Abraham, fathers no longer had to sacrifice their sons. Occasionally I heard parents threaten that they would make a *kurban* of their children if they misbehaved – a perverse way to keep children in line.

Although I had had a long-standing interest in the story of Abraham and had visited Haran, I was not aware of the extent to which the sacrifice was embedded in Turkish Muslim thought and life. But my interest helped me come to a much deeper understanding of the hajj, its place in Islam, and the meaning it held for the villagers.

In addition to the sacrifice, the hajj is intimately involved with Abraham in other ways. In Muslim belief, Abraham is one who first established the pilgrimage. First, he cleansed Mecca of its polytheistic deities and completed building the Ka'ba (Temple of the Lord) on the very place believed to be where the first bit of earth appeared. It was marked by a black stone, held to be the 'eye of

God on earth'. Then, God told him to call all people of the earth to make the pilgrimage. Over time people forgot or abandoned that original faith and began worshipping idols again.

Muhammad, who was born in Mecca, was distressed by this turn of events and had a vision that his role was to recall people back to the original religion given to Abraham. Thus, Muhammad is considered merely the conduit, the Messenger, not the founder of a new religion. However, many of the people in Mecca were not happy with his message. So he gathered a group of believers and, together, they moved to the town of Medina. Their emigration in CE 622 is referred to as the *hijra* (Turkish: *hicret*) and is the date from which the Muslim calendar (AH: after the *hijra*) begins. The word *hijra* has also been used to legitimate a Muslim's emigration from a land of disbelief. After the community of believers was consolidated in Medina, Muhammad revisited Mecca. Like Abraham, he is said to have cleansed the area of idols, rebuilt the Ka'ba, and declared the pilgrimage – the hajj, but he never again lived in Mecca.

The hajj is one of the five conditions (Turkish: *şart*) of Muslim faith. The others are: making the testimony of faith, performance of the prayers five times a day, keeping the fast during the month of Ramazan, and paying alms. But going on the hajj is much more than simply fulfilling one of the conditions of faith. It is meant to signal that one's devotion and obedience to God is reminiscent of Abraham's. Of course, whether that is true in the case of every pilgrim is something that demands investigation, but that is not possible for non-Muslim researchers.

With this background in mind, I will now discuss the preparations for the hajj that I witnessed in the fall of 1981. Although I have written about the hajj in several places, for this chapter I have also consulted my three large type-written (on a small manual typewriter – in days before computers!) notebooks from my fieldwork. I must stress how important it is to keep a daily journal of events both large and small. You never know when something seemingly insignificant will reveal a clue to something much broader. Furthermore, rereading them takes you back to the experience and helps you remember things you may have forgotten.

Muslim holidays (holy days) are not fixed because the Muslim calendar is a lunar one which means that the dates of the holidays move back about 10 days every year. Thus, the date for departing on hajj changes every year. In addition, people must consider the time needed for the travel to Mecca in order to be able to participate in all the rituals.

For villagers, the hajj is usually undertaken only toward the end of one's life and only if one can afford it. In our village, one elderly couple sold their entire flock of sheep and did so with equanimity, perhaps thinking they might not return. It is considered a great blessing to die in Mecca, for Mecca is not only the *axis mundi* – the still center of a turning world – it is one's original home and represents an image of one's ultimate home, namely Paradise. In 1981 eight villagers (five men and three women) decided to make the pilgrimage. Before they could leave, however, it was customary for the *hacılar* (those going on the *hac*) to give a feast for the entire village – a huge and expensive undertaking. They do this, they said, not only to pay off any social debts but also to earn *sevap* (a blessing that brings its own reward).

The day before the hajj meal was to take place in our village, my closest neighbors asked me to attend one in another village where they had relatives. I didn't really want to go, partly because the road down the mountain was a dirt one, deeply rutted, and there had been several serious accidents with overturned wagons. But I realized that this would be an opportunity to compare their *hac* meal with ours. We careened down the mountain in an open wagon attached to a tractor driven by the male head of my neighbor's family. In the front part of the wagon sat the *muhtar* (headman of our village), the imam, and several old men; in the back were the women and children. On the way I learned that the village we were visiting had been established by the government for Turkish immigrants from Bulgaria and that only four or five families from our village lived there. It turned out that the family going on the hajj was the *muhtar*'s brother and his wife, and they would be providing the meal.

Before the meal I was told that we were expected to go to the *cami* (mosque) for the *mevlud* (prayer ceremony) and that I must make an *aptes* – the ritual ablution required before each of the five daily prayers and before entering the mosque. The ablution consists of washing one's hands, rinsing one's mouth three times with water, then nose, head, arms, ears, and finally feet. When they saw I had nail polish on my toenails, some of the women said I would not be permitted to enter the mosque, but others persuaded them to let it pass.

When we got to the mosque the men put up a fuss, I was *gavur*, an infidel, and it was *günah* (a sin) for me to enter. But again, the women prevailed and led me up to the balcony where the women sit, behind a screen. It was very crowded and we could not see anything taking place below. I was never sure whether our separation was because our presence was somehow defiling or distracting for the men praying below. Women generally prayed at home and only on rare occasions were they allowed in the mosque. One woman stood in front facing us and led us quietly in prayer. When the *mevlud* was over, rose water was sprinkled on our hands and candy was passed around. We did not stay for the extended prayer.

Some of the women superintended the cooking in large copper cauldrons. This was a small village and they needed only about 20 kilogram of rice for the pilav and two sheep for the meat dish. Outside, two large canvases were spread and five *sofras* (low round table-trays) were set. The men would eat first. They ate as much as they wanted, calling for seconds, and with little regard for all the women and children yet to eat. I realized that in the United States we are more likely to serve the children first so the adults could eat in peace. Here, the children hovered hungry and were whining as they had had nothing to eat since early morning and it was already 2:00 p.m. The meal consisted of yogurt-rice soup with tomato-butter sauce on top, tomato salad with onions and green peppers, bread, green beans, lamb meat in sauce and, for dessert, grapes in syrup along with *tel kadayif* (looks like shredded wheat suffused with honey).

As I sat with the women, they began to tell me how everyone was related. It was very confusing, and I wrote in my journal that I wished my professor was here to explain the kinship relations. We returned to our village late in the afternoon and I had a headache. Many villagers believed that they get sick whenever they leave the village and enter a different environment, which I just had. Despite the similarity of the water and food, clearly I was becoming *tam kodblac; yludblac; —* a true villager.

That night there was a full moon but the morning dawned cold and overcast. It was September 13, one day after the first anniversary of the military coup but no one mentioned it. Instead, some of the men began the preparations for the send-off meal to which all villagers were invited. Men usually did cooking if it was done outdoors but, on this occasion, rain threatened so they moved the cauldrons into the laundry house and the women took over. Although there were 850 people in our village, more than half of them children, not everyone partook of the feast; some people were away from the village or ill. On the other hand some had visiting relatives. Regardless, this feast consisted of gallons of soup, 100 kilogram of rice for pilav; eight sheep (120 kilogram of meat), and 26 kilogram of *horşaf* (fruit compote). While the cooking was going on all the men of the village proceeded to the mosque for the noontime prayers. (This time I was not invited.) Coming out of the mosque, they were led by the imam and all were chanting 'God is great'.

As in the other village, canvas sheets had been spread on the ground and *sofras* set out for the food. Similarly, the older men were served, then the younger men and boys, all of whom were served by women and girls. When they had finished, the women and girls ate whatever was left, but no one waited on them. Because there was meat, a relatively rare occurrence, everyone grabbed pieces, including me, relishing this treat. The pilav was excellent as was the meat but, because we ate with our fingers, it was quite messy. Some of the little boys, however, went around offering us bread to wipe up. A week later the *hacılar* would leave.

The *hacı* were recognizable because they were dressed in pale blue suits with a tiny Turkish flag sewn on the pocket. This would be their uniform until they reached the sacred precincts of Mecca when they would have to don the ritual garment of white unsown cloth. The three women going on the hajj had long pale blue dresses and head coverings, but they were not included in the circle of men, nor would they shed their local identifying clothing. They stood outside the circle, behind the backs of the men, thus they were rendered invisible. Only after the circle had broken up and farewells spoken, did the imam come over to wish the women *hacı* a safe journey.

It was an emotional morning as everyone was aware that some of the pilgrims might not return. The journey is arduous and people are liable to get sick. They were not accustomed to trying or eating foods different from their own. Although all of them had packed provisions for the journey, these would eventually run out, and then the villagers would have to drink unfamiliar water and eat unfamiliar food. They joined an arranged bus tour that was composed of people from nearby villages. They told me that they were afraid to fly because if the plane crashed, they would not be able to have a proper Muslim burial. The cost of this modern caravan to and from Mecca was about US$1,500 and would last about 32 days.

Since no non-Muslim may enter Mecca for the hajj, I can only report on what took place from the accounts the *hacı* gave when they returned, late in October, to the village. As soon as they arrived, resident villagers ran to greet them; I was called to join a small group visiting a *hacı* couple who were also my neighbors. We learned that several of the *hacı* had been sick in Mecca and a few days after their return, one man died.

Those returning are expected to bring small gifts from Mecca to their friends. I was surprised to receive not only a metal ring (that I wear as an amulet whenever I fly), as did many others, but also a string of plastic beads and a lovely paisley 'silk' scarf. Other villagers became a little jealous of these tokens bestowed on a *gavur*. The couple offered us some dates and asked me to put my fingers in a vial containing myrrh, but when they offered me a drink from what was considered sacred water from the well in Mecca, I declined worried about getting sick.

On the trip to Mecca, they had slept on the bus or on the ground but in Mecca they had a tent. They claimed they drank only water that had been boiled and, while it lasted, cooked some of their own food. They regaled us with stories about how hot it was (40–50 degrees Centigrade), about date palms which they had never seen, and about all the foreigners speaking languages they could not understand, not even Turks from other countries. They had thought that being in Mecca with other Muslims would be the supreme experience of the Muslim community, but instead the diversity threatened their sense of identity. When too many people began to crowd the room, the couple invited me to return later and have dinner with them.

Then they told me about circumambulating the Ka'ba counterclockwise seven times as angels are said to circulate around the Throne of God, about praying at the Maqam Ibrahim, a stone thought to hold the imprint of Abraham's foot, and about touching or kissing the black stone wedged in the corner. Other rituals include running between al-Safa and al-Marwah that commemorates the story of Hagar seeking water for her son Ismail, stoning three pillars in Mina to remind them of Satan's attempt to divert Abraham from his duty. (Others say the three pillars represent the three pre-Islamic goddesses to whom, in 1980, Salman Rushdie referred in his book, *Midnight's Children*, and sparked a worldwide Muslim backlash against him that caused him to go into hiding.) One of the last rituals is standing on the plain of Arafat from noon to sunset, praising God. Finally, at the end of the hajj, the rituals culminate in the

Figure 5.1 Delaney in her village outfit

Feast of the Sacrifice when each male head of household sacrifices a ram (or substitute) as Abraham did.

In addition to talking about the prescribed rituals, villagers made several striking observations. First, in the village they pray in one direction – facing Mecca toward the Ka'ba, but in Mecca they could pray toward the Ka'ba from any direction. That implied that there were many paths to God, an idea that is heretical and contrary to what they had been taught. They had thought they would become more oriented in Mecca, yet their experience was just the opposite; it was confusing and unsettling.

Second, they were more appreciative of my situation in their village and drew an analogy between their experience and mine. 'You came here and didn't know the language, didn't have the same customs, or eat the same foods. ... You have respected our customs and tried all our foods. We went to Mecca and didn't try anything. And you are not afraid.' No longer did they make fun of my linguistic mistakes or cultural faux pas, but instead treated me with a kind of awe and respect as befits a *hacı*!

After their return, the *hacılar*, especially the men, gain a special status; henceforth they would be referred to as *hacı* and would be treated with more respect. The men are allowed to let their beards grow as they were required to as they entered the sacred precinct of Mecca. No longer will they shake hands with women or let women kiss their hands, a customary sign of deference and respect to elders. Now such a gesture would be polluting to their pure status. They began to spend more time sitting with their friends in the precinct of the mosque (a space where women did not go). At home they can expect to be waited on as they expect to be attended by the *houris* in Paradise. For the women, little had changed. The first time I was able to return to the village was in July 1986; at that time three men and three women were preparing to go on the hajj. Since then, I have returned many times, and many more have made the journey.

Before my first return, I finished my dissertation and received the PhD in 1984, but there were no openings for academic positions in my field. Instead, I applied for and received a Fulbright Fellowship to conduct research among Turks in Belgium from September 1984 through August 1985. Through the fellowship, I was affiliated with the anthropology department at the Catholic University in Leuven, which arranged for me to live at the Groot Begijnhof, formerly the secluded residence of a community of religious women, now turned into a beautiful living space for visiting scholars. I was also provided with an office. While pleasant this arrangement was problematic. Leuven is a Flemish speaking area of Belgium but the Turks were living in Brussels, where French is the major language.

Because of my prior background and experience with counseling and therapy groups, these psychologically oriented anthropologists wanted me to help them conduct 'self-help/therapy' groups for Turkish women who were experiencing a wide variety of psychological and physical ailments, whereas I expected to conduct my anthropological research in the Turkish community – visiting people in their homes and accompanying them in their activities. Since the group sessions were held in Brussels, it meant we had to commute to the city, and though I participated for a while, I soon began to feel not only that the psychological model being used was too narrow and did not take into consideration the very different culture from which these women came, but also I was cut off from the lives of these people. I considered moving to Brussels but that was not possible because the quota for foreigners living in that quarter was full.

In order to conduct my own research I had to take the train from Leuven into Brussels and make contact with the Turkish community. It was an exhausting endeavor – transiting between two Belgian linguistic groups in addition to Turkish, and especially because I had no place to rest in that community because the tea houses, as in Turkey, were for men only. In winter this became even more problematic due to the cold. My study was not turning out the way I had hoped, but I persevered, determined to salvage something from it.

Most, but not all of the Turks in Brussels had come from villages, though not from 'mine', and were also Sunni Muslims. In a sense, my move from a village to the city paralleled theirs, and I feel that my prior experience in a village was a huge benefit in understanding their lives in a city in a different country. Generally, Turkish immigrants to European cities have been studied under the rubric of 'migration studies' which tend to be informed by theories that focus primarily on economic factors, for example, the 'push and pull' factors that encourage them to migrate. In addition, these studies often rely on notions of the 'working class', a class to which such Turks may be ascribed in Europe but one with which they rarely identify. Such researchers fail to recognize the cultural baggage these 'urban villagers' carry with them from the village to the city and, thus, misunderstand many of their actions.

Contrary to my expectations, Turkish women were more secluded in the European city than they had been in their villages in Turkey. Because they were living among foreigners and infidels where, if they went to shop, visit friends, or take their children to school, they would encounter unrelated men. Their husbands, many of whom were out of work due to the economic downturn at the time, had more time to exert control and surveil the women. They demanded that they remain at home. Sadly, teenage girls were taken out of school and kept at home until a marriage could be arranged. In such confined quarters, it is no wonder the women began to have psychological problems.

A prominent effect of this isolation was expressed as '*gurbet*'. This was a turning point in my research for it echoed things I had heard in the village. *Gurbet* is a feeling of being in exile, longing for one's real home, and is expressed in songs and poems and in seemingly mundane situations. Back in 'my' village, I heard this expression used by young married women living with their husband's family in a house only a few streets away! And men spoke of it during their military service. But it was also used to talk about their true, original home – *öbür dünya*, the other world or heaven. I remembered some village wall hangings with inscriptions stating that life on earth was exile, the true, original home was *öbür dünya* – a glimpse of which was thought to be available on the hajj in Mecca.

The Turks I met in Belgium were in an acute state of *gurbet*, longing for their home back in Turkey. Although they lived and worked in Belgium, they were not citizens, they did not assimilate; their 'real' home was in Turkey. This notion helped to explain one of the most significant yearly events that had barely been mentioned in the migration literature. I observed that against any rational calculus, thousands of Turks living in Europe undertake the arduous journey back to Turkey year after year, at vast expense, in physical discomfort, and at risk of life. Instead of spending money to invest in houses and better living conditions in Belgium, they spent it on the journey home and on building a house back in Turkey which they would add to, in stages, each year. In addition, they bought carpets, appliances, and furniture which they never used in Europe, in order to provision these 'eventual' homes in Turkey.

Just as the journey to Mecca takes place at a specific time on the calendar, so too did these journeys home. They generally occurred during the month of Ramazan – the month of fasting that Turks in Brussels managed to claim as their 'vacation' time, using it for the journey. But the trip was hardly a vacation; these travelers were not tourists stopping to take in the sights, they made the

Figure 5.2 Elderly men sitting in the 'garden' of the mosque

journey as quickly as possible. On the route to Turkey, they had to traverse communist countries which they referred to as the Dar el Harb – the land of unbelievers – since communists were assumed to be atheists.

Unlike the trinkets brought back as gifts from Mecca, these 'pilgrims' were expected to bring substantial secular gifts symbolizing their worldly success – gifts such as machinery, electronic equipment, and household appliances and, rather than sharing them with the whole community, they bestow these luxuries on their own relatives, a gesture which created envy and enmity in the group. Such gifts were felt to be obligatory, a kind of repayment of a debt. Villagers have no comprehension of what the European salaries actually mean for, no matter how meager, to them they seemed otherworldly and, thus, they had no idea of the huge sacrifice the migrants made in order to bring these gifts. Yet, in another sense, they can be seen as the price the migrants must pay to maintain their own sense of self-esteem and respect back home which they so lack in Europe. If the visit went well, migrants and their families in the village celebrated together the holiday that marks the end of Ramazan – Şeker Bayramı or Sugar Holiday, when candy and sweets are distributed. Often relatives would sacrifice a sheep in their honor, and for the short duration of the visit, they were treated almost as *hacı*.

Back in Belgium they reminisced about their visit. In their conversations, Turkey, especially their village, came to seem like *Cennet* (heaven) as they idealized the warmth, the sun, the clean air, the clear water, and the delicious fruits and vegetables grown in their own gardens. In contrast to their lives of hard labor in Europe, they fantasized about a life of ease where they would eventually be waited on by adoring relatives (as they imagined the *houris* in Paradise). Turkey, but more specifically, their home village is their original and final home as the bodies of Turks who die in Europe are sent back to their natal villages to be interred in their native soil.

Discussion

The more I thought about all this, a pattern seemed to emerge. The journey the Turks in Europe made to their home village seemed to me to be a kind of pilgrimage. It was hardly for fun but almost obligatory if they could afford it. They yearned for their homeland, *Anavatan* (motherland) and especially their home village which they talked of as almost *kutsal* (sacred, holy). They spoke of its hallowed ground with reverence and claimed it was *kapalı* (closed), as are their women. There seemed to be a sense in which the home village had taken the place of Mecca, though I doubt this thought came to consciousness. If it did, it could not be articulated for it would be heresy. In other words, the journey home seemed to be symbolically and meaningfully informed by the

Figure 5.3 A wall hanging that says 'What are you? From where are you coming? To where are you going?'

structure of the sacred hajj so that I began to see their emigration as a kind of secular *hijra*, and the journey back to their villages as a secular hajj. Although these migrant Turks assume they will eventually return to live in the houses they had been building in the village, sadly, that is rarely the case.

Beyond my thoughts about the hajj, I also realized that all pilgrimages are not the same. For example, the traditional pilgrimage to Mecca is a very different notion from the one that informs Christian pilgrimages. For Christians the archetype is Pilgrim's Progress, that is, a notion in which life, itself, is imagined as a pilgrimage. It is a 'going forth' not a return. Of course, some Christians make pilgrimages to sites holy because of Jesus or because of saints or healings, but it does not carry the sense of 'going home' in the way that both the pilgrimage to Mecca and the one back to one's village is for these Muslim Turks.

Migration and pilgrimage are rarely brought into meaningful conjunction in academia; one is generally studied in economics or politics while the other is studied in departments of religion. Hopefully, this study raises the question of whether academic boundaries prevent us from seeing connections between seemingly very different things, as well as keeping us from recognizing differences between superficially similar things.

Readings

A good starter to overview this topic is my own *The Seed and the Soil: Gender and Cosmology in Turkish Village Society* (Berkeley: University of California Press, 1991). Focusing on the significance that Muslims assign to pilgrimage, Juan Campo's 'Shrines and talismans: domestic Islam in the pilgrimage paintings of Egypt' (*Journal of the American Academy of Religion* 55 (1987): 285–305) is an interesting read. For more information about the hajj, please see William Roff's 'Pilgrimage and the history of religions: theoretical approaches to the hajj', in Richard C. Martin (Ed.), *Approaches to Islam in Religious Studies* (Tucson: University of Arizona Press, 1985).

Author

I first heard the story of Abraham's sacrifice when I was about eight or nine years old. I was both shocked and repulsed; this feeling resurfaced many years later when I had a child and wondered how anyone could think of sacrificing their child, even if they felt God had commanded it. I began to wonder how or why was Abraham's willingness to go through with it the model of faith at the foundation of the three Abrahamic religions? I had to explore this question in more depth. I first went to Harvard Divinity School, not to become a minister but to pursue an academic degree, delve into explanations of the story, learn more about the context of the ancient Near East through written work and archaeology. But I also began to realize that the story had to do with notions of paternity, maternity, procreation, that is, gender, especially when I learned that the name Abraham means something like 'the father is exalted'. Yet notions of reproduction are rarely studied in the context of 'religion'. As you read, I first thought of becoming an archaeologist, and imagined I would dig up something in Haran that would help my interpretation! But rather than the past, I became more interested in ways these notions persisted in the present. Thus, I turned to cultural anthropology to study theories of procreation among a variety of peoples and ultimately decided to do work among people who did not know the modern theory of procreation but who were, nevertheless, members of one of the Abrahamic religions. From my prior experience in Turkey, I knew I would find answers in a village. Despite my criticism of the story of Abraham and of religion more generally, my time at the Divinity School was one of the most productive of my life, and my fieldwork in Turkey most rewarding. My book about that fieldwork has been translated into Turkish and is now being taught in a number of universities. This has resulted in more contacts, discussions, arguments, and invitations to speak. I continue to return to Turkey and maintain contact with the villagers, now sometimes through Facebook!

Chapter 6

Studying Islam and the city

The case of Istanbul

Christopher Houston

Preamble

Like many who have lived in Istanbul for any length of time, I both love and am exhausted by the city. The glitter of its waters and the messy intricacies of its built environments; its plural and proliferating ways of being wealthy and its monochrome way of being poor; its antagonistic social movements, propelled by atrocities brought to the fringes of people's consciousness in the heat of protest and forgotten just as quickly; and its (literally) countless inhabitants – all make researching Istanbul and its denizens' lives fascinating and overwhelming in equal measure. Its security apparatuses terrify – passing massed ranks of helmeted and truncheoned special forces for the funeral of a journalist beaten to death by police, fearful of being caught in a new burst of violence – yet Istanbul is familiar too, homely with favoured places and beloved friends even more than my own city.

Like many anthropologists, I am also a frustrated novelist (failed would be too unkind). During my fieldwork in Istanbul I used to read local novelists with an admiring envy. Here were writers who recalled the smell of an apartment stairwell, the picture on a childhood lolly wrapper, the congratulations exchanged between relatives upon hearing news of a military coup, the melancholy that the Odeon Cinema used to make them feel. In their dallying in the private experiences and perverse perceptions of their characters, novelists luxuriated in the uniqueness of individual's lives and emotions in wilful disregard of their shared dimensions. No one condemned them for failing to place those perceptions in a structural context. I felt that my anthropological writing too often did the opposite, leaping to the institutional conditioning of the moment that ordinary souls were unaware of, or to that moment's evolution in the historical development of the political economy. In my doctoral thesis I examined the burgeoning Islamist movement's thinking about the Kurdish problem. The issue was internal to itself, as many religious Muslims were also self-aware Kurds. The theoretical question was the possibility of Islamist multiculturalism.

In this chapter I want to write something different about my fieldwork on political Islam in Istanbul in the years 1994–6, pursued in the tense aftermath of the victory of the 'Muslim-friendly' Refah (or Welfare) Party in elections for the Greater Istanbul Municipality in 1994, and of the spread of the armed rebellion of the Kurdish Workers Party (or PKK) in the country's southeast. Each sent shock waves through Istanbul's secular and nationalist residents. I want to tell you about my two best friends, one a *bilinçli* (knowledgeable) Kurd, the other a *şuurlu* (conscious) Muslim – both self-descriptions. I'd like to tell you their real names, if I could be assured that no one would hold what I say against them. But they themselves have given me reasons to give them pseudonyms, so let me name them Ömer and Hüsnü respectively. I met Ömer on a basketball court in Istanbul in 1992, as I was contemplating postgraduate anthropology. I learnt from him about being Kurdish in Turkey, and consequently formed the idea for a research topic. I met Hüsnü two years later on my first day of fieldwork in Istanbul (1994), editing his English in an essay written for his master's degree in sociology at Bosphorus University, a task agreed to in return for the department's sponsoring of my research visa. For nearly 20 years I've caught up periodically with each of them, listening as their loyalties and practices have changed, transforming my understandings of Istanbul and Islam in the process.

Narrative

Grace

What is the most beautiful word in any language? *Lütuf* in Turkish: in English, grace. Both of my friends have shown me much undeserved favour, not just in welcoming me as if I was special every time I came to Istanbul but also by smoothing out in myriad ways my dealings with the city's alien systems of local life – phone line, furniture, water heater, flat repairs, tradesmen, gas bill, and so on. Ömer found an apartment for me in Kuzguncuk in 1994, a suburb cramped up hard against the Bosphorus, arguing down the rent with Uncle Mevlüt, the landlord who lived upstairs. Inflation being high, we would take up a wad of notes once a month. He also went with me to the foreigners' section of the police to renew my residence permit every six months, each time a trial for him because Bingöl, a city in the southeast where the PKK was especially active, was printed on his ID card as his place of origin. 'Where are you living in Istanbul?' the officer would bark; 'what does your family do'; 'how do you know the Australian?' Not that Ömer with his long hair and perfect Turkish, learnt at boarding school in Izmir, conformed to their stereotype of the average Kurd. But perhaps they were right to suspect him: once when he heard that back in Bingöl someone had informed on his family he brought over two carpetbags of prohibited books with dangerous titles like *Doğu Anadolu'nun Düzeni: Sosyo-ekonomik ve Etnik Temeller* ('The order of eastern Anatolia: socio-economic and ethnic foundations') and *Şerefname* ('On the history of the Kurdish principalities'). They turned mouldy in my 'sunroom'.

Ömer's parents were not particularly religious, although both came from well-known Kurdish Muslim families. Neither was Ömer, who anyway disliked the Turkish nationalism of the country's mosques, whose clergy are all paid functionaries of the State. By contrast, Hüsnü was pious, and I remember feeling nonplussed when, drinking tea together for the first time in an outdoor café, he suddenly disappeared to do his prayers. For different reasons Hüsnü, too, was critical of the Republic's system of managing Islam, partly in the name of a desire for religious revolution but equally for what he felt was the mocking of the religious mores of Muslims by middle-class and secular Turks in their desire for cultural distinction.

When I first met Hüsnü he was engaged to a fellow student, but there was a hitch in their plans. He insisted that his partner cover her head and Deniz's family, being secular, was upset with their relationship. Deniz herself did not care one way or the other, a blasé disdain for the veil's political symbolism that disturbed her mother. She refused to come to their wedding ceremony because Deniz wore a headscarf. Yet all the way through his master's degree, and even more so as he wrote a PhD in Turkish politics, I noticed Hüsnü changing, distancing himself from the black and white views of the broader Islamic movement even as he became sociologist of his own Muslim identity and politics. By contrast Deniz began to read devotional writings by Sufi masters, developing her spiritual interests and gently teasing Hüsnü for a new lack of attention to his prayers. 'You're becoming like Chris', she'd joke. But it wasn't true: Hüsnü and I would sometimes join her for the evening ceremony at her Sufi lodge, one of the few *tekke* that had not been shut down by the State in the 1920s, for occasions of devotion and whirling. Sitting cross-legged and squashed beside the other men, I would sing the simple, sometimes lovely hymns from the page, rocking back and forth to the music. Hüsnü, however, was easily bored. 'Shall we go', he would murmur when we'd only just begun, and I'd jab him in the ribs to stop his fidgeting. 'I should have been the Muslim', I'd say on our way home.

On the other hand in the mid- to late 1990s, Ömer and I stopped going to Kurdish activities and events, but for entirely different reasons. It had become too dangerous, especially after the simultaneous bombing by State security agents of the offices of the Kurdish paper *Özgür Ülke* ('Free country') in Istanbul and Ankara in late 1994. Whereas the visibility of Muslim actors in Istanbul's public spaces was common, most strikingly of course in the gendered self-presentation of 'covered' women like Deniz, the embodied performance of Kurdish distinction – say in the display of symbols of Kurdish national identity – was heavily and often violently policed by the State. The difference in State response revealed the political bedrock of the republic: threats to the domination of Turkish nationality were taken more seriously than challenges to its pristine secularism. For practical reasons of safety, more of my public fieldwork was then spent attending and participating in events aimed at generating and mobilizing an Islamic identity, from the crowded

Figure 6.1 The anthropologist at work

public rallies of the Refah Party, to workshops and conferences by Muslim intellectuals on a huge range of topics, memorial and solidarity evenings for suffering Muslims in Bosnia and Chechnya (which always made Kurdish Muslims squirm), and events organized by Refah-controlled local councils during the month of Ramadan (mass-public *iftar* meals, competitions in the call-to-prayer (*ezan*) and Qur'an reciting). I also read the 'Islamist' newspapers faithfully, both the more intellectual and liberal *Yeni Şafak* and the hard-line *Akit*, over time interviewing many of their journalists.

Sometimes Hüsnü would come with me to these events, but I had also started going to them with a girl from Kuzguncuk – later I became her husband. Once we went to a rally at Abdi Ipekci Stadium on the other side of the city, planning to meet up at one of the side entrances as the buses provided by the Refah Party shunting us to the venue were segregated according to sex. In the chaos I got lost, was rounded up by a sympathetic official and made to sit in the 'protocol' area, missed my ride home and had to come back on one of the women's buses. In Kuzguncuk I also attended a twice-weekly Qur'an study group organized by local men, some of whom were shopkeepers, others of whom owned their own minibuses ferrying children back and forth to school each day. How compelling it was to read the Qur'an verse by verse with a commentary, under the assumption that it is God's Word: one wanted not to rebuff it but learn from it, discuss life with it, think in its categories. Then it seemed not only true but also to be addressing us.

And there were many pressing problems facing people in Istanbul that the Qur'an was made to address. Making a living was one, in a huge city with too much insecure, badly paid and informal work, high unemployment, and exploitative relations between workers and employers. I met one young man who had taken a loan at high interest to buy a truck from which to sell watermelons. But as a person with few skills, no resources, and no contacts at the council, Erdoğan was having trouble getting a permit to set up a truck stall on a street corner. He also couldn't marry, as marriage meant money for rent, electricity/gas, food, and so on, not to mention for the expense of furnishing a household with new white goods as well as certain expected gifts of gold for his wife. His father was dead and he was supporting his mother. 'Imagine', he said, 'you can't even marry in Turkey'.

Erdoğan thought Turkey's problems were a result of the weakening of religion, traceable back to Atatürk and the policies of the Republic. Şeriat (Islamic law) was seen as the antidote: it would give people their due, both between genders as well as between employer and employee. For him and many others, Islamic politics was a promise of the abolition of class and gender conflict, and the ümmet or Muslim community symbolized an order where rich and poor, men and women, could live peacefully and justly together: to each according to a combination of their need (i.e. poverty) and their nature (i.e. sex).

An equally compelling issue of course was the Kurdish question. For many religious people only the application of Qur'anic principles could solve the problem. Islam instructed ethnic tolerance between Muslims, and allowed everyone to speak their own language. As a verse in the Qur'an says, this is how Allah created ethnic groups: as different. But there was an emerging tension between Turkish and Kurdish Muslims that I came across all the time in my research – for Islamists, Muslim multiculturalism was applicable only in so much as ethnicity was not allowed to become an organizing political principle in competition with Islamic identity. On those grounds they condemned Kurdish nationalism, what they called Kürtçülük. By contrast, for religious Kurds Islam was not felt to cancel ethnic identity but to give them space and permission to be Kurdish within a religious framework. Here Islam was a discourse of liberation not assimilation. 'We want a democratic state in which whatever rights Turks have, Kurds have them too – that is, our own schools, TV, media, books, and magazines', said one of my Kurdish interviewees, leader of a religious group. 'That's what Islam gives'. Kurdish Muslims suspected Islamists of using the rhetoric of Islamic brotherhood and Muslim essence to deny the reality and legitimacy of Kurdish identity and the history of their repression by the republic. They also felt betrayed by Islamist claims that Kürtçülük was fabricated by 'outside forces' intent on fracturing the Muslim community, the very same charge made against 'knowledgeable' Kurds by Turkish nationalists as well.

My fieldwork encompassed a third group of political actors too, seeking not only to comprehend the motivations and historical imagination of Islamic and Kurdish groups but also to give attention to the identity politics of militant secularists. When the leader of the Refah Party became prime minister in a coalition government in 1996, the bitter war of words and symbols between Islamic and secular activists escalated. Not surprisingly, secularists, who were also firm supporters of the State's official ideology of Kemalism (named after Kemal Atatürk) and therefore hard-line Turkish nationalists, were blind to political differences between religious Turks and Kurds. 'Reactionary Muslims are all the same and there are no Kurds in Turkey', was a common sentiment. By chance, in 1997, I was in the small seaside town of Kaş with Ömer, on the official celebration of Republic Day (29 October). Schoolchildren paraded, recited nationalist poetry and songs, and folk-danced in front of their teachers, State officials, and military officers; the whole event orchestrated in the shadow of a large Atatürk statue erected in the town square. The main opposition party hung a huge banner across the street emblazoned with just two words, *Laik Cumhuriyet* (Secular Republic), testimony even then to a disastrous long-term political decision to concentrate their electoral campaigning around the supposed threat of Turkey's Islamization.

Change

They should have read the times. A month earlier Hüsnü had published an article in a Muslim newspaper, entitled 'An Islamist sociologist's conflicted state of mind' (my translation). In it he made a distinction between the certainties and purities of Islamists in the 1980s and of himself (and by extension other Muslims) in the present. When he began to study sociology, Hüsnü relates, he wanted to be an Islamic sociologist. Rather than reconciling Islamism and sociology he sought to Islamize sociological knowledge. But he changed his position, Hüsnü concluded. From making an Islamic sociology he now seeks to write the sociology of Islam. He is not spooked by the word 'modernity.' Pursuing his profession in Istanbul, he encounters so many different people and places that he cannot remain pure. He appreciates people with different ideologies. He loves his irreligious friends and his foreign colleagues. As he says, these affections have transformed him. He has become a new subject, and his Muslim identity has mixed with his modern profession. His comments caused a stir. Hard-line secularists and committed Islamists alike frown upon the compromises and contaminations of their respective cadres: secularists who sought to learn the *ney* (Sufi bamboo flute) were as bad as Muslims who took off the headscarf to go dancing. And yet that's what some people did. Militant intellectuals did not like personal or ethnographic accounts of contradictory practices in inhabitants' lives that fieldwork in a global city such as Istanbul forced the anthropologist to describe. Ömer felt the rightness of the moral cause of the Kurdish nationalist movement keenly, but he too chafed at the ceaseless commitment and responsibility it demanded from its activists. Even *bilinçli* Kurds had to relax, and sometimes late at night we'd flee to a rock-bar for relief from what felt like the neverending nationalist, secularist, or Islamist identity politics constituting so many civic activities. Like Hüsnü,

Ömer was a brilliant participant-observer of urban life, an anthropologist of Istanbul's banal Turkish nationalism who joked about people's prejudices against Kurds even as he managed his family's affairs. To the disappointment of his committed older sister, Ömer discovered scuba diving in those years, and for a number of summers took a job as a dive instructor on Turkey's Aegean coast. She wished that he would be more selfless. But Ömer had an ulterior motive, one that didn't affect her so deeply; given the declaration of martial law in many of the Kurdish provinces, and their occupation by tens of thousands of troops, he was determined never to do his compulsory military service. His intention was to leave Turkey and only ever come back again as a permanent resident or citizen of another nation. He met a couple while teaching diving who agreed to sponsor him to study at university in Germany, and in 1999 another phase of his life began.

I shouldn't give the reader the impression that politics made the city joyless. Unlike some Islamist movements elsewhere, Muslim politics in Istanbul did not disparage the arts. In the article cited above, Hüsnü described one of his habits: far from the Islamist newspaper criticizing leisure in the name of Muslim morality, he went to the plays and films recommended in its culture pages. In Istanbul there was an ongoing cultural politics, forms of art and performance that expressed contending political attachments and projected contesting political positions. Social movements lionized their own beloved writers, poets, and musical genres: Necip Fazıl Kisakürek for Muslims; Nazım Hikmet for Left Kemalists; and Yahya Kemal for Kurds. Each assured their own distinction by denying their resemblances. Istanbul itself facilitated sonic and visual action and was acoustically saturated: its streets afforded parades, chanting, clapping, its squares reverberated percussive sound, and music resounded in the enclosed urban spaces of minibuses, ferries, waiting rooms, and cafés.

There were everyday pleasures to be had in less exalted places and activities too. It was fun to make çiğ köfte (raw meatballs) together at the Qur'an study group, and drink endless cups of tea afterwards as we chatted. Often we played football as a team on the half-size outdoors carpeted arenas. Being pious, they ran out from the changing rooms wearing long, baggy, brightly coloured shorts draped over their knees. The opposition was amazed. 'Thank God I'm a Christian', I said to them. Indeed, practices of fun were an intrinsic aspect of the generation of Muslim cultural distinction in Istanbul, which meant my fieldwork on Islamism's various dimensions was also highly enjoyable. Islamic fashion shows, Muslim boy bands, Islamist cafés facilitated new modes of selective consumption and commercialization. Intellectuals enjoyed vital debates about 'Islam and democracy', conferences on the 'Islam of Ottoman society', and panels on 'Women in Islam'; students flocked to Muslim youth group picnics; young lovers smoked narghile (hookah or water pipe) in restored Ottoman medrese as the city allowed its parts to be recruited by the Muslim utopian imagination; everywhere fellow travellers shared satisfying even pleasurable feelings of outrage, persecution, and resentment at their lot in the world.

Discussion

Hüsnü's thesis on Muslim novels was published in 2007. Through studying Islamist fiction he traced a revolution within Islamism, a transformation that applied to himself as well. In the 1980s and early 1990s Islamists wrote 'salvation novels', fictional stories by religious Muslims that deliberately sought to Islamize the novel. This was not art for art's sake but ideological fiction, novels that sought to prove a thesis through their story. Did Islamist novels stay at the level of ideological fiction? Hüsnü described how in the mid-1990s Islamist novels diversified, reworking their criticisms of Kemalism to include new grounds (such as its lack of proper democracy, not its lack of Islam) and criticizing various aspects of the Islamist movement itself. For Hüsnü, these new novels were characterized by more self-reflexive narratives of Islamic actors, revealing aspects of conflicted, inner selves.

Art imitates life, which imitates art, which imitates life … Fictional accounts of Islamism in Turkey may have been primarily literary conceits but they also mirrored, with endless transformation of detail, newly emerging Muslim subjectivities in the public sphere. True, fiction is not biography, even as it tells the stories of characters whose lives are parasitic upon everyone yet identical to no one. Yet novels express what people feel, and people feel what novels express. And not just Islamists of course – in the fiction of Orhan Pamuk, Turkey's most celebrated writer, the disintegration of the integrity of his secular characters echoes the fracturing of the homogeneous Islamist subject in Muslim fiction.

Movement

In 2006, I came back to Istanbul with my seven-year-old son for a sabbatical. Anxious and confused, I felt like a character from a novel. Hüsnü took me to a tea garden overlooking the Bosphorus. While I was in Australia, Deniz had taken off her headscarf, sick of the assumptions that people made about covered women, including pious Muslims. Her unveiling resembled Nisa, a female character in one of the Islamist novels who made the same decision, frustrated by Muslim pressure on veiled women to act as the storm troopers of the Islamist movement. Nisa tries to make her angry husband understand that her identity as a believer was firm, that she still felt 'veiled'. By contrast, Hüsnü was supportive of Deniz's decision, a far cry from his pressure on her all those years ago to don the headscarf.

That sabbatical I visited Ömer in Germany, who with his typical quickness and skill had learnt German, married a local belle, and set up his own business. While diving Ömer had taken up underwater filming, and in Cologne he was now a well-known wedding and portrait photographer. As a Kurd in Turkish society, Ömer had developed an acute ability to observe, flow with, and even gently direct the currents of social exchange. I watched as he put the wedding party at ease, touched the elbows of the bride and groom while moving them into position, took more standard photos for their family – standards different amongst Turks, Indians, and Germans, his main customers – and more playful ones for the couple: got the groomsmen to jump in the air, distributed bridesmaids around a garden feature, shot the lovers from below or above, made them gaze past each other. 'At 2:00 p.m. you have the possibility to shoot the couple', he explained. 'You have an hour. You analyse the light, you analyse the situation, you have to be quick, you decide on a type, you decide on a style, on how you want to take the photos that day. It depends on the location, on the time, on the religiousness of the couple.' 'My big fat Turkish weddings', he said.

Back in Istanbul I began a new research project, an exploration of urban politics in Istanbul in the 'crisis' years 1977–83, the period fractured by a brutal military coup on 12th September 1980 that continued on for nearly three years in the form of martial law.

For many analysts, the 1980 *coup d'état* and its instituting of the third Turkish republic ushered in a new era in Turkish politics, a period dominated by an ongoing struggle between Muslims and secularists, between pro-Kurdish movements and a bloody-minded State, in the context of a newly liberalized, consumer-oriented and globalizing economy. This was the context of my first fieldwork (1994–7). Even as that research facilitated some comprehension of Kemalism, political Islam and the Kurdish movement in those post-coup decades, my historical knowledge of Istanbul's *longue durée*, of what was new and of what was enduring, was weak. I wanted perspective, to fill in the gaps in my education, to make better links between Istanbul in the late 1970s, the mid-1990s, and in the present. And yet, how to do fieldwork on a place that apparently no longer exists, made invisible in the decades since by breathless discourse about the transmogrification of Istanbul into a 'global city' as much as by real change?

I learnt of the sketch of a body drawn in ink etched on the courtyard flagstones of Fatih Camii, one of the monumental Ottoman mosques dotting the historic city's skyline. During my first fieldwork in 1996 I had become friends with a brilliant Kurdish scholar, a historian of Kurdish Islam and, like Hüsnü, a regular contributor to Muslim publications. During the sabbatical he told me that his older brother, a well-known activist in an Islamist youth group, had been murdered in 1979, shot dead in a notorious attack by Turkish nationalists while leaving Fatih Camii after doing his prayers. Metin Yüksel has no State-sanctioned memorial or official 'site of memory' (*lieux de mémoire*) but he has not been forgotten: the outline of his slain body painted on the 400-year-old paving stones by his friends marks his martyrdom, and there on the anniversary of his death each year they do commemorative prayers. You, too, now know his name.

This project on activists' relations with, perceptions of, and experiences in the pre-coup city, an urban version of the anthropology of the senses, entailed a different sort of research. Alongside a trawling of 'archives' – the journals, often short-lived, of the different political factions, and the daily newspapers – the major fieldwork tool was intensive interviews with ex-activists, hours-long sessions complemented by follow-up conversations on other days. Because I had no opportunity to participate in activists' activities, the research began to focus on inhabitants' memories of the city, of acts of occupation or appropriation of space, of sit-ins and strikes, and of conflict and violence. What relationship between the apartheid character of Istanbul, divided up and controlled by different political factions, and the distributed memory of their members? And what of the interview process itself: in asking activists to recall the sounds, appearances, and textures of a politically chaotic Istanbul, how did it facilitate their re-imagining of perception, providing an opportunity to re-order memories in the present? I noticed that even as activists recounted 'raw' experience, present interests and intentions led to the foregrounding of certain memories of the city and the relegating of others to the edges of consciousness. Pre-coup Istanbul has not disappeared: the co-makers of its great urban chaos, aided by the city itself, continue to create the meaning of their present through a reflective and emotional engagement with their historical activism.

Graceful habits

I still go to Istanbul when I can, a few weeks of research here and there in the semester break, a flying visit to a conference, a trip to visit the in-laws. I take my sons too, so they can know two cities and their myriad histories, experience two religions (or none), practice *lütuf* with their friends and relatives in both places and become, like Ömer, connoisseurs of action and talk in each.

Whenever I'm in Istanbul I go to the Cumhuriyet Meyhane every Friday evening. It's a noisy tavern, photographs of old film stars on the walls, the same waiters there from year to year, with smoke from cigarettes and grill wafting over the meze plates and fruit platters. Regulars leave half-finished bottles for the waiters to store for the next visit. Hüsnü meets there each week with his four oldest friends from high school, once all very pious but now middle-aged and my confidantes as well. We drink *rakı* mixed with water and ice and get loquacious not drunk: Hüsnü and I, know-alls about political Islam; two psychiatrists treating depressives with Sufi music therapy and electric shocks; a writer of mathematics textbooks bitter from a custody dispute with his ex-wife but popular now with covered girls who appreciate his radical mathematical method; and a schoolteacher, religious enough to refrain from alcohol still, sipping coke. 'What type of Muslims are you?' says Hüsnü, proposing a toast. Like the teacher, I don't drink much, unconvinced by *rakı*. 'In Istanbul's psychiatric wards no one thinks they're Muhammad', said one of the doctors, 'but there are many Isa (Jesus)'. We talk on and on, and at the end of the night and after all these years they still don't let me pay.

Fieldwork is this and more, and ethnography its artful recounting. Anthropology as a discipline treads this fine line: it orients itself to empirical reality even as it cannibalizes social and philosophical theory to conceive and communicate its full dimensions. Many of the remarkable things it records evaporate, forgotten in the flux of living by both anthropologist and locals, revivified briefly, perhaps, if stumbled upon in a jotted-down field note. Sometimes unimportant things are remembered and endured, switch-points of conviction or meaning that index development in a life or its change of direction: Deniz's veiling and unveiling is like that, or Hüsnü's imbibing of *rakı*. Although Islam may not change, Muslim activists – and their interlocutors – do: in our convictions and our practices; our bodies and our memories; our friendships and the quality of our relationships; in our perceptions and knowledge of the built environment as it transforms before our eyes; and through our experiences of subordination, domination, or empowerment. If there is a secret to the passion of our lives together, it lies in our exchange, not just of grace but of our needs as well.

Readings

For most of its history Istanbul has been a world city, and as such the subject of an innumerable amount of writing testifying to its superlative nature. Shelves in the Greater Istanbul Council bookshop in Beyoğlu groan under the weight of a hundred Istanbul titles, from local histories of each of the city's older suburbs to examination of its representation in 1001 novels, songs, films, and poems. Almost every edition of Middle Eastern studies journals includes new material on the social history, sexual practices, religion, labour relations, architecture, consumption habits, sartorial dress, and so on, of Istanbul in any one of its many manifestations. As well as the material listed above, for readers of English interested in the way Muslims live out an Islamist commitment in Istanbul, Jenny White's *Islamist Mobilization in Turkey: A Study in Vernacular Mobilization* (Seattle: University of Washington Press, 2002) is a good place to start; a more theoretical but shorter analysis is Nulifer Göle's article, 'Islam in public: new visibilities and new imaginaries' (*Public Culture* 14, no. 1 (2002): 173–90). For a discussion of the Kurdish question in the context of Turkish, Arab, and Persian nationalism, see my *Kurdistan: Crafting of National Selves* (Bloomington: Indiana University Press, 2008).

Author

Christopher Houston is head of the Department of Anthropology at Macquarie University, Sydney, Australia. He is currently researching the recent history of Istanbul, focusing specifically on the years 1977–83 (the period before and after the 1980 military coup) and the spatial politics of leftist and rightist activists in those years. He has published his work in a number of journals, including *Thesis Eleven, Political Geography, Critique of Anthropology, Theory, Culture & Society,* and *JRAI.*

Chapter 7

Study of Shi'a Muslim women in Southern California

Bridget Blomfield

Preamble

While in graduate school, I decided to study Arabic. A few miles from my house was a mosque and, on the other side of the street, a school for Muslim children. For whatever reason, I turned left into the school and inquired about taking classes in Arabic. At the age of 50 I started to attend the school and was placed in a fifth grade class. Most of the children attending the school were from Iraq, Iran, and Pakistan. Of course I was quite the oddity and the children, especially the girls, hovered around me asking me if I had converted to Islam. They offered to teach me to wash before I pray, taught me the prayers offered throughout the day, and instructed me on etiquette in their cultures. At the time, I would never have imagined that I would spend years researching this community for my PhD dissertation. I would become a scholar of Shi'ism and professor specializing in Islamic studies.

Narrative

Although the school stated that it was open to all Muslims only Shi'a attended. Shi'a are to Islam what Catholics are to Christianity. They observe specific rituals that are not shared by all Muslims. Many of the rituals are culturally specific. I was asked to tutor children in exchange for my lessons. I had only been teaching at the City of Knowledge School for a few weeks when Muharram started. Muharram, the month-long ritual observance Shi'a Muslims practice, commemorates the martyrdom of the Prophet Muhammad's family.

As I entered the school, I was greeted by the principal who agreed to allow me to study Arabic. When I asked her if I needed to cover my hair she said no but that it would be nice if I did. I didn't own a single scarf so went across the street to a shop that sold hair products for African Americans. I purchased a tiny satin scarf and wrapped it around my head, tying it in a small knot under my chin. The woman working at the store giggled and told me that this type of scarf was tied on top of the head and was used to sleep in, so that one's hair would stay smooth. I had already put it on so I shrugged my shoulders and said, 'it will have to do'. I went back across the street and entered my first Arabic class. Of course, I looked ridiculous and by the next day was given a dozen scarves and directions to an Arab clothing store where I could purchase a long dress called an abaya to wear with my scarves.

Soon after I started attending the classes I was invited to participate in the afterschool rituals. I was told to wear black and was given a chador to wear over my abaya. A chador is the billowing black, tent-like cover seen so often in Iran and Iraq. Finally, I had the appropriate clothing. The school, a converted bowling alley, was located in Southern California. On the outside it was stark and plain with the exception of large black flags hung as a reminder of the suffering of the Prophet's family. Inside the prayer room the floor was covered with carpets. The walls were wrapped with black fabric, some of which had sayings written in Arabic. To my surprise, I sounded out the Arabic letters 'Ya Husayn'! I was so excited, I told the girls, 'This is the first thing that I have ever read in Arabic!' This was seen as a very positive omen and from that moment on I was called Sister Bridget. I was told that Husayn was one of the great imams the martyred grandson of the Prophet Muhammad.

The first day that I attended these lamenting rituals President Bush bombed Iraq. This only added to the anguish of the participants. They wept for the holy family of the Prophet and also lamented for their own families oppressed by Saddam Hussein. Now their relatives were dying in the crossfire of American intervention. The women sat and wept, sobbing and beating their chests. Of course, I wept too. It was impossible sitting in a room of 200 wailing women not to cry. There were mothers and grandmothers, sisters and cousins, all who still had relatives in Iraq. What was their fate? Would they be martyrs too? I was told to try to cry and if I did, I would receive *thawab*, merit, in heaven. It was easy to cry just hearing them cry. I felt a tremendous sadness for all those who have suffered and are still suffering.

Most women used Kleenex to wipe their eyes but I watched a few women wipe their tears away with small cotton handkerchiefs, then put them into a plastic baggie and into their purses. I was told that these handkerchiefs would be saved for years, collecting tears. Upon death, the hankies would be buried with the women proving to Fatima, the Prophet's only surviving child, that the tears were wept on her behalf. One of the women told me that Fatima has a scroll seven yards long, and on it are all the names of the pious believers. Fatima will stand at the gates of heaven, and if you have been a believer your forehead will be stamped 'believer'. If you are not a lover of Fatima, you will be stamped 'sinner', but no matter how many mistakes you have made in life if you have loved Fatima and her family, she will stamp your forehead with 'lover' and intercede on your behalf, asking God to allow you into heaven.

Muharram lasts for one month but the rituals peak on Ashura, the tenth day of Muharram. Each day holds a specific meaning and purpose, and is dedicated to a martyr. On this day of Ashura I would experience the intensity of sorrow as the practitioners lamented the death of Imam Husayn, the Prophet's grandson. That first day I was there the ten-year-old girls sat by my side translating and explaining every thing to me. What is it called I asked. 'It is azadari', she replied, 'I guess in English it means sorrow. Please stay with us for the ritual. Even if you cry one tear for Lady Fatima she will love you.'

'Come, sit', my friend called out to me. She motioned for me to sit next to her and that she would explain everything to me. As the room filled women started the ceremony by taking turns reciting and chanting the poetry of lament in Arabic. After a few bars of the lament the women started to beat their chests with either a closed fist or opened hand. They pounded with one or both hands, or alternated with the right hand hitting the left upper chest or vice versa. As the participants become immersed in the grieving process they formed a circle and began, in unison, the rhythmic ritual movements, stepping in unison, bending back, and then thrusting their heads toward the center of the circle. In unison they beat their chests, slapped their cheeks and foreheads, all the while chanting and crying out 'Ya Husayn!' (Oh Husayn), chanting in unison.

Their bodies bent back and forth and they thrust their heads down, then back, their hair flailing dramatically. Sometimes one woman entered into the center of the circle to encourage the others to participate more fully. She made eye contact with one woman at a time, as she intensifies her movements as encouragement. At this point the energy in the room felt intense yet some women remain seated, rocking back and forth while they watched, gently slapping their thighs or chests. It is as if there were two different movements in a piece of music – one maintaining the rhythm and the other improvising the melody. This intimacy shifted the energy of the women and they started to weep.

The elegy stopped and the women sat down and pulled the upper folds of their black chadors over their heads and held white Kleenex over their faces while they cried.

After ten or fifteen minutes of crying, it was over. Women got up and attended to their children, who wandered around playing, seemingly unaffected by the sobs of their mothers. Tea and sweets were served and women spoke softly to each other. Then the process started all over. The woman next to me looked a hundred years old. Draped in black, only her face was visible and it was covered in wrinkles and tiny tattoos on her chin and under her eyes. I wondered if she had lost a husband, children, grandchildren. I imagined the sorrow of living for decades of oppression and war.

Suddenly I felt a wave of energy in the room and started to cry. It felt like the suffering of humanity was in this room, here in California, and was the microcosm of human suffering globally. As I sat and cried I felt a hand take mine and pull me up off the floor. The woman holding my hand led me to the circle of women. I started to move, copying their gestures in a rhythmic step, slapping my cheeks and bending back and forth, throwing my hair down and up as they did. I wasn't crying anymore but was uttering 'Ya Husayn' like they did. I felt as if my personality was gone and I had entered into a sea of movement that was spiritually sustaining. My heart felt radiant and full of love and I felt an incredible peace. I sat back down and pulled my black chador over my head and cried but these tears were of a different nature. I actually had no idea why I was crying. After all, I wasn't Shi'a and didn't cry for the martyrdom of the Prophet's family anymore than the martyrdom of Jesus. My tears, however, felt good, really good. I felt tremendous gratitude to be alive and to cry. I felt cleansed and purified. The entire evening was therapeutic.

A few days later I was invited to a house for a gathering. These gatherings started around 9:00 a.m. then occurred every two hours or so until 3:00 p.m. when we went to the school for the afternoon rituals. We would stay at school late and then sometimes go to a special prayer hall called a Zaynabiyah or Husayniyah in honor of Zaynab, the Prophet's granddaughter and daughter of Fatima. The Husayniyah was dedicated to Fatima's son, Imam Husayn. On these nights we would easily stay out until 1:00 a.m.

Today we started at the home of a Pakistani woman. Like others, she had a formal dining room where we sat and were offered tea and samosas. There were plates of sweets and fruit on the table as well. After a short visit we entered a room that was painted soft beige. On one wall was an altar or *imambara* as the Pakistanis call it. There were beautiful embroidered velvet banners covered in gold embroidery. I could read the names Fatima, Ali, and Husayn written in Arabic and embroidered in gold. Tiny jewels and sequins dotted the velvet and each banner was trimmed in gold braid. Next to them were *alams*, tall staffs draped with flags and adorned with garlands of flowers or prayer beads. The carpeted floor was covered in white sheets that were tightly stretched across the floor. On the wall was a miniature version of what is found in the larger centers. The long shallow closet at the end of the room was painted black. Tiny holes had been drilled into the wood and light poured through them as if they were little twinkling stars. There was a tiny silver replica of a baby's coffin. This, I was told, was to represent the death of a tiny baby who died in his father's arms. After we finished crying we went to the living room and were served refreshments, an important custom.

During Muharram, after every ritual, food is served and I gained weight. Today, in the Pakistani home, a mixture of milk, ground pistachios, almonds, and *rooh afza* was offered. This special drink is served in memory of the babies that suffered without milk when their mothers were murdered or taken to prison. At every occasion there are nuts and dried fruits as part of the offering.

After we had a gathering at her house we all piled into our cars and headed to the prayer hall attended mostly by Pakistanis. Tonight everyone wore black. They had not lined their eyes with kohl or covered their lips in red lipstick. 'We don't wear make-up or perfume during Muharram', I was told, 'and we are supposed to be sad because the holy family has been martyred. After all, when you are depressed are you feeling like getting all dressed-up? No, you just feel sad and you look plain.'

Pakistanis differ from the Iraqi and Iranian communities. They have altars in their homes and their rituals are important for different reasons than other

Shi'a. My friend explained to me that in Iran and Iraq Shi'a could visit their sacred sites whenever they chose but because none of the imams are buried in Pakistan they build special shrines in their homes. 'In some ways', she said, 'our ziyarrat [pilgrimage] is done through imitation and action and has a very symbolic meaning.' She went on to explain to me that their pilgrimages were 'an affair of the heart. We must imagine that we are there with them, that they are close to us because in reality whether we are in the US or back in Pakistan it is difficult to make these journeys to the holy cities like Karbala. We must have our journey through symbols. That is why we act out the processions here in the center.' That night I witnessed women walking around the room carrying large *alams* and leading a procession inside the building. Some young women carried in a mock coffin covered by a black cloth. They set it on the floor and women took turns walking over to it touching their foreheads to the cloth that covered the mock coffin.

Months later I was invited to one of the Pakistani centers to speak about Bibi Fatima, the Prophet's daughter. I dressed in what I thought would be the appropriate color, black. When I arrived I entered a room where there were dozens of women and children dressed in beautiful, colorful shalwar kameez. In contrast to the somber occasions where the women wore black and no jewelry, this event offered the opposite. The outfits were covered in elaborate embroidery on the finest silks in every color imaginable. Each outfit was beaded with tiny jewels, sequins, and pearls. Dozens of gold and jeweled bangle bracelets wrapped around their wrists and necklaces embedded with diamonds, rubies, and emeralds dangled from their necks. Some women had huge dangling earrings to match and some even had matching hair ornaments draped across their foreheads. Of course, I looked ridiculous and out of place in my shabby black abaya.

The next day I was invited to the Iraqi imam's house. When I arrived, I was surprised to see a modest home in a lower middle-class neighborhood. There were dozens of cars parked everywhere. I entered the house and, after removing my shoes, was greeted by dozens of women. The living room was completely emptied of furniture. Sheets were spread across the floor and women sat against the walls. After a fairly short gathering reciting the laments, shedding tears, and offering salutations, we sat down to eat. As usual, the food was delicious. The hostess told me that much had been cooked the day before but that she had been up since four in the morning. 'We say prayers over the food', she said. Her friend giggled and added, 'these are superstitions but they really do work. When we cook, we ask Allah to answer our prayers and then of course we pray in thanks, when our prayers have been answered.'

I excused myself and wandered into the kitchen. I was approached by a young woman who asked me if I was the teacher writing the book. I said yes and she grabbed my arm. 'Sister, you must help me. I can't get a job because I wear the headscarf. Please take me on the Oprah show to tell my story.' I explained that I didn't have connections to the popular Oprah Winfrey television show. The woman told me that she had been a hairdresser in Iraq for years. When she moved to the United States no one would hire her because she covered her hair. 'In Iraq, we have ladies only shops, but here in the United States men and women are in the same room working together. In Iraq, when I was at work I didn't need to cover my hair at the salon but here in the United States men and women are in the same room working together.' Can you help me she begged? Can you go on Oprah and tell my story? This was a familiar conversation. The Shi'a women often told me that they felt misunderstood by everyone including other Muslims. They were happy to have a non-Muslim represent them. 'After all', one woman told me, 'everyone will listen to you because you are an American and a teacher with very white skin.'

I had a favorite teacher at the school who was Iranian. She was very pious, very intelligent, and very affectionate. This woman held a master's degree in biology and taught many of the science classes at the school. She was also in charge of teaching ethics to the high school students. I loved to listen to her lectures because they were truths from the heart, not canned, memorized lectures offered as a warning to those who sinned and would be sent to hell. She had a great sense of humor and taught from the perspective that as Muslims, students should be good for 'goodness sake'. After all, what would make Allah more satisfied than a truly good human being following the ways of the Prophet himself?

During one such class she told a story of two women at Friday prayers. One woman was young and beautiful, a recent convert to Islam. The other one was old and pious. Born and raised a Muslim, she knew the teachings of Islam perfectly. The young woman, prayed piously and sincerely, from the depths of her heart asking Allah to hear her prayers and accept them in his grace. As she bent over in prayer her feet peaked out from under her abaya revealing bright red toenail polish! The old woman, seeing this took great offense and chastised the girl telling her that wearing toenail polish in the house of God was a terrible sin and that her prayers would not be heard! There I sat, with my own bright red toenail polish on my toes. I curled them under my abaya feeling like the wicked witch in the *Wizard of Oz*. The teacher asked the students, who is the better Muslim, which woman? She went on to explain that one's *niyyat*, or intention, is what is most important. A greater sin is to judge another person and act arrogantly like the old woman did.

I immediately went to her after class and apologized for the times that I had worn nail polish during prayers. I was truly ashamed and never meant to be disrespectful. She laughed and said, 'Oh sister, you are just learning our ways but now you know better.' From that day on, I always wore black socks. Years later, I would make my own pilgrimage to Iran and be turned away from Imam Reza's tomb because I had toenail polish on. Fortunately, my friend pulled off her black socks gave them to me and we were allowed to enter.

Another night I was invited by some Iraqi women to attend a gathering, or *majlis*, as they called them. It broke my heart to hear these women talk about their families still in Iraq. The suffering that they had been through, the guilt they experienced leaving relatives behind so that they could move to the United States for a better life. Here I sat in a room with 150 other women from the ages of newborns to old grandmothers that looked 100 years old. Some had tattoos on their faces and they were as wrinkled as old apple dolls. This communal grieving was different than anything that I had ever seen. As an American when I grieved, I did so alone. Curled up in bed, wrapped in a flannel nightgown, I could sob over my personal sorrows. Or, I could pay a therapist to help me process my guilt, shame, or grief. Here, there was a collective grieving process that was inviting. It allowed us to participate and lament the death of the family of the Prophet Muhammad but also gave space to the acknowledgment of personal suffering. Such suffering made me feel deeply connected to this community and for that matter all of humanity. I felt what it is to be human, to suffer, and to experience joy and how that was experienced and shared by every human being. In this environment, such human suffering was given voice and space. It was acknowledged and honored. It made sense to me that Shi'a lamented the injustice in the world and I realized that we should cry. Every time we witness something sorrowful we should weep and acknowledge the human condition. As Americans we become numb to sorrow because we see suffering daily in the news. All we need to do is turn the channel of our television to another station to avoid it. Most of us do not experience loss on a level like the Iraqis and Iranians have. It made me feel that my own suffering was silly and self-indulgent and I cried really hard that night. I cried for all the suffering in the world.

Finally, at one in the morning, everyone was exhausted from the crying and there was a deliberate quiet in the room as we pulled our scarves over our heads and bundled up small children who had long been asleep. There were hugs and kisses goodnight as everyone departed. I drove home passing Denny's restaurant and 7–Eleven stores, their neon lights blinking invitations to have one last snack. I continued home feeling bewildered at what I was experiencing. Here in Southern California, only a few miles from Hollywood and Beverly Hills, I was participating in an ancient religious ritual with women from countries I had never visited. It felt surreal to me. I had grown to love them and their expression of sorrow. I would grow to love their music, food, and customs even though I knew I would never be as religious as they were.

One afternoon I attended a *majlis* at the home of a wealthy woman. As I arrived I saw many Mercedes, Jaguar, and Lexus cars as well as minivans. The neighborhood was full of million-dollar homes. The chairs were put up against the walls creating a huge circle with the center of the room wide open. Older women sat in chairs and on couches while the younger ones sat crossed-legged on the floor. As usual, everyone was wearing black. The hostess took my arm and walked me around the circle as she spoke Arabic to the women. I assumed that she was introducing me as was commonly done. 'This is the professor that is writing the book about us.' Or, 'This is Sister Bridget who works at our school and is studying our religion.' This time, however, when she spoke, instead of nods and smiles, kisses on both cheeks, the women burst into tears. A few jumped up and hugged me saying Mashallah!

I asked her what she had told them. She explained to me that she had told them that I had been diagnosed with skin cancer and that some of the women had rubbed some sacred soil from Karbala on my cheeks, praying that I would be healed. It was true, I had been treated with a medication to remove skin cancer. I had a terrible reaction to the medication and my skin bubbled up and looked like an oozing cheese pizza. I was in incredible pain. Wherever I went no one said much. In polite American society we pretend not to notice, yet in this community they all asked me what had happened. They held my hands, got tears in their eyes, and exclaimed, 'you were so beautiful, this is terrible, I know a doctor for you to see. Don't worry, we will pray for you.' One of the women came to me and offered to rub the sacred soil on my face telling me not to worry that it was pure and clean and had no pee-pee in it. This dirt came from Karbala the place where Imam Ali was martyred so it was pure and sacred. They stood around me uttering prayers as she sprinkled the dirt from a small glass bottle on to her palm and dabbed it on my horribly infected skin. I expressed gratitude but inside I was cringing. My dermatologist is going to be furious, I thought to myself. Now, a year later my skin was healed. The acidic medication had not only burned away the cancer but gave my overall skin quality a vibrant glow. Who was I to argue with dozens of women as they had proof of the miracles possible through prayer and the holy soil of Karbala? Only my dermatologist was skeptical.

Once Muharram was over we could stop mourning and get back to daily activities. I was invited to attend the day that a nine-year-old girl received her scarf. I had known this family for a long time. He was Iranian and she an American. They had been married since she was seventeen and had three daughters. Now, nearly forty years old, the mother devoted all of her time to the girls. I met them at the school and we became close friends. The mother and two older daughters wore hijab but they had discouraged the little one from wearing it. Little Nadia wanted to wear one so that she could be like the other girls in her family but because she was an ice skater her parents insisted that she wait. Commonly, girls start to cover at the age of nine but she was already eleven. She asked her parents to let her cover saying that she was ready to make the commitment. Her parents told her that she could still ice skate but that they doubted that the team would let her compete. After all, she couldn't wear a frilly costume with a scarf on her head.

I was invited to attend the hijab ceremony and after party. It was held at an old church that had recently been purchased by the Iranian community. It would later be transformed into a beautiful *masjid* covered wall to wall with Persian carpets but for now it was a church with pews still in place. The invitation was similar to a wedding invitation. This time, I knew I didn't have to wear black so I bought a peach colored abaya and matching scarf. As I entered the church I was given a small gift and ushered into the hall. There were well over a hundred guests – women only, of course. People sat and visited until the mother of the new hijabi walked up to the front of the church. There was no altar in place, only a large chair where the imam sits and gives the Friday *hutbah* (sermon) after the community prayers.

My friend announced that the ceremony would start but to please be mindful not to video or photograph women who did not have their hair covered. At women-only functions many women remove their veils as they enter, others do not. At any rate, it would be inappropriate to take photos. I could hear movement in the back of the church and whispers of Mashallah! I turned to see 20 little girls walking down the aisle. They all wore floor-length satin dresses in white, ivory, or pale pink. Each girl had a crown of flowers on her head and carried candles. One young girl led the group as she sprinkled flower petals across the floor. Nadia was the last one entering, wearing a floor-length satin dress and matching veil. With an enormous smile on her face, she walked to the chair that was now draped in satin. She regally perched herself on the chair and looked out at her guests as if she were a royal princess of some sort. All the mothers were crying and I, too, had tears in my eyes. This reminded me so much of my first Catholic communion and of Christian weddings. One by one, female family members and friends stood up and spoke lovingly about Nadia and her commitment to Islam. Her sister recited a poem she had written for the occasion and her mother hugged and kissed her. When the event was finished we left the church and moved to a large dining hall in the next room. There were tables set for all of us. The men had prepared a feast and they passed it through doors so that they would not disturb our privacy.

One afternoon when I was at the school I was approached by a woman who asked me if I would be willing to wash the body of an Iranian woman. The woman had died the day before and had no daughters to wash her. She explained that it was difficult to find people in the community to participate. I told her that I would be honored to help with the washing. I met the other women at a Christian funeral home. The woman was well into her eighties and had very fair skin. Her body was brought out and very cold to the touch as she had been kept in a cold room. Dressed in special garments we worked in silence while one woman read the Qur'an out loud. I followed the women as they unwrapped the corpse. They were gentle and caring and whispered to each other. 'We will wash her three times, just copy what we do and pray.' I was told. The first washing was with soap and water. We washed her entire body and her hair with a bar of soap. The table she was on had a slight angle so that the water could run down. Her skin was pinkish white and she had a long scar across her chest. Clearly she had had some kind of surgery. Did she have a lung replaced? Did she have tuberculosis? I knew that she only had two sons. What was her life like? Had she been religious or was she one of the many secularized Shi'a Iranians in Southern California?

I thought about my own mother's death. Would I be allowed to wash her or would she end up in some antiseptic environment touched and prepared by strangers. I could feel tears welling up in my eyes. I had never really thought about my own mother's death. Now I thought to myself, this is a wonderful way for closure. I imagined that I could weep as I washed her body and how intimate and real it would be. How I could lament the times I had been unkind and critical of her. I fantasized saying good-bye to her and how much I would miss her. All her small faults that irritated me seemed so silly and tri-vial. I sat down, crossed my legs and cradled my head between my arms and started to cry. My friend came to me and touched the top of my head. 'Is it too much for you, sister?' 'No', I replied with a slight smile, 'I am just thinking of my own mother and how much I love her. I hope that someday I will have this honor with her.' We wrapped the woman in muslin, fashioning a scarf to wrap around her head. When we finished we all went home to shower before attending the funeral.

The next day was the funeral. I drove past archangels and giant flower arrangements as I entered the cemetery. As I drove around the corner my Muslim friends couldn't be missed. The Iranians were dressed in long black chadors that billowed in the wind. I could see some of them crying. The Muslim cemetery had no angels or statues, no poetry or flower arrangements. There were just plain markers on the ground. Because I was writing a book about the community I was allowed special privileges that most women in the community were not. I was escorted to the grave, dragging my black chador in the dirt trying to keep from stumbling. I watched as the men carried the woman a few feet and set her on the ground. This was repeated three times. 'Why do they do that?' I whispered. My friend said, 'Oh sister, we do not want her to feel that we are rushing her to the grave so we stop and let her rest for a moment.' The dead woman was placed in the ground, in no casket, by her sons. From dust to dust, I assumed. Her head was set on a pillow mounded from dirt facing Mecca. Prayers were offered and tears were wept. My favorite prayer was uttered, 'inna Lillahi wa inna ilaihi raji'un' (we belong to God and to him we shall return).

A week after the funeral I was invited to a baby shower. 'Please come', my friend insisted, 'There will be lots of food and dancing.' I had attended female-only dance parties and celebrations before weddings and I knew that they were really fun! Women came dressed in evening gowns covered in sequins and heavy gold jewelry. Even though it was a baby shower, by Wes-tern standards, it would look more like a female-only cocktail party. 'What will I wear?' I asked. 'Don't worry', my friend answered, 'I will find some-thing covered in sequins for you to wear so that you don't look so drab.' It had never occurred to me that publicly they were always shrouded in black or dark colors but in private their clothing was sexy and beautiful. In the private world, inside their homes, they dressed in all kinds of colorful clothing. I was the one that looked drab in my T-shirts, capris, and flip-flops.

I would end up spending six years in this community of believers, meeting more Shi'a after I moved to Nebraska and finally making my own pilgrimage to Iran. As a professor of Islamic studies, I would defend Shi'ism to my Sunni students, many who were from Saudi Arabia and were prejudiced against the Shi'a. I watched as my Shi'a students sat quietly in class, afraid to defend their beliefs. On more than one occasion Saudi Shi'a students came to my office with tears in their eyes, 'You are the only teacher that has ever taught about our religion. In Saudi Arabia we are ignored or tormented. Are you Shi'a?' I explained that in the United States academic system we are required to teach about all the different versions of Islam. For scholars, there is not one true Islam but many ways to interpret and live the religion. As a professor, I couldn't offer a class on Christianity and only teach about Catholicism. I had to give lessons on the many different kinds of Christianity in the world. The same was true of Islam. I explained that my interest in Islam was from a Sufi perspective, the mystical dimension of Islam, yet another way of interpreting the teachings of the Prophet Muhammad. As I studied through the years, I read over a hundred books about Shi'ism but my real lessons came from the women I researched. Now I can say yes, I am Shi'a in my heart. As I witnessed their joys and sorrows as well as my own, I became more fully human. Like them, I will stand forever against oppression and be an activist for justice. This is what the Shi'a women taught me.

Discussion

Witnessing the sacred and ordinary aspects of the women's lives, I was able to obtain a rich insight into their lives and religious experiences. As part of this study, I examined the religious rituals of these women, their spiritual role models, how they engaged feminism, and how their religion established agency and authority in their lives. I attempted to dismantle Western stereotypes of these women as passive victims in a patriarchal Islam. With them, I explored their daily lives and how they created sacred space in the United States. By using ethnographic research techniques I was able to give insight into the women's lives through their own voices and to show the diversity of these voices. Through personal interviews and my own observations an entirely different perspective from the typical stereotypes portrayed by American media became apparent.

I used feminist ethnographic research methods with the aim of putting each woman at the center of her own experience. It was therefore easy for me to tell my own story and see the academic and non-academic validity to my research. Ethnographic methods allowed me to let the women tell their stories in their own words, attaching meaning to each experience. Because of the intimate relations we shared through the years I was able to become friends with the women I interviewed and, visiting them years later, I was invited to stay in their homes.

Feminist researchers influenced my methodology. They helped me to critically question what, why, and how I was studying the women and how my presence affected the women in the group. Their research helped me to place my own work academically and intellectually, using critical thinking to balance my overflowing heart. I kept announcing that my methodology was love but as time went by I was able to see that my motivation was love and my methodology had to faithfully represent 'women's worlds'. The use of multiple voices showed the diversity of each individual woman even if she was a part of a cohesive community that tried to gender and define her. For this reason, Shi'a women must speak for themselves. The addition of my own voice had taken me away from the academic, supposedly unbiased researcher to a person who really cared and maintained a long-term relationship with the group.

In the case of the Shi'a women I studied, they created their own rituals placing them as knowers of their own, separate experience. The Shi'a women in the study had their own venues of creating, implementing, and analyzing their rituals and the experiences that manifested from such ritual enactments. They therefore stood as agents of their own identity. They authored their own 'truths', with rituals done by women, for women, and were agents of their own religious knowledge.

I argue that these Shi'a Muslim women's experiences define their religious experience, giving them personal agency and religious authority. As a result of that authority, they dominate certain institutions like family and school, directing themselves religiously through Qur'anic studies and women's gatherings. Their religion flows throughout every aspect of their lives.

It took years to build trust in the community. I tried to gather information that was gained through explicit recording and analysis of such information for the purpose of social science research. Participant observation used interviewing formally and informally to collect data. Through participant observation, I became a part of the group I studied because I participated in the rituals with the women. This acceptance did not happen immediately. The women that I studied needed time to know and trust me before personal interviews were granted. The longer I participated in the community, the more invitations I received and the more intimate and expressive the interviews became. By participating in the context for long periods of time, participating in numerous activities with the group, using everyday conversation as an interviewing technique, and observing leisure activities, I was able to collect data.

Allowing for non-verbal communication shaped our interactions and especially shaped our interpretation of the situation. As a student in the Arabic class I had one experience but four years later as I sat weeping and beating my chest at a funeral, I experienced another dimension of intimacy. When my Arabic teacher taught us to sing in class one day, giggling and winking at me, I experienced a lovely happy teacher. As time went by, and she told me about her breast cancer and her fears of dying and leaving her two small children without a mother, I began to know a completely different person. This person, as we sat face-to-face with tears rolling down our cheeks, was no longer an 'interviewee' but someone I loved dearly. We had shared too many special times to reduce her to a statistic or piece of data. I was not just doing research; I was actively participating in the community of women, we were participating in each other's lives.

From this research I was able to analyze material and develop a thesis and theory from a perspective that would never have happened had I popped in with a questionnaire that the women could fill out and return to me. I sat face-to-face with the women that I interviewed, laughing and crying with them. Their joys became my joys and their sorrows were mine too. It was a reciprocal relationship. When I had skin cancer they prayed over me and rubbed my face with sacred soil that had been brought from Karbala. They petitioned Fatima to heal me and a year later I was paraded around a circle of women as my friend jabbered in Arabic. Suddenly all the women started to weep and cry out. She had told the women that I was proof of Fatima's miracles because my face had completely healed. When she translated this for me, I too, burst into tears.

From my perspective in good ethnographic research, the ethnographer and the interviewee should be able to share a piece of themselves. They must both bring to the community something fresh and new, and be able to take away something that enriches their lives. Deep listening, trust, and sincere caring are the components of a commitment made by both parties to relatedness, to the 'I that is we', to the human condition, and to the present moment whose memory lasts forever and whose future is an unfolding mystery. There must be a shared spiritual commitment, even if there is a different religious tradition between the research partners. There must be mutuality, and respect, an engaged heart and an authentic affection between the two parties.

Readings

Unfortunately there is very little scholarship on American Shi'a Muslim women's ritual practice and their daily lives. Working toward closing this gap, I have published 'From ritual to redemption: world-view of Shi'a Muslim women in Southern California', in Zayn Kassam (Ed.), *Women and Islam* (Santa Barbara, CA: Praeger, 2010) and 'The heart of lament: Pakistani–American Muslim women's Azadari Rituals', in Peter Chelkowski (Ed.), *Eternal Performance: Taziyah and Other Shiite Rituals* (Chicago, IL: University of Chicago Press, 2010). For research on Shi'a Muslim women internationally, see Lara Deeb's *An Enchanted Modern: Gender and Public Piety in Shi'i Islam* (Princeton, NJ: Princeton University Press, 2006) as well as Kamran S. Aghaie's edited collection *The Women of Karbala* (Austin: University of Texas Press, 2005). A general study of Shi'ism can be found in Moojan Momen's *An Introduction to Shi'a Islam* (New Haven, CT: Yale University Press, 1985) as well as Liyakat Takim's *Shi'ism in America* (New York: New York University Press, 2009) and David Pinault's *The Shiites* (New York: St Martin's Press, 1992).

Author

Bridget Blomfield received her PhD from Claremont Graduate University where she specialized in Islamic Studies and Women in Religion. Her areas of interest are Shi'ism and Sufism. Currently an Associate Professor of Religious Studies at University of Nebraska in Omaha, she teaches Women in Islam, Islam, Muslims in America, and Sufism. Dr Blomfield is the director of the Islamic Studies Program at UNO and takes students to study abroad every year in Muslim countries. She has a dear love for children, dance, and food.

Chapter 8

Studying Indonesian Muslim masculinities in Indonesia and Australia

Pamela Nilan

Preamble

This chapter provides the reader with some views on conducting research with Indonesian Muslim men. It draws on my long experience of ethnographic and mixed-method research in Australia and Indonesia. In keeping with the theme of this book, a narrative approach is taken, with emphasis on researcher experience and the actual practice of fieldwork. Perhaps the first and most important thing to be said about studying Indonesian Muslim men in these two countries is that social science research should always be rigorous, ethical, and respectful, and never more so than when conducted by a tertiary-educated, white, female, non-Muslim researcher with Muslim men from non-Anglo backgrounds. Equally important is the fact that conducting research in Muslim communities inevitably touches on political sensibilities at both the local and the global levels.

Unfortunately, Islam suffers from bad press in the West. In Australia, for example, this amounts to a moral panic about Muslims. Consequently, not only are Muslims per se seen as a suspect group by non-Muslims, but Muslims themselves are strongly aware of this, and are thus likely to regard non-Muslim researchers with suspicion. In Indonesia, many Muslims are mistrustful of Australians and other Westerners, which complicates the research process. So studying Muslim Indonesian men can be a politically sensitive project in many ways.

Narrative

Between 2006 and 2012, I conducted research on masculinities in Indonesia. Those studies used qualitative methods: embedded fieldwork, interviews and focus groups, and a survey. Up to 2008, I also conducted research on Indonesian Muslim masculinities in Australia using interviews. All those projects meant collecting data from Muslim Indonesian men. As a female, non-Muslim researcher, I have worked in collaboration with male academic colleagues, both Indonesian and Australian. I greatly value this collaborative approach because I am not a man and I cannot see things as men do. At the same time though, ultimate responsibility for interpretation of data has rested with me for publication.

There is much debate on the ethics and politics of who is best positioned to carry out research with Muslims. Some argue that only Muslims should research other Muslims since they are less likely to pathologize or stereotype 'their own'. However, there is no guarantee a Muslim researcher will provide a more consistent or 'authentic' account. While sameness may yield valid information on a particular topic with particular informants, difference may give an advantage on other topics, with yet a further set of informants. I feel that applies in my case.

The researchers' training and background influences what they research and how. As a youth sociologist, I started researching Muslim youth in Indonesia in 2002 not because they were Muslim but because they were young people, and over 85 per cent of Indonesians are Muslim. I already had the language, and a knowledge of youth and youth culture forged over a decade, but found that there were still gaps in my knowledge about what it meant to be a young Muslim of either sex in a rapidly Islamizing Indonesia. I not only needed to learn more about Islam, but about global Islamist movements and the online Muslim youth communities that link countries across the world. I began to fill this gap by: (a) finding out more from my own Muslim nephews in Australia about how they saw the world; (b) reading the Qur'an in translation; (c) reading Al Jazeera and Indonesian newspapers every day; and (d) investigating some notable websites where 'hot' issues for young Muslims were debated. Later during fieldwork in Indonesia I lived in Muslim-majority cities for months on end and got to know families in which young people were growing up. I reached out to young men who were good at explaining things and could bridge the gaps in my own understanding. I worked on improving my knowledge of polite greetings (e.g. *assalamu 'alaikum*) and always dressed conservatively, wearing long pants and shirts with high necks and sleeves. I acknowledged that at times I would need to cover my hair and always packed a suitable scarf.

Collecting data, I have to constantly keep in mind who I am, where I come from and how I am perceived by Muslim informants. Most Muslim-majority countries, including Indonesia, are located in what many call the global 'South'. The politics of the very research process itself are skewed by the circumstances in which I, a well-paid researcher from the global North, attempt to study Indonesian Muslims who struggle to prosper in a precarious labour market in the global South.

As a woman researching Muslim men, the complex gender politics of collecting data should not be underestimated, to say the least. Any female researcher collecting data about men and masculinities faces certain critical challenges, especially in 'embedded' fieldwork. However, the inherent difficulties for me as a first-world female researcher studying the lives of men from a developing country are further complicated by the gender order of Islam. In fact, throughout masculinities research to date, religion as an aspect of masculine identity and practice has been often ignored even though it is vitally important.

There is guiding theology and regulation for Muslim men about interacting with unrelated women that must be acknowledged and respected if communication is to take place at all, let alone flow effectively. In my experience, for some men, and in some situations, it is better to get a male researcher to collect data, even while guiding and developing the project. As this advice suggests, piety and regulation vary greatly between men and between different strands of Islam. Moreover, Indonesian Islam is astonishingly diverse across the archipelago, and the commonly recognized divisions may not be always relevant. In Indonesia, I found that some Muslim men would not shake hands or make eye contact with me as an unrelated woman, but were happy to chat with me as a foreign researcher and discuss even sexual matters quite openly. A few would not agree to participate in the research interview unless conducted by a male interlocutor. Most men though, were warmly welcoming and keen to talk with me and tell an outsider about their lives and their views. The fact that I speak Indonesian and know the country well was a crucial factor in this regard.

Indonesian Muslim masculinities

Religion matters a great deal in Indonesia. It is not only enshrined in the constitution but an integral part of who people take themselves to be. Religion is often left out of masculinity studies, but in Indonesia this would be a major interpretive error. For many Indonesian Muslims, Islam infuses every aspect of their lives. Some celebrate their faith by consumption and display of

Figure 8.1 Pam Nilan interviewing during fieldwork with Muslim men in Indonesia in 2012

the 'parallel universe' of Muslim popular culture: Arabic dress, illuminated Qur'anic calligraphy wall hangings, Qur'anic phone ringtones and calligraphy wallpaper, halal potato chips and cola, hajj pilgrimage board games, Saladin's victory video games, *nasjid* boy band hit songs, film Islami, and so on. Others manifest their faith in ascetic terms by eschewing consumerism and centring their lives simply around prayer, the holy texts, and a spiritual leader.

In general, the teachings of Islam promote the responsibility of men to maintain the moral order in both the private and public domains and this dovetails with the strong patrimonial traditions of the Indonesian archipelago. Ideals of masculinity were entrenched by centuries of colonization and monotheistic religious influence. Subsequently, second president Suharto's authoritarian New Order government (1966–98) defined narrow, normative roles for Indonesian men and women that enshrined conservative gendered power relations. The 1974 Indonesian Marriage Law, still in place today, states that the husband is head of the family and protects his wife, who is defined in her domestic role. Polygamy is allowed and wives must obtain their husband's consent to get a passport or to take up night employment.

The question of homosexuality is a vexed issue in Indonesia given that Muslim religious discourse warns against it. Yet Indonesia has no national laws proscribing transgender behaviour or sex acts between men. In fact, pluralistic gender formations have long been represented in the Indonesian cultural landscape and still find expression today, not least in films and literature. For example, the first gay cinematic kiss featured in the 2003 film *Arisan*. Since then even popular teen films such as *Coklat Stroberi* (2007) have followed gay themes, and the most recent winner of the prestigious Maya film awards was *Lovely Man* (2012), which explores the first encounter between a transgender sex worker and his pregnant teenage daughter. Intriguingly, the extensive Islamization of the country in the past 30 years has been both repressive and productive in relation to transgendered and gay men. I have met devout transgendered men (*waria*) who proudly wear women's pious attire and the Muslim headscarf (*jilbab/hijab*). There certainly are Islamist vigilante groups who intimidate and attack gays, lesbians, and *waria*, and fatwas have been issued against Indonesian gays and lesbians by some Muslim clerics. On the other hand, there is some openness within liberal Islamic discourse about non-heteronormative masculinities.

As indicated above, I have frequently collected data directly from Indonesian Muslim men. Yet for some men, being interviewed by a Western woman, even in their own language, is unacceptable on grounds of gender segregation and perceived racial/religious hegemony on the global stage. And sometimes the environment has simply been too dangerous. For instance, once while walking to an interview at midday in Makassar, South Sulawesi, a rifle was pointed at me by two young men wearing Muslim skull caps who came out of a house. I ran away. They did not follow and the gun was probably not loaded. I have exercised caution ever since. It should be noted that gun ownership is not common in the country. In fact, urban Indonesia is quite peaceful and orderly for the most part and I rarely feel threatened. Yet there are some jihadi groups of whom almost everyone lives in fear. I noted the following show of strength on the street one afternoon during fieldwork in Solo, a city that has long been a hotbed of Islamic radicalism.

> Laskar Jundullah were *berkonvoi* – motorbikes, trucks, banners. The young men were wearing the black and white Arab headcloth and black Arabic clothing. They were very loud and threatening. Ordinary locals seemed cowed by them and people were leaving the street and ducking off into side streets and lanes. People were saying, 'Don't look at them, don't make contact.'
> (Field notes, Solo, Central Java, 31 August 2007)

I followed my Indonesian friends into a street-side café, where we all sat quietly until the jihadi gang had passed. One of my friends said she knew one of the gang and he was 'not all that bad'. She offered to arrange an interview with him if I wanted. This would have been an ideal way to find out more about the (now outlawed) Laskar Jundullah group in Solo. However, I declined because that was not really the focus of my investigation in 2007. I wanted to look at ordinary young Muslims in Solo, not members of 'spectacular' youth cultures, Muslim or otherwise.

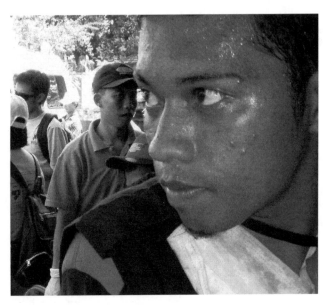

Figure 8.2 Angry young Muslim activist following urban street protest, taken during field-work in Indonesia in 2007

Researching Muslim Indonesian masculinities in Australia

I turn now to conducting research with Muslim Indonesian men in Australia. Having done both kinds of studies, I can say that researching Indonesian Muslim men in their own country and in Australia is certainly different. As anyone who has spent long periods in another country can tell you, the experience makes you very aware of the distinctiveness of your own culture. Some of the men were enjoying their time in Australia because it was so different to Indonesia, while others disliked it for the same reason. In either case though, the men were keen to talk reflectively about the contrast.

Unfortunately, the period of research took place in the long shadow of 9/11 and the aftermath of the Bali bombings. At that time, negative public discourse about Muslim Indonesians in Australia was running high. It was in this context that I began data collection on Indonesian Muslim masculinities with two Australian male colleagues. I began by interviewing some male postgraduate students. To encourage openness, I started by asking what they thought about Australian men, so that an easy bridge to their own self-perceptions might be made. This proved very successful. The men did not just talk about Australian men, but comparatively about themselves as Indonesian Muslim men.

For many, the sexual openness they witnessed in Australian media and culture was at odds with Islamic teaching. They reflected on their own sexual practices, for example,

> I have seen some very vulgar movies here [...] the man behave to the woman very like, only animals do that. Animals can do that, but man just do that to the woman – sex! But in Islam we cannot do that. We cannot do oral sex, we cannot bring ... We just have sex in a very good manner. I mean we have some Hadith from the prophet, saying how to do sex with our wife.
>
> (Uki, Newcastle, 10 May 2005)

Uki explained this cultural contrast at some length. He began with Islamic doctrine – 'it's prohibited for not married couple to doing sex, even just kissing [...] even we have limitation for look at each other, because we must avoid the free sex. It is forbidden from our religion.' He made a direct contrast with the public sexual behaviour of Australian men – 'Here men just like happy to show that he has like girlfriend and he can just kiss. He can hug even in the public area.' He implied that he knew he had no right to judge this culturally different behaviour, but it made him feel uncomfortable – probably because of the sexual thoughts it prompted; 'Sometimes I feel like embarrassed myself if I get close to them and they just like ... like kissing and hugging [...] I feel embarrassed if I look at a couple who are doing sex in front of me. I just get away from that situation.' However, later in the interview Uki admitted that he would quite like to kiss his wife in public – 'kiss the wife in front of people. I can't, I can't do that. I can't do that. I want to do that [laughs] but I'm afraid if they feel just like I feel when I saw people here, so it's not comfortable.'

Budi too was offended by depictions of sexual activity in Australia. Like Uki, he referred to Islamic teaching about how a man should have sex, 'Like if you want to have intercourse, this is the limit, this is the way, and this is what you gonna do [indicates the missionary position]' (Budi, 12 May 2005, Newcastle). Budi was not particularly enjoying his time in Australia because so much of everyday culture and lifestyle offended him. As a very pious Muslim he was longing to return to Indonesia. In the meantime, he indicated that the local mosque was a haven, 'We are a very strong community […] Lucky that I am very strong. I have a relationship with my mosque – we have a big community in Newcastle.' Budi implies the mosque as a place not only for men to pray, but to socialize and maintain moral strength with other men. Praying at the mosque, where all men are equal before God, reinforces not only Muslim cultural identity, but also lateral bonds of masculine solidarity.

As these two examples show, the Indonesian Muslim men that I interviewed in Newcastle were keen to talk to me and quite open in expressing themselves. When I chatted to them before and after the interviews, it was clear that they felt I understood Indonesia, because I spoke the language and went often to the country.

Indonesian encounters

Much of my Indonesian data on Muslim men was collected informally and ethnographically; not as formal interviews or focus groups. Information and insights were written up later in the form of reflective field notes. I often spoke to young men and women in the shopping mall or while waiting for public transport. In general, Indonesian people are very sociable and like to chat to strangers, especially if they can practise some English. In such chance encounters, I met a range of young Indonesian Muslim men, from the secular to the pious. The following profiles give a sense of this contrast.

Basudi

Basudi was a young man from a Muslim family who favoured a secular lifestyle. I met him in the main street of Solo, Central Java, when he and his brother were admiring a Harley-Davidson parked outside a motorcycle shop. They were smoking clove cigarettes, laughing, and joking. I asked where they were going – *Mau ke mana?* This is a very common way to address someone in Indonesia and reflects a polite cultural concern with the doings of people in everyday settings. At 23, Basudi was employed in a real estate agency. He was engaged to be married. His father was a businessman. For weekend wear, Basudi was wearing jeans, a dark T-shirt, a wide leather belt with a big buckle, and pointed leather shoes. He had two mobile phones, one for work and the other for personal communication. He had a very trendy hairstyle. That evening he was wearing coloured contact lenses which made his eyes electric blue.

Saifuddin

Fifteen minutes later, Saifuddin was waiting for the bus. He was going to the mosque to attend a lecture on the Qur'an. His father was an imam. Saifuddin was 18 years old and still at school. Very pious, he was wearing a white collarless shirt, a white skullcap, and trousers cut off at mid-calf. He was attempting to grow a beard. He did not have a mobile phone but always carried a small Qur'an in his pocket. He said his marriage would be arranged by his parents. He vowed that he would marry the woman chosen for him no matter what. He did not wish to meet his future wife until the day they marry.

The differences between these two young Muslim men might seem profound. They seemed to inhabit two completely separate lifestyle worlds. Yet on reflection I concluded that this is a primarily relational contrast. Saifuddin's lifestyle choice takes its cue from Basudi's lifestyle choice (and the reverse) in a double game of identity performance constructed through the dialectical relationship between Islam and the West. Moreover, it is really Saifuddin who represents an extreme position, not Basudi. Saifuddin's decision not to own a mobile phone is the most striking antithetical choice relevant to contemporary urban Indonesia. Regardless of religious piety, very few young urban Indonesians do not have a mobile phone even if they are very poor. Saifuddin's father led a large and prosperous mosque, and had a Blackberry in constant use. His son was making an ascetic statement in choosing not to own a cellular phone. It signifies that his desires are not those of ordinary young men. Mobile phones offer young Indonesians a degree of freedom and they permit social exchanges of every possible kind, including flirting. So in refusing to own a mobile phone, Saifuddin is effectively distancing himself from moral risk, and from secular modernity. In contrast, Basudi owns not one but two mobile phones. He wears bright blue contact lenses, contradicting his Indonesian appearance, making himself exotic. In 2007, coloured contact lenses were popular with young Javanese, especially those who favoured nightclubs and dance parties. Everything about Basudi's appearance was oriented to a consumerist Western lifestyle.

In terms of sexual relations, the contrast is striking. Although Basudi did not actually tell me where he and his brother were headed later that evening, given their appearance I imagine it was to a place that Saifuddin would not have approved of, such as a karaoke bar, a nightclub, or a billiards hall. Such places in the urban night-time leisure economy are frequented by men and women of dubious sexual morality, or at least as far as pious Muslims like Saifuddin are concerned. Saifuddin distances himself entirely from that 'immoral' world by stating that his parents will arrange his marriage and he will meet his wife only on their wedding day. This is far from the usual pattern of courtship and marriage in Indonesia today, even among devout Muslims. In other words, the majority lifestyle choices of young Indonesian Muslim men lie between the two polarities represented by Saifuddin and Basudi.

Extreme views: interpreting hard-line statements from Muslim men in Indonesia

In 2011, 86 interviews were conducted with 'ordinary' men from a range of socio-economic and ethnic backgrounds, the majority Muslim. The questions were about men's attitudes to violence. Some made explicit statements that defended their negative views on women from a Muslim theological viewpoint. It was then important for me to interpret those statements in a culturally sensitive way. For example, one informant stated bluntly, 'If I were to beat my wife, I would have the right because I was teaching her how to behave properly … the husband is supposed to be like the imam [Muslim preacher] in the family' (P4, 31, Military, Muslim, married, Pekanbaru, 4 August 2010). The implication is that if the woman breaks the theological rules of wifely conduct in the eyes of the husband, violent consequences are justified. Another man offered a similar kind of justification,

> In Islam the ruling says that in the family women are supposed to be protected. However, the wife is weak and accepts information without filtering it. She also dismisses information in the same way, without filtering it. But if the woman has the proper understanding of what a wife should be, God willing, this will lead to clear communication and not mutual cursing at each other. I mean that's why it [domestic violence] happens.
>
> (MT3, 28, Political Party Activist, Muslim, unmarried, Mataram, 20 June 2010)

From a feminist viewpoint these statements seem to use Muslim theology to blame the wife for provoking the husband to violence. Yet rushing to judgement is unwise. Indonesia has long been, and remains, a patriarchal society. Even now there are not only religious, but national and traditional discourses that enshrine the 'natural' authority of the man in the Indonesian family, so it is not really surprising that misogynist views were expressed. And while theological justifications were given, this is not the whole story. To avoid demonizing Indonesian Muslim men, or Islam itself, in writing up such data, it is judicious to counterpose some very different statements from other men who seem equally devout, for example, 'there are certainly beatings [of women] … Now we have laws against [domestic] violence, so I hope and pray that that will make people more readily condemn it' (S7, 50, Political Party Secretary, married, Muslim, Solo, 28 July 2009). Another man also deplored violence again women, 'it is really taboo to strike women and female children' (R1, 40, Private Sector Clerk, Muslim, married, Pekanbaru, 3 August 2010). Even one local gang member, fond of fighting with other men, was able to identify verbal abuse of a woman as violence, 'It IS violence if a guy yells at his girlfriend that she is a whore, a prostitute. That often happens to women' (MK1, 28, Gang Member, unmarried, Muslim, Makassar, 20 June 2010).

Indonesia has ratified CEDAW (The United Nations Convention on the Elimination of All Forms of Discrimination against Women). In 2004, Law No. 23 on the Elimination of Domestic Violence set out procedures to protect victims of domestic violence and punish perpetrators. It is this law to which S7 refers above. As a result, men do seem to have more awareness that domestic violence is unlawful,

> Domestic violence? That would not be carried out by any man who knew about the regulations against it. It is possible such a man who would conduct violence on members of his family might not be aware of the rules and regulations. It sometimes happens like that.
>
> (MK2, 38, Security Police, Married, Muslim, Makassar, 25 June 2010)

In my experience, it is important to meet the challenge of interpreting contentious statements from Indonesian Muslim men without condemning them, given that they have obliged me by frankly engaging with the request for information. To some extent, extreme statements speak for themselves and do not need much authorial elaboration. It is important though not to tag the religion of Islam with every sexist or extreme comment made by a Muslim man. That is why I advocate the interpretive practice of juxtaposing different discourses from men on the same topic.

Discussion

My stories of data collection and data interpretation show that working effectively as a non-Muslim researcher in Muslim-majority contexts should embody the first principles of good intercultural and cross-cultural research. Fieldwork in particular benefits from constant deep appraisal of the moral dimensions in how the researcher and the project might be 'read' by Muslim informants. It is appropriate to get fully acquainted with the basic beliefs of Muslims and the five pillars of Islam that guide everyday orthopraxy. I also think it is crucial to read the Qur'an carefully. There is a great deal of misunderstanding about what the holy text contains. Often what is claimed about Islam by non-believers comes not directly from the Qur'an itself, but from the Hadith, which were written at a later date, or even from the work of Wahabi scholars. And in any case, every Muslim-majority country is culturally different.

While the brotherhood/sisterhood concept of *ummah* covers all Muslims, Islam is not understood or practised the same way in all Muslim-majority countries. I have found it sometimes quite unhelpful to use material on

Muslim men from the Middle East, North Africa, or Turkey to illuminate my research on Indonesian Muslim men. Even close neighbour Malaysia does not match the peculiarities of Indonesian Islam. Moreover, Indonesian Muslims do not always follow the same 'strand' of Islam throughout their lives, and their levels of professed piety can also alter over time and location. For example, I have noticed that university students from Muslim universities are often more liberal and tolerant in their attitudes than their zealous counterparts in secular state universities. Yet, ten years after graduation there is little lifestyle difference to be found between professional Muslim men.

Throughout my years of investigation in Indonesia I have never researched Islam as such, but it is always present as a consideration in the data. I find that the way not to lose focus in the minutiae of claims that reflect theological and personal variations in the country is to keep my independent research aims uppermost. It has also been vital to develop key informants with a transcultural perspective who can tell me whether someone's Muslim beliefs are germane or not to my topic of investigation. There is a strong need to untangle theological and political identity claims in informant accounts. This is important for developing interview schedules, research questions, and, later, for developing interpretations. The researcher needs to be aware of sensitive topics. Not only are trusted key informants central to this endeavour, it is also important to triangulate, to discover and use data sources of different kinds that bear upon the same set of claims. In particular, when researching Indonesian Muslim masculinities, blunt, direct questions should be avoided.

Finally, decisions about what to present and how to present it in publication inevitably have political implications for the wider sphere of relations between Islam and the West, even if the setting is highly local. Almost every time one of my articles on Muslim youth or Muslim men in Indonesia is published in an international journal, I am contacted by one branch or another of the US government security complex. My findings that pertain to Muslims in Indonesia are not contentious, yet nevertheless I am asked to share my raw data, for example, or contribute to a US report on radicalism in the region. I do not cooperate with such requests. I have also been contacted by a number of international news websites, both pro-Muslim and anti-Muslim, to elaborate further on my findings. Once again, I politely refuse. I take the view that if someone wants to read my research findings, they are available as academic resources, and there is no point in muddying the waters with informal comments that could be misinterpreted. These instances do, however, focus my attention on the need to represent my findings on Indonesian Muslim men in the most objective way possible in academic publications.

Readings

The English language literature on Muslim masculinities is limited but of high quality. A good starting point is the book *Islamic Masculinities* edited by

Lahoucine Ouzgane (London: Zed Books, 2006). The reader could follow this up with the chapter by Gerami on the difference between Islamist masculinities and Muslim masculinities in *Handbook of Studies on Men and Masculinities* (M. Kimmel, J. Hearn, and R. W. Connell (Eds), Thousand Oaks, CA: Sage, 2005). A more recent book that explores the same topic, but in a less scholarly way, is Maleeha Aslam's *Gender-based Explosions: The Nexus between Muslim Masculinities, Jihadist Islamism and Terrorism* (New York: United Nations University, 2012). My own research findings on Indonesian Muslim youth can be accessed in the following journal articles: 'Contemporary masculinities and young men in Indonesia', in *Indonesia and the Malay World* 37, no. 109 (2009): 327–44, 'The "spirit of education" in Indonesian Pesantren', in *British Journal of Sociology of Education* 30, no. 2 (2009): 219–32, and 'Youth transitions to urban, middle-class marriage in Indonesia: Faith, family and finances', *Journal of Youth Studies* 11, no. 1 (2008): 65–82. My jointly authored work on Indonesian masculinities in Australia can be found in the chapter by Nilan, Donaldson, and Howson in the edited collection *Migrant Men: Critical Studies of Masculinities and the Migration Experience* (London: Routledge, 2009). Useful contemporary sources for conducting research with Muslim informants can be found in the Ryan *et al.* article titled 'Insiders and outsiders: working with peer researchers in researching Muslim communities', in *International Journal of Social Research Methodology* 14, no. 1 (2011): 49–60, and in the Abbas article 'Muslim-on-Muslim social research: knowledge, power and religio-cultural identities', in *Social Epistemology* 24, no. 2 (2010): 123–36. Excellent reference sources giving an overview of Indonesian Islam include Robert Hefner's *Civil Islam: Muslims and Democratization in Indonesia* (Princeton, NJ: Princeton University Press, 2000) and Azyumardi Azra's *Indonesia, Islam, and Democracy: Dynamics in a Global Context* (Jakarta: Equinox, 2006).

Author

Pamela Nilan is Professor of Sociology at the University of Newcastle, Australia. She has been a visiting researcher at SOAS in London, at KITLV in Leiden, and at La Rochelle University in France. Her books include *Adolescents in Contemporary Indonesia* (New York, Routledge, 2013, with L. Parker), *Australian Youth: Social and Cultural Issues* (Melbourne, Australia: Pearson, 2007, with R. Julian and J. Germov), and *Global Youth? Hybrid Identities, Plural Worlds* (London: Routledge, 2006, with C. Feixa).

Chapter 9

An ethnographer among the Ahmadis

Learning Islam in the suburbs

Marzia Balzani

Preamble

About a decade ago, while teaching in London, I came to know of the difficulties that a few Muslim students on campus experienced in the Muslim prayer room. It appeared that some Muslim students were making it clear that other Muslim students were not welcome. Some Sunni Muslims had decided, following politically motivated practice in Pakistan, that Ahmadi Muslims were not really Muslim at all and so had no place in the university's Muslim prayer room. At this time my fieldwork in Rajasthan with a Hindu community had come to an end, my work and family in London made extended research visits to India impossible, and I was looking for a new research topic to keep in touch with South Asia, even if in the very different world of the South Asian diaspora in Britain. The context was post-9/11. Islamophobia was evident in the media, and the diverse student body to whom I taught such subjects as the anthropology of religion motivated me to learn about local forms of Islam ethnographically to help me better understand not only the background to the inter-Muslim tensions on campus but also those in the local area where I lived and worked. Below I explain how I came to do this and what I learnt.

Narrative

Who are the Ahmadis?

Early in the course of my research I was to find that Ahmadi Islam was founded by a charismatic leader, Mirza Ghulam Ahmad, in late nineteenth-century India. Ahmad had been educated by tutors from different Muslim sects and traditions, Sunni, Shi'a, and Sufi, and had taken from each aspects of the faith that he was later to synthesize into what became his prophetic vision of a reformed and purified Islam. This new religious movement was, in part, Ahmad's counter to the active Western missionary proselytization campaigns to convert Hindus and Muslims to Christianity then taking place in the

Punjab. During an unsettled period of rapid change and modernization in Punjab's history, Ahmad was able to attract followers from both towns and rural areas of the state. In a matter of years he had gone from requiring his followers to pledge their allegiance to him to declaring himself to be the *mujaddid* (renewer of Islam), a *muhaddath* (person spoken to by Allah or an angel), the *mahdi* (the rightly guided one, the messiah), and *masih* (the promised messiah). Further, in the same way in which he claimed to resemble Jesus in spiritual form, he also claimed to be the spiritual incarnation of the god Krishna for the Hindus. By the time of his death in 1908 Ahmad's claims had led to protests and opposition from other Muslim groups, Hindus, and Christians.

Had Ahmad's followers remained in India they might have provided an interesting study for anthropologists working on new religious movements and the social conditions necessary for their formation. Ahmad, however, had learnt from the tactics and strategies of Christian missionaries in India and in the early decades of the twentieth century the movement sent its own missionaries west to convert the British and others to Ahmadi Islam. From village origins, Ahmadi Islam had embarked on a global mission to convert the world. The first mission to the UK arrived in 1913 and by the early 1920s a small Ahmadi mosque, built with funds raised by Ahmadi women, had been established in south London. But this was history and I wanted to know about the Ahmadis living in London as my neighbours and how their past not only shaped their present but also how it shaped the ways others understood and interacted with them. At the south London mosque, so key to Ahmadi history in the UK, my first encounter with the Ahmadi community took place.

Below I outline some of the events and activities that took place in the Ahmadi mosques where I conducted my research, and also the events in the local area that Ahmadis engaged in or which had an impact on them because of their faith. In the process of setting this material out I also discuss why the Ahmadis are treated as they are by some Muslim-majority states and non-state actors and how they deal with hostility and persecution. My gender, professional ethics, and research methods are considered when working in a complicated social environment that encompasses local politics, religious and community relations as well as national and global religious divides which are played out not simply in the religious space of the mosque but in local shops, schools, libraries, council offices, and in cyberspace to name but a few. But that is to jump ahead to my discussion when I have yet to introduce London's Ahmadis as a community.

Entering the 'field'

My first 'official' encounter with the Ahmadi community was one that seemed to augur well for future work. I simply turned up one morning at the first UK purpose-built Ahmadi mosque, a small green-domed white building with adjoining halls and offices, which the community had grown out of and had unsuccessfully sought planning permission to expand, located in a quiet suburban residential area. With no reason not to present my intentions directly I knocked on the door unannounced and uninvited and asked if I could conduct my research on the Ahmadi community. It is only in hindsight, after learning of the difficulties encountered by other researchers and the suspicions people have as to their motivations when seeking to conduct research with Muslim groups, that I realized just how well I was treated. I was received politely, led to an office, and asked to wait while the person who first met me set off to find someone more senior with whom to discuss my research plans. In a short space of time and with the exchange of a few details, the proffering of a cup of tea, biscuits, and snacks, I found myself invited to meetings organized by Ahmadi women, loaded down with a selection of leaflets and books about Ahmadi Islam and informed of the Ahmadi website on which I was told there would be all the information I could possibly need.

In the years that followed, I have attended many meetings in mosques and other meeting places, including meetings organized by the Ahmadi community for non-Ahmadis, or community meetings organized by local councils and groups to which Ahmadi representatives are invited. These meetings include gatherings for women who have converted to Ahmadi Islam or are consider-ing conversion (and where I too was gently nudged towards joining the faith by ever hopeful Ahmadi women who consider this not only their duty but in my best interest); the regular monthly women's meetings; iftari gatherings (marking the end of a day of fasting during Ramadan); Eid al-Fitr celebrations (celebration to mark the end of the month of fasting during Ramadan); spe-cific Ahmadi occasions such as the three-day Jalsa Salana (annual gathering) that is held for members of the community to meet and renew their faith together; the now well-established annual peace symposium; committee meetings where Ahmadi and community representatives discuss and seek to resolve local matters; the annual women's event that is held at the mosque where the final rounds of competitions in reciting the Qur'an, religious spee-ches, and so forth are held for the country as a whole. I have joined tours of the mosque designed for schoolchildren learning about Islam, tours for non-Ahmadi visitors that are held on open days or whenever non-Ahmadis attend the mosque for functions. I have occasionally even taken the minutes for the Ahmadi women's liaison committee; visited displays set up by Ahmadis in local libraries; joined in Ahmadi celebrations for the wedding of Prince William and Catherine Middleton in 2011; attended Ahmadi charity events and the very many small-scale local gatherings that take place across the capital and across the country; and I have joined Ahmadi women and men at the Houses of Parliament where their Khalifa (spiritual head of the community) has spoken to MPs – to name just a few of the very large number of meetings catering to women, men, children, and professional groups such as engineers, doctors, and lawyers in the community.

In addition to all the face-to-face meetings there are also the television programmes made in the mosque studios and broadcast on the Ahmadi television channel (MTA, Muslim Television Ahmadiyya) and now also on YouTube. Ahmadi websites include recordings of Friday sermons (*khutbah*) with translations into several languages, digitized journals dating back to the early twentieth century such as the *Review of Religions*, the Ahmadi flagship journal, books, speeches, photographs, documents on persecution against members of the community, historical and educational materials used to teach Ahmadi children about their faith, and considerably more. Then there are all the informal social gatherings, visits to the homes of individuals, some of whom have become friends, and the impromptu chats when I happen to meet people I know as I go about my everyday life in the locality. As an example, I describe below, using notes taken during and just after the event, one meeting where Ahmadi representatives were invited to present their faith to a wider audience. Following this, I discuss what it was possible to learn from this meeting and how I moved from a 'front-stage' to a 'back-stage' understanding of the event and its participants.

An inter-faith meeting (the front stage)

On a dank Wednesday evening at the end of January in 2004, I trudged through London's snow-slush to attend what was billed as Wandsworth Council's first public event showcasing the borough's multifaith subgroup with faith representatives each talking on the importance of 'family life' for their faith and then answering questions from an invited audience made up of teachers, social workers, senior police officers, charity representatives, council policy paper writers, voluntary group representatives, and worthy others. The multifaith subgroup was set up following 9/11 to promote inter-faith dialogue and understanding. The group first met in February 2002 when representatives from the main faith communities in the borough were invited to meet with the leader of the council and the chief executive. All the main faiths in the borough were represented and in some cases different people represented subdivisions of the same faith.

The speakers on this particular night included a rabbi (the only woman faith representative), a Buddhist monk, a Hindu *pandit*, two Christian ministers (one Methodist and one from the New Testament Assembly Church), a speaker representing the Sikh community, and two Muslim speakers (one a Sunni Muslim and the other an Ahmadi Muslim). The evening started late, mainly because the leader of the council and chair of the Wandsworth Local Strategic Partnership, which oversees the multifaith group, was delayed by the snow and only made it to the relative warmth and post-Victorian opulence of the council meeting rooms at 7 p.m. Still, this delay gave me a chance to introduce myself to a group of Ahmadi women, recognizable by their style of modest dress. I sat with this group for the rest of the evening, listening not only to the official speakers but also to the comments of the audience around me.

The eight speakers were divided into two panels and after the first panel a brief interval allowed the council's photographer to take the official record of the event. I noted in my account of the evening that the two Muslim speakers were on separate panels and also that they stood one at each end of the line of speakers for the official photograph, as far from each other as it was possible to be. Given the occasion, and despite the wet umbrellas and soggy raincoats scattered about the council chamber, there was a certain amount of formality during the evening and the council officials seemed to have dressed up for the occasion. Some people appeared to be caught up in the moment and paid close attention to every word spoken as though a great deal was at stake, while the police officers present mostly just looked bored. At one point in the proceedings the Ahmadi women I sat with simply dismissed the female rabbi with a curt and disapproving 'how can a woman represent the faith?' A comment I assumed to be both about the place of women in faith and society and also, perhaps, about liberal Judaism.

My notes for the talks and question–and–answer sessions that followed each panel noted how the Muslim speakers seemed to be most concerned with presenting their faiths as tolerant and just to women, tolerant of other faiths and of those among whom they had chosen to live in the UK. The Christian speakers, by comparison were more conservative in their attitudes towards women (who should stay at home, have children, and obey the male head of household as one speaker pretty much put it). However, while the Christian speakers felt that they could accept those who chose to leave Christianity for another faith, the Muslim speakers answered such questions by saying that, if raised properly in the faith, a Muslim would never even consider such a change. It was interesting to see just where the overlaps and also the dividing lines were on that evening. I was left to wonder if the general public's typically less than positive view of Islam had led the Muslim speakers to focus on tolerance and the positive roles of women in the community and household while the general acceptance of Christianity had given the Christian speakers the confidence to assert some rather conservative views about women. As it happens, the Ahmadi women with whom I sat made it clear that they approved of these latter views.

Following the council leader's concluding remarks we were invited to continue our discussions informally over a buffet where tables were considerately labelled 'halal', 'vegetarian', and so on. The different faith groups had brought along some of their own foods and so I hovered, cold and tired after a long day at work and an extended evening of concentrated listening and taking notes, over the samosas. At this informal gathering where, of course, everyone was on their best behaviour and professional networking was much in evidence, I met some young Ahmadi men, one of whom, when told of my interest in the community, proceeded to give me what I now know to be the 'official line' on the community. This is not to say that this version of who the Ahmadis are was not true – just that it is a fairly formulaic and standard rendition of who they are, what they stand for and what their place in British society is. As this young man reached the point in his outline of Ahmadi Islam where he recited the well-known Ahmadi refrain, 'Love for all, hatred for none', another Ahmadi young man standing nearby jokingly added 'Love for all, except for Man United fans!' This second young man then engaged me in a conversation which ranged over Ahmadi attitudes towards education (everyone should be educated and Ahmadi women are particularly well educated, often more so than the men), Darwinian evolution (mostly right but with some issues here and there), and how he had been treated with respect when, as a child, he had asked the Khalifa if aliens existed. Soon, warmed by tepid coffee and revived by the food brought by the Ahmadis I felt able to contemplate my bus journey home and said so to my new acquaintances. To my surprise the young man, who by then had introduced me to his wife, offered to give me a lift home and as we all got into his sport's car, his wife remarked to me that her husband, and father of their infant daughter, had chosen a particularly apt model as a family car. On the way home we agreed to keep in touch and, until the family moved to the Middle East, that is exactly what we did.

Discussion

Front-stage frustrations, back-stage complications

This description of the inter-faith meeting made up of brief extracts from my notes exemplifies what I consider to be some of the issues with 'front-stage' ethnographic data. I have chosen this example to show how getting beyond the front stage helped me to understand how the inter-Muslim politics, some of it dating back decades, of the subcontinent continues to be played out today in London.

Following the sociologist Goffman, the front stage is an arena in social life where we present ourselves as we would wish to be viewed by others. This is where impression management comes to the fore as in this front-stage space we tend to avoid the conflicts, contradictions, and the rehearsals for our social performances that we would prefer others not to see. All of us have front-stage personas when we know others are watching and listening to us, and where we are careful to be the best we can be. The front stage is real and the truth of who we are, but it is not the only truth or the only reality and if a researcher stays at the level of the front stage then any analysis and interpretation is necessarily limited to this one aspect of reality.

Despite the friendly welcome I received from the Ahmadi community it soon became clear to me that I was being kept in the front-stage area where visitors and outsiders remain unless they choose to become Ahmadi or in other ways manage to develop relationships of trust with community members who may then allow them access to the back stage (which, however, is also another kind of front stage, as even in the back stage, impression management and the presentation of self and community are performed). Another issue for me was my gender which allowed me reasonably easy access to the women in this segregated community, but less ready access to the men who organized much of the community, made policies or approved those put forward by the women's organization, and put into practice the decisions of the leadership.

Therefore, with a clear sense that I was missing something in my research but not really knowing what this something was, I focused on developing further what I had already been a part of and knew. I set about asking those who had been at the inter-faith meeting how they would assess the success of the event. I asked not just Ahmadis but anyone I could think of who had been at the event or had some knowledge of it. Most people blandly stated that the event had been positive in bringing together different faiths to share knowledge and understanding. None of this was particularly revelatory until someone happened to mention, almost in passing, that the whole event was almost called off and that the calm, polished well-orchestrated evening I witnessed was in fact the result of a last-minute deal brokered by diplomatically skilled council officials who managed to agree a truce between the Sunni Muslims and the Ahmadi Muslims. After some now more focused questions directed at different groups so as to build up a nuanced understanding of events in the run-up to the inter-faith meeting, I discovered that my notes had inadvertently picked up on some of the points that could be explained by the tensions between Sunni and Ahmadi Muslims in this local context. As I reconstructed events from different accounts of the evening, it appeared that the Sunni Muslim group had threatened to boycott the inter-faith meeting if the Ahmadis were described as 'Muslim' on any event publicity or programmes. For these Muslims, the Ahmadis were not to be considered Muslim. The Ahmadis, for their part, appear to have informed Wandsworth Council that if they were not described as Muslim, which they consider themselves to be, then they would contact the press to let them know just what was going on under the guise of inter-faith community building.

From what I have pieced together the council officials, at the last moment possible, managed to get an agreement between Sunni and Ahmadi for the inter-faith meeting to proceed. Some of the features of the agreement seem to have included not defining any speakers explicitly by faith so as to avoid describing any individual by a faith designation that another speaker might reject. Further, on the printed programme for the evening the speakers were listed by name and so was their organization but again no one was explicitly described as 'Jewish', 'Hindu', or anything else that might classify them by faith. And during the event, as I had noted, the two Muslim speakers were on different panels and so never had to sit together, nor did they take questions together as each panel had its own question-and-answer session. The official photograph of the speakers was also arranged to keep the embattled Muslim speakers as far apart as it was possible to be.

This was my route into a back-stage understanding of Ahmadi Islam and the local politics in which the Ahmadis were involved. Without this back-stage knowledge and grasp of the details of the divisions between different Muslim groups, their histories, and how they each tried to assert their own position in a local context, drawing council officials and others into managing their disputes, the full meaning of the multifaith evening in Wandsworth, and indeed the remarkable success of the council in handling what has been historically a contentious and sometimes violent encounter between Ahmadi and Sunni Muslims, might have eluded me.

So where did the idea that the Ahmadis are not Muslim come from? After all they describe themselves as Muslim; the Qur'an is their most sacred religious text; their children are taught to recite this in Arabic as well as studying the Hadith (reports of what the prophet said, did, or approved of) and Sunna (teachings and example of the prophet); they adhere to the five pillars of Islam; men and women dress modestly and remain in sex-segregated groups whenever possible; they are scrupulous in observing Muslim food restrictions; their places of worship are officially listed as mosques in all town planning documents in the UK; and for all intents and purposes they live as practising Muslims do. To the non-Muslims of south London, the Ahmadis look like 'typical' Muslims, to such an extent that local non-Muslim groups inevitably organize campaigns to protest against plans to build mosques in their areas and the British National Party (a far-right white supremacist anti-migrant party)

Figure 9.1 Baitul Futuh Mosque in Morden, London. The mosque view from the car park. Photo courtesy of Mr T. Khokhar

even staged a protest against the Ahmadi Muslims when they sought to build their state-of-the-art mosque in Merton.

The answer to the question is not to be found in the UK at all but in the history of the subcontinent and particularly in the history of Pakistan from the 1970s onwards. The Ahmadis have experienced problems with other faith groups such as the reformist Hindu Arya Samaj and other Muslim groups in India from their inception in the nineteenth century. There are doctrinal differences between Ahmadis and Sunnis and these include the Ahmadi belief that the promised messiah has already returned in the form of their founder Mirza Ghulam Ahmad. They also believe that he is a prophet, but not of the same kind as the Prophet Muhammad as Ahmad has not brought any new knowledge or laws to the faithful; his task was merely to draw them back to the correct way of practising and understanding their faith. Therefore, for Ahmadis, while the Prophet Muhammad was the last prophet to bring the word of God to humankind (hence seal of the prophets), he was not the last of the prophets, as reformers and renewers of the faith are still needed to guide the faithful. The Ahmadi interpretation of jihad (literally, striving) is another point of difference from mainstream Islam in that the Ahmadis only believe in peaceful jihad using the pen rather than the sword to achieve their goals, and this interpretation, while overlapping with more orthodox views, does require some reworking of Islamic notions of jihad. In addition, since the very early days of Ahmadiyyat, Ahmadis have not considered it acceptable to pray behind a non-Ahmadi imam, citing the hostility of non-Ahmadi imams to their founder as the reason for this. When other Muslims declared the Ahmadis to be *kafir* (unbelievers) the Ahmadis referred to a Hadith that anyone calling another Muslim *kafir* becomes himself *kafir* and the application of this Hadith effectively rendered the non-Ahmadi Muslims who did not accept Ahmad as the reformer and promised messiah themselves *kafir*. Confrontations between Ahmadis and Sunnis, and between Ahmadis and Hindus, occurred during Ahmad's lifetime and accusations and counter-accusations have been a feature of Ahmadi history ever since.

This fractious situation continued in the new Muslim-majority state, Pakistan, which came into being in 1947 and to which most Ahmadis migrated from India at partition. While much of the hostility directed at the Ahmadis remained verbal or invoked legal recourse to achieve the goals of the anti-Ahmadi groups, occasionally violence erupted and lives were lost. This happened in rioting in 1953 in the Pakistan Punjab and resulted in a judicial report which concluded, after taking evidence from many and diverse individuals and groups, that it was not possible definitively and to everyone's satisfaction to define what a Muslim is. Therefore, it was not possible categorically to state that the Ahmadis were not Muslim. However, by the 1970s in Pakistan things had changed. Conservative religious leaders were still calling for the Ahmadis to be declared heretics and the leader of the country, Zulfikar Ali Bhutto, for his own political reasons, acquiesced to the calls of the mullahs (religious scholars) and changed the constitution of the country in 1974 explicitly to discriminate against Ahmadi Muslims by declaring them to be non-Muslim. In 1984 more legislation passed by the ruling military dictator Zia-ul-Huqq effectively criminalizing all Ahmadis. Such changes in legislation made clear that the state was sanctioning discriminatory treatment of Ahmadis. Ahmadis with jobs in the military or positions of seniority in government and even in the private sector found that they were dismissed from their positions, others were routinely insulted, students expelled from schools and universities, and Ahmadi places of worship, burial grounds, and homes were increasingly targeted by people incited to violence and swayed into believing that aggression is an acceptable way to deal with difference. Among many discriminatory acts, the Ahmadis were not permitted to call their places of worship mosques. As a result of increasing persecution in the subcontinent the leader of the Ahmadis, the Khalifa, left Pakistan in the 1980s to live in south London and so make this the global headquarters for the movement. Since then more and more Ahmadis have been forced to leave Pakistan and seek asylum in Western countries.

As a result of my research, I have sometimes been asked to write 'culture reports' setting out the context and conditions in which Ahmadis live in Pakistan. These reports have been used by Ahmadi asylum seekers in their appeals against the refusal of refugee status in the UK. Writing these reports has meant that I have read the often harrowing accounts of those seeking asylum and have become familiar with the levels of daily abuse and discrimination that Ahmadis endure and which, in some cases, reaches the threshold of persecution as defined in international law. While the level of violence against Ahmadis in the UK has certainly never equalled that faced in Pakistan, and has never led to incidents such as the mass murder of almost ninety men and boys as they prayed on a Friday afternoon in May 2010 in Lahore, there is continuing evidence of discrimination and harassment of Ahmadis taking place in the UK and certainly so in south London.

In the months following the attacks in Lahore, London Ahmadis found that they were increasingly the targets of discrimination and abuse in the diaspora. A member of Khatme Nabuwat (an organization set up in the early decades of the twentieth century specifically to persecute the Ahmadis and calling itself 'Finality of Prophethood' in reference to the prophetic claims of the Ahmadi founder) gave a speech at the Tooting Islamic Centre denouncing Ahmadis and calling on Muslims to boycott their businesses and to refuse to interact with them. Ahmadi women reported they were refused service in local restaurants as waiters informed them that they could not serve Ahmadis, and Ahmadi shopkeepers lost income because of the boycott. At least one Ahmadi man in Tooting lost his job during the year because of his faith, though he later won a case for unfair dismissal at an industrial tribunal, and shops had notices in Urdu in their windows stating that they would not serve Ahmadis who were described as infidels, heretics, and unbelievers. It was reported that leaflets denouncing Ahmadis and calling on Muslims to use violence against them were distributed in parts of the UK. During the UK election campaign in April the non-Ahmadi Conservative candidate was mistaken for the Ahmadi Liberal Democrat candidate when he went to speak at the Tooting Islamic Centre and had to be locked into a room for his own protection against an angry mob which had gathered believing him to be Ahmadi. On satellite television a Muslim channel broadcast material which media regulators, Ofcom, described as a breach of broadcasting regulations because of its 'abusive treatment of the religious views and beliefs of members of the Ahmadiyya community'. These forms of abuse and calls to use violence against Ahmadis replicated patterns of harassment that are routine in Pakistan and have now found their way to the UK.

In October the MP for Mitcham and Morden, Siobhain McDonagh, secured a debate in Parliament on the Ahmadiyya Community and announced the formation of an all-party parliamentary group for the Ahmadis. Yet, despite the monitoring of the situation by Parliament, the police, and local council officials, discrimination and boycotts continue. In January 2013 an Ahmadi woman told me of a conversation she overheard a few days earlier in Tooting between a shopkeeper and a man dressed in what she described as 'Islamic clothing'. In Urdu the bearded man in shalwar kameez (traditional clothing of baggy trousers and loose overshirt) asked the shopkeeper if any Ahmadis were still working in a shop opposite. The shopkeeper told him that there were no longer Ahmadis there so he could buy goods from this shop without any worries.

As the Ahmadis have migrated from South Asia, so too have those who oppose them, including a few who advocate for their eradication as a faith group. Global movements of people are also matched by the rise of global media ensuring that no place in the world remains free from the consequences of historical clashes that originated over a century ago and continue with persecution and suffering in Pakistan today. The result of this is that in the UK today public officials, the police, and members of the wider community who have to engage with a multifaith general public have had to learn not only about an abstract and often idealized Islam in order to carry out their jobs, but also about the realities of sectarian divides within Islam located in the specific histories and politics of particular nations, and to find strategies to deal with the historically rooted and entrenched positions that have been transplanted from the subcontinent to the UK.

Part of my work as an anthropologist has been to make sense of this complex situation by starting with the events taking place around me in London and then through observation, interview, and participation in meetings to try to understand not only what people do but why, from all the possible options available to them, only particular actions are chosen and only particular explanations are put forward to make sense of events from their own particular perspectives. And while the Ahmadis, just as much as the Muslims who oppose them, identify themselves in terms of their faith, these religious identities are ones that cannot be separated from their historical origins, the politics of the sub-continent and the global politics of recent decades that has resulted in the current opposition between the minority of Muslims who define themselves as anti-West and an equally intransigent element in the West determined to portray some over-generalized Islam as the cause of the world's woes. While most Muslims and most of those in the West (and these are far from being mutually exclusive categories) would not identify with or support the extreme positions of either radical Muslims or radical anti-Muslims, the Ahmadis have been caught up in this politics as Muslims who have been declared non-Muslim, as a group their enemies consider to be pro-Western, and as a group that looks like Muslims to non-Muslims unaware of or uninterested in inter-Muslim sectarian rivalries. As a consequence, Ahmadis are subject to the same Islamo-phobia as any and all Muslims in the West today and also to anti-Ahmadi harassment and discrimination from some other Muslim groups.

In this complicated local–global, historical–contemporary, religious–political situation I have found that steering a path that does not limit me to a front-stage, women-only understanding of south London's Ahmadis requires careful negotiation. There are advantages to my gender in that I am able to mix with women in a way a male anthropologist would find difficult to do and still, as an outsider female, interview male Ahmadis or take part in mixed gatherings so that, with time and patience, I am sometimes able to gain more than a front-stage knowledge of events. Certainly, getting to know Ahmadi women has been one of the pleasures of this research, and learning about the women's organization, the committees, hierarchy, elected offices, and the equal space devoted to women's prayer halls in the mosques makes clear that, while con-servative in many respects, the Ahmadis are progressive in others. Indeed, Ahmadi women had their own organization in India in the 1920s and today take for granted things that many other Muslim women continue to campaign for such as equitable access to and leadership positions in mosques. Yet in other respects they remain deeply conservative and my work seeks to find a way to explain, in terms that start from the perspective of the Ahmadis themselves, just how they view their world. However, my task is not that of an advocate, partly because it would be patronizing of me to speak on behalf of the Ahmadis when they are more than capable of doing that for themselves (and do so), and partly because my role is to learn about Ahmadiyya Islam and everyday Ahmadi life from the Ahmadis. I seek to present the practices and beliefs of those I study fairly but not to stop at this as I must also interpret and analyse my data as an anthropologist. This means that my task is not simply to reproduce the views of those I study, but nor should I add to material that might be taken out of context and used against those I work with. This is particularly important given just how much hostility and violence Ahmadis are subject to in the subcontinent and increasingly elsewhere. And here research ethics becomes a problematic issue. Beyond the usual requirements to render anonymous and protect the privacy of individuals, how do I discuss some of the issues that certainly exist within this community, as they do in all communities, without providing yet more ammunition for their detractors?

Some of the issues raised in representing and understanding the position of the Ahmadis, while also taking into account the sensitivities of other Muslim groups in the local area, can be hinted at using one small ethnographic example. In recent years the Ahmadis have funded an advertising campaign on London's buses proclaiming 'Muslims for Loyalty, Freedom & Peace' with 'www.LoveForAllHatredForNone.org, Ahmadiyya Muslim Community' also clearly visible on the advertisements. While the Ahmadis present this campaign as a way of getting across the message of the peacefulness of Islam to the general British public, a message that has been praised by local councillors and politicians, some Muslims have interpreted this and similar Ahmadi campaigns as an attempt to claim that only the Ahmadis are peaceful Muslims and to imply, therefore, that the others are not. Such an interpretation would, I am certain, be rejected by the Ahmadis but it does serve to show how delicate the local situation is and while any form of harassment, discrimination, or violence is never justified, there may be scope for understanding just how sensitive any statement, encounter, or intervention is, and just how open to misinterpretation it may be, fuelled by many years of hostility in a country to which many London Ahmadis no longer have a direct connection. Lastly, while I do now know why some students tried to prevent others from entering a Muslim prayer room I am still struggling with how to write up many thousands of

Figure 9.2 One of the many buses displaying the message of peace from the Ahmadiyya Muslim community passing through central London. Photo courtesy of Mr T. Khokhar

pages of field notes so as to further understanding of the Ahmadis while minimizing misrepresentation and scope for misusing my work. But that is probably what any anthropologist would say.

Readings

There is a wealth of material available from the Ahmadis themselves on their website at www.alislam.org (not to be confused with a very similar website address by a non-Ahmadi group and perhaps designed to mislead those looking for Ahmadi information). However, as this is the official Ahmadi perspective, researchers need to supplement this with material from other sources. There are also many anti-Ahmadi sites and these too need to be read in context and with an understanding of the conflicts that mark the positions taken. Often anti-Ahmadi sites describe Ahmadis as 'Qadianis' after the name of the village in which their founder was born. This term is considered insulting by Ahmadis. For a general introduction to the Ahmadis with a focus on their history as it relates to the USA but much other relevant historical and doctrinal material too, see Yvonne Haddad and Jane Smith's *Mission to America: Five Islamic Sectarian Communities in North America* (Gainsville: University Press of Florida, 1993). For a general introduction to the issues of persecution, see Antonio Gualtieri's *Conscience and Coercion: Ahmadi Muslims and Orthodoxy in Pakistan* (Montreal: Guernica, 1989). The Ahmadis also have a website, www.persecutionofahmadis.org, where they collate material on persecution including reports and articles by national governments, organizations such as Amnesty International, newspapers, and others. For detailed theological explanations of the Ahmadi position in Islam, see Yohanan Friedmann, *Prophecy Continuous: Aspects of Ahmadi Religious Thought and its Medieval Background* (Berkeley: University of California Press, 1989). For more on the front-stage/back-stage metaphor as applied to social practice, see Erving Goffman, *The Presentation of Self in Everyday Life* (New York: Doubleday, 1959).

Author

Marzia Balzani is Research Professor of Social Anthropology at New York University, Abu Dhabi. Her current project is on the Ahmadi Muslims of London and she is completing an ethnography on the Ahmadis which considers the community as a charismatic new religious movement and global organization. Her previous work has included an ethnography of political ritual in Hindu South Asia (*Modern Indian Kingship*, Oxford: James Currey, 2003) and work on gendered violence, the asylum system, and dreams in Islam. Her future fantasy project is an ethno-history of the medieval Tuscan town where her mother was born.

Chapter 10

Gender, sexuality and inclusivity in UK mosques

Dervla S. Shannahan

Preamble

Prayer is one of the five pillars of Islam and is a foundational part of religious practice for Muslims. The Qur'an itself insists that the daily ritual prayers bring believers closer to Allah, and there are numerous supererogatory, or extra, prayers. Whilst Muslims can pray almost anywhere, praying with others is considered preferable to praying alone; across the world, Muslims pause their lives every Friday for the *jummah*, congregational prayer, preceded by a *khutba* (sermon) at a mosque. Mosques are particularly busy during Ramadan (the month of fasting), and religious holidays, such as Eid. All Muslims, women and men, are required to pray; there are different views on whether women are also obliged to pray in congregation.

The fieldwork account presented below is from a pilot project exploring how gender and sexuality shape women's mosque experiences in the UK today. It is part of a larger two–year research project into gender and mosque spaces which seeks to provide an overview of inclusivity issues in mosques, involving mosque managers and administrators, regular attendees, stakeholders, and non-practising Muslim women. This shorter pilot study foregrounds the larger research project, focusing particularly on LBTQI (Lesbian, Bisexual, Transgender, Queer, and Intersex) Muslim women and single mothers.

Narrative

In what follows I present one example of a fieldwork experience. Thus far (late January 2013), I have conducted eight interviews for this pilot, and expect another ten before any conclusions can be drawn. For the purpose of this chapter, however, I will focus primarily on the content and experience of the first interview, which took place in December 2012.

It was a chilly Sunday morning when we met outside a tube station in central London and, as we walked to a suitable location for the interview, exchanged pleasantries about the Christmas break. The streets were unusually quiet; we both wrapped up against the cold and soon found a suitable café, off the main street, and chose a table. The respondent, let me call her Aabidah (names changed to protect anonymity), chose a table; it is important that researchers do everything that they can to keep respondents at ease, comfortable, and feeling safe and respected during the whole research process. This begins from the first contact and continues right until after publication; it is a general courtesy to send interview transcripts to respondents, if they are interested, and proof versions of the final write up, even if names have been changed beyond recognition.

I went up to the counter to fetch drinks to warm us up. I should add here that although I have conducted numerous interviews such as these, on previous research projects, this was the first one I had ever attempted with my eleven year old son present. Whilst he is very self-contained (and used to occupying himself in a book while I work at home), I felt a little nervous about how the following hours would be. As I waited in line to buy our drinks, and saw him and Aabidah animatedly chatting away, I self-consciously wondered about the clashing of roles (researcher and parent) and how I would maintain the necessary clarity to focus upon the task in hand. Perhaps one of the biggest challenges of off-site fieldwork is the management of roles that is required, the importance of keeping focused upon the work, while staying aware of how one's own subjectivity as a researcher impacts upon the research topic, process and respondent.

Returning to the table, I explained that our interview was about to begin and settled my boy down with his book and hot chocolate and enough napkins to keep the two separate. I then turned to Aabidah and we smiled at each other. I explained the context of the research, as she had seen the summary in the call for participants but not the whole research plan. She seemed interested and we discovered that we have shared interests; we were both in second year psychotherapeutic training courses. She also worked full time, had many family commitments, and was due to travel abroad in the following week with a lot to do before departure. I found myself immediately warming to the respondent and respecting her multiple commitments. Although the setting was all quite informal due to the public setting, our table was quiet enough, I could hear her very well, and fortunately she seemed keen to talk; it is difficult when respondents are shy and you have to pry each syllable from them. I began with the first question and Aabidah seemed like a very self-assured, articulate, smart woman who evidently considered issues of gender and sexuality very deeply, especially through having therapy. She seemed happy with herself and had a balanced and full life. I told her that I appreciated her time, and meant it, too. This respondent was sociable, relaxed, amicable, open, and gave well-considered, detailed answers.

She had lived in London for six years; before that lived in a variety of countries and had a range of experiences of how Islam was practised and framed differently around the world. Despite this, or perhaps because of it, she was very well able to articulate about her own faith journey and how inclusivity issues in mosques vary tremendously depending on the context and pressures on local Muslim communities. She told me that she lived in the Middle East, Yemen, UAE, Syria (was born in Sudan, left at seven months), parents made sure that our [Sudanese] culture travelled with us ... anywhere where I am is home. Religion has always been part of my life, as a child it was forced, wasn't really given chance to explore it, just passed down through generations ... Therapy helped me break away from that [understanding of religion], learning the religion in my own, also living in Nebraska with my brother, he is quite religious but it gave me a chance to look at Islam more for myself.

Whilst this research is focused upon UK mosques, the respondent spoke a lot about mosque experiences in other parts of the world, and brought a refreshingly cosmopolitan perspective to the specificities of the UK context – a point I will return to in the following discussion. I have long been interested in this topic and was very happy to hear her expound on her experiences and understandings of the differences between mosques around the world. She brought a huge range of life experiences to the topic and I enjoyed how she was able to jump across continents verbally, seeing the issues on a global scale, and making links between spaces. Then I asked Aabidah about the differences between her experiences of different (global) mosques. She replied,

In Sudanese culture women just don't go, even for Eid prayers, they stay at home and pray. In Syria and UAE we always went, there are bigger spaces there for women, it's not frowned upon [female attendance]. I remember in Oslo, looking through [the mosque] at the men's section; it was very, very clean, the section for women was like second class. They [mosques] are really different in different places. It's interesting, the one in New York, we went a lot, and to Sunday school, Qur'an classes and events. At social events there was mixing, but with a buffer zone in the middle, a big space between men and women ... Here in the mosques there are divides, ethnic and gender. In Mecca there is no divide between men and women, it's different.

Although she had been in London for six years, Aabidah reported that she did not attend one mosque regularly and reflected upon the reasons why.

I haven't been to many [mosques] here, mainly Regent's and Finsbury Park [mosques], there is always a divide, Egyptians sit on their own, Somalis sit on their own, different areas ... although Finsbury Park mosque is more mixed, Regent's Park is more Arab. I get the impression that [smaller UK mosques are] not always open, not always have [a] full-time imam. There's one off on Holloway Road, a small mosque, I've walked past it a few times, always lots of Somali men, maybe doesn't have a women's area, I don't even know if they do. I don't really go to them that often here, I went at Eid, found that people were very friendly, giving. I was happy, as hadn't been involved in going for a while, it reminded me of when I used to go, I guess.

As well as having found her own path within Islam, Aabidah gave a lot of thought to questions of interpretation, of culture, of contexts, really, in religion. She seemed able to think about a variety of perspectives when responding to each question, her answers contained an interesting mixture of self-reflective thought and awareness of how societal and psychological forces shaped individual experiences. This was particularly evident when the discussion turned to gender and mosques:

> Some people say that women don't need to go, it really depends on culture; [some are] not allowed to go, some who don't want to go, some women don't feel a need to go, or don't always feel like they are welcome. It's psychological in that sense, if you don't feel welcome, you don't want to go. When I was younger I always went with my family, I felt that if I went alone, it felt strange.

Related to these culturally located interpretations of Islam is the issue of attitudes (and perceived attitudes) within the spaces themselves. As a mosque can be the hub of community life, it can also be a space where behaviour is regulated by the community. As Aabidah talked, I found myself recalling an experience praying in a central London mosque; I just stumbled upon it during a walk and, my phone having recently alarmed the prayer time, spontaneously decided to go in. After making *wudu* (ablution), I followed the staircase up to the women's section (really a large balcony constructed so that women could see and hear at least some of the *khutba* (sermon) given below, but not be seen by male worshippers). Maybe a handful of women were already there, in varying stages of prayer, and I found an empty space, made my intention, and began to pray. It was lovely, and I was really enjoying the sense of peace and serenity that some, especially larger, spacious mosques offer; there is something very different about praying in a specially designed building than in one's own living room. Anyway, after the first two *rakats* (cycle of prostrations), as I rested, I found myself hastily returning to this earthly realm by a gentle tapping on my shoulder. Looking up, a kind-faced older woman was trying to get my attention. I felt concerned and asked if she was okay. It turned out she wanted to tell me that my prayers would be invalid as I was wearing nail varnish. I looked down at my lightly painted nails and felt annoyed that she had interrupted my prayer to tell me this. Aabidah's words reminded me of this frustration:

> In mosques, you do feel judged, people automatically have an idea when they see you, Islam is very much interpretation according to culture.

People act like there is just one way to pray, people feel like they are saving you. Also, Arabs are very racist people, I can say that 'cos I am Arab, and some mosques stop women coming in altogether, by barricading door, if you are wearing jeans. I remember one time I was praying, a woman actually moved me during my prayer, I was so shocked I just said thank you! It is a whole mentality, of 'my way is the way', people feel that they understand God better than anyone else, I'm like 'really, really?' In mosques, people expect you to pray as they do, be as they are. Some people have this idea that there is only one way to pray, women are always expected to be quiet, to quiet down, women's voice is *awra*, needs to be concealed, not heard [by men] ... Mosques always vary according to culture, and how women are seen in that culture.

Later in the discussion I asked Aabidah, 'do you think sexuality matters in mosques?'

I don't think that sexuality does matter, it shouldn't ... but it does. When you pray beside someone else you don't have to know [their sexuality], it doesn't matter, in that sense it's fine, it's maybe safer to be in a space there. But it's about acceptance ... It's like if it's not spoken it doesn't exist, in mosques it doesn't matter, but people feel like it is their duty ...

Whilst Aabidah is right, of course, that sexuality should not be a factor when worshipping in mosque spaces, sometimes it can be. One respondent suggested that, 'sexuality is not relevant in mosques, maybe it's easier for women, but ... if it's a known entity, then [it] definitely would be a problem'. Another respondent explained that gender expression can be much more noticeable than sexual orientation; when I asked her if sexuality is relevant to mosques, she said something similar:

It is not important. [But] if you were gonna ask a camp man, probably get different answers ... in terms of going to a mosque, and the issues that come out of it, it is. I went with a friend who had very short hair, a lesbian, she looked very boyish, as soon as we walked in the security guy said, 'put something on your head', she put a hat on, so there were issues there. She didn't look like a typical girl, it was very brave of her, I was shocked, she is [a] timid person but did it 'cos she wanted to go to the mosque.

In this case, gender expression crossed over with sexuality, and might be a more visible marker than anything else; transgendered individuals, effeminate men, or masculine looking women, for example, might face prejudice therein. As mentioned above, race, dress, style of prayer, and physical appearance could be raised by other members of the community, in mosques, as in other communal spaces. The issue we arrived at is one of acceptance and community policing along gendered lines, and this was one raised by Aabidah. Even for a feminine looking woman such as Aabidah, whose sexuality was not necessarily visible in a mosque, it was the sense of not being accepted that was a problem. She tells me,

> I still believe in the teachings of Islam, I would want to teach my kids about it, I'm not going to use it to terrorize, to control them … If I have kids I would like to take them to the mosque, if they can be accepted for who they are. I'd like them to be able to learn about Islam in that environment, and see different sects of Muslims praying together, Sufis and Sunnis too.

It was the question of acceptance to which we continually returned. If Aabidah and her partner were to have children in the future (and this point is also often raised by single mothers), the possibility of complete acceptance by the Muslim community within mosque space was a challenging one.

After the questions were done, we chatted a little, maybe ten minutes, about her interest in the Inclusive Mosque Initiative (IMI). I told her that the group is having a dinner and prayers later on that day. She reluctantly said that she couldn't come as she had so much to do before travelling, but hoped to come to an IMI event once she was back and would check the website. Then she said she had to leave and I thanked her again for her time; I felt the interview had gone well and been enjoyable (for me, at least). After she left I got more coffee and spent 40 minutes going over the notes, adding bits that came back to me, making it more legible, expanding on abbreviated words, and generally trying to record as much as I could remember before I forgot. I also wrote two pages of reflections and general observations on the interview content, for my own reference. These reflections greatly contributed to the account presented above, and reminded me that spending time with the interview content, as soon afterwards as possible, is a really vital part of accurately remembering and recording fieldwork findings.

Discussion

Once upon a time a man and his handful of supporters were persecuted for their religious beliefs and driven from their city. Another city offered them refuge. They humbly accepted, relocating women, men, children – even the little ones. A new way of conceiving time, and space, began. This is no new story but what happened next is remarkably radical. The man was Muhammad, and upon arriving in Medina he built a humble building that irrevocably changed human history. Al-Masjid al-Nabawi (the Prophet's mosque) became the blueprint for all later Muslim places of worship and, in many ways, set the tone for Muslim community structure. The Prophet's mosque housed, and functioned as, the natural 'heart' of Muslim community building. Living literally next door to the mosque, the Prophet's family and personal life was entwined, from the very beginning, with Muslim social and spiritual life. During congregational prayers, children (including the Prophet's grandchildren) spilled through the rows and clambered across prostrating backs. When the Prophet passed away, in the room of Aisha, it was here that he was buried.

Whilst we cannot map exactly how gender originally intersected with spatial experience in this mosque, it has been noticed by scholars that there appears to have been no walls or partitions to separate men and women. Today the Prophet's mosque remains on the same site but is larger, vaster, shinier. It is also supposedly gender segregated, an official stance that stumbles under the sheer weight of praying bodies during the hajj (pilgrimage) season, and is hardly perceptible in the countless courtyards that surround it. Although internal sections of the Prophet's mosque are clearly gender segregated, when the *adhan* (call to prayer) descends, clusters of praying, gendered bodies are formed wherever they are standing.

Inclusivity in UK mosques

I began this research initially interested in how sexuality might affect women's mosque attendance, yet it soon became clear that inclusivity issues also arise around race, gender, mobility, and sectarian differences. Although every mosque is, on paper, inclusive, in practice and experience this can vary immensely. Inclusivity in UK mosque spaces deserves further exploration as gendered patterns in mosque attendance and involvement around the world are changing.

I would like to end this chapter by considering inclusivity issues beyond sexuality, and end by thinking about intentionally inclusive mosque spaces. In 1889, the first purpose-built mosque was built on UK soil. Just like the early Muslim community, it drew together all ethnicities, ages, and degrees of Islam. Unlike the mosques of early Islam, the first UK mosques saw a significantly higher proportion of male worshippers than female, reflecting the specificities of British Muslim history more than it does anything intrinsic to global mosque design. Fast forward 120 years, and estimates of the number of existing UK mosques are set around 1,600, with many more places used as temporary mosque spaces (such as during Ramadan). There are more than three million Muslims in the UK today, of which about half would be women, and as a whole, existing mosques do not reflect or accommodate this. Some mosques do not provide any women's space at all.

As Aabidah pointed out, mosques vary tremendously globally, and the intersection between gender and rituals is filtered through culture in every religion. My interview highlighted the importance of interpretation in religion, and how localized, cultural views of women shape expectations of religious performance. At this point in time, UK mosque management committees seem to privilege male involvement, decision-making, and leadership roles. This obviously influences the physical spaces and facilities available to female worshippers, and may make them less keen to attend. That said, many British Muslim women do frequently attend mosques; conditions vary immensely and women's experiences are in no way monolithic. Tayyiba's description of the women's sections in UK mosques was common, '[I've] usually found them to be much more inferior, dingier, at the back, like we're some kind of second class citizens', yet on another occasion I was told '[m]y experience of this, the mosques were ok, they were nice actually. I like Regent's Park mosque, it's nicely carpeted, all the facilities ... I thought they adequately provided space for women.' Some respondents spoke at length about the services and activities provided specifically for women at their local mosques, mostly in larger UK cities.

Everyone I spoke to agreed that mosques are important for the British Muslim community, in the sense that they need to exist as communal spaces. Respondents differed on their importance in their own lives. When I asked Tayyiba, a practising Sunni, 'Why do you go?' she laughed and said, 'My mum ... I don't feel I need to be in religious institutions to pray, or in that environment. The things that happen in mosque, the patriarchy, 'cos I'm a staunch feminist, those things irritate me.' This was echoed by other respondents, such as Sukina's summary, 'They're important for the community, but not necessarily important for your faith. You can practise Islam anywhere.'

As Aabidahs's interview highlighted, inclusivity issues are not limited to sexual identities or gender expression. Like all communal spaces, UK mosques can be divided along racial, sectarian, ethnic, economic, social, and linguistic lines.

One woman that I spoke to, a practising Shi'a, explained how her background and beliefs influenced how she used existing mosques. She reported that frequent attendance simply was not part of her childhood (as her Shi'a family was not made welcome at the local Sunni mosques) and that she remained uncomfortable praying in Sunni-majority spaces.

> [It] would be good to have a space where people can pray however they like ... but people are very defensive ... I think my issues [with attending mosques] stem from being Shi'a, it's really the fear of praying in a Shi'a manner, so it's the complete inclusivity thing. It's not about who leads, I can do either [prayers], its a big fear of mosque culture ... I have this idea in my head, I know I could probably go there and do it how I want, its just at the moment I do *khanut*, I worry ... having fear in prayer is so bad, I feel like I have to do it really quick so no one works it out.

A space where people can pray however they like and, as the subtext reads, feel accepted by other Muslims, despite whatever differences they bring to their Islam. It is worth mentioning two related points here: first, debates over gender and prayer, gender and religious leadership, or even gender and mosques are not in any way new. Indeed, they stretch back to the time of the Prophet himself. Second, aspirations for such inclusive spaces, where people can pray 'however they like' are dynamically being realized by Muslims

Figure 10.1 Norwich, © Ahmed Krausen Photography

around the world. This is linked, in subtle and overt ways, to the process of rethinking gender and mosque spaces; we increasingly see groups creating spaces and places where women and men can worship together, and where female-led prayers can occur. In North America there are multiple resources, activist campaigns, and physical spaces which facilitate inclusive Muslim worship (MPV Unity Mosques and el-Tawhid Juma Circle Mosques, for example). For British Muslims there is the Muslim Education Centre of Oxford (MECO) which consciously attends to inclusivity on all levels, identifies as feminist and offers female-led prayers. However, it does not have a permanent space for prayers, is run by one man, and being based in Oxford, cannot serve the whole of the British Muslim community.

This research project was designed through consultation with the Inclusive Mosque Initiative (IMI). Whilst it takes time to fund and build a mosque, responses to the initiative have been overwhelmingly positive so far, and working groups are already established around the UK. IMI hopes to create a space where every understanding of Islam can be explored and practised, and where women like Aabidah, Tayyiba, and Sukina are welcome with their differences intact.

Readings

A good classic to begin with, for anyone interested in this topic, would be Leila Ahmed's *Women and Gender in Islam: Historical Roots of a Modern Debate*

(New Haven, CT: Yale University Press, 1992). For more information about women's relationship to mosque spaces and religious authority, Masooda Bano and Hilary Kalmbach's edited collection *Women, Leadership, and Mosques: Changes in Contemporary Islamic Authority* (Leiden, Netherlands: Brill, 2011), Julianne Hammer's *More Than a Prayer: American Muslim Women, Religious Authority, and Activism* (Austin: University of Texas Press, 2012), Jamillah Karim's *American Muslim Women: Negotiating Race, Class, and Gender Within the Ummah* (New York: New York University Press, 2009), and Amina Wadud's *Qur'an and Woman: Rereading the Sacred Text from a Woman's Perspective* (Oxford: Oxford University Press, 1999) are all interesting reads. Furthermore, for a look at Muslim religious aesthetics in the United States from a historical viewpoint, see Akel Kahera's *Deconstructing the American Mosque: Space, Gender, and Aesthetics* (Austin: University of Texas Press, 2002).

Author

Dervla Shannahan is an independent researcher who has published a variety of words in a variety of places (academic journals, book chapters, websites and elsewhere). She has an MA in Islamic Studies (from the University of Wales, Lampeter) and an MA in Queer Studies in Arts and Culture (from Birmingham City University). Her research interests include Islam, faith-based feminisms, queer theologies, and postcolonial theory. Since completing her last MA, she has taken time out from formal study to focus on writing, parenting, and

Figure 10.2 Birmingham, © Ahmed Krausen Photography

psychotherapeutic training. She has also done bits of activism around gender and sexuality in Islam, and she is on the management committee of the Inclusive Mosque Initiative, discussed in this chapter. She recently realized that she will never get a proper academic job without a PhD, so will start at Goldsmiths shortly (2013).

Chapter 11

Where heaven meets earth
Music and Islam in everyday life and encounters

Carin Berg

Preamble

All over the Middle East music is played – in taxis, buses, restaurants, homes, demonstrations, commemorations, political events, and religious feasts. Simultaneously, music is being banned and concerts and festivals are closed down with the motivation that the circumstances might exhort sinful acts or thoughts. This chapter derives from my experiences and understandings of the complex relationship between music and Islam, particularly in the Lebanese and Palestinian contexts where I lived for approximately six years. The chapter will render discussions with religious Muslims and leaders, sheikhs, on how they make sense of music and Islam in contemporary times. It will also describe my involvement in how religiously accepted music (*anashiid*) is produced and used and how members of religiously correct bands argue on the matter of music. The following narrative and discussion, for example, will consider why religious Islamic practitioners consider certain lyrics of love and atheism as blasphemous (haram) and why songs that, for example, encourage battle are in line with Islam (halal).

Narrative

Putting music and Islam on the scene

During an extraordinary hot day in May a few years ago, I was invited to a family in Baalbek in the Bekaa Valley mid-west of Lebanon. Baalbek is considered to be a political hot spot due to its strong Hezbollah support. The area is also built upon a family clan system, which basically makes Baalbek a no-man's land in terms of official security. My purpose of visit that time was not deliberately to understand the relation between music and Islam. Nevertheless, this visit came to me as a realization of how one should make sense of its complex coherence. I had previously met the father of the family on a couple of occasions. The father is a sheikh, meaning that he is either an elderly person who has much knowledge and experience or, as in this case, an Islamic scholar. In both cases a sheikh is a respected and honoured person who can govern a society but cannot be in direct leadership, as that is the task of an imam. I arrived in Baalbek after a rather humid three-hour trip in an overcrowded minivan permeated by loud Arabic pop music. As it was not considered safe for me to be wandering around alone in Baalbek, the sheikh and one of his sons met me at the bus. As is the religious custom, neither of them shook my hand, but put their right hands on the chest and nodded slightly while saying salaam (peace). I got used to this custom after meeting a few more religious men, and did not reflect upon it any more. I even began to feel more respected when men kept their religious customs even when meeting a European like myself.

The entire family had been waiting for me. The women greeted me with three kisses and the men all lifted their hands towards their chests. Coffee, sweets, and fruit were served immediately on the floor in the living room. As I had told the sheikh that I wanted to take the opportunity of visiting the famous Roman temples of Baalbek, he had organized that the same son who picked me up from the bus would take me there. I was very excited as we left in his car, just about an hour later, for the temple ruins. His English was rather non-existent and my Arabic at that time did not reach the level of keeping long conversations alive. So after some genuine attempts to communicate, he began searching among some CDs and apparently found the right one. A loud authoritative man's voice guttered from the speakers, and I felt embraced and somehow touched by the sound. There were no accompanying instruments but nevertheless the message was so powerful and I only wished that I could under-stand the lyrics. My companion must have anticipated my wish as he pointed at the CD player and said repetitively, 'Anashiid, anashiid'. I did recognize the style of the music but had just not heard the term before. I wondered if it was political, religious, or perhaps the name of the singer. As if he could read my mind, again, he said, 'Hamas'. OK, political, I thought, probably including some religious messages and elements as well then. I never got to see the temple ruins that day, but we did drive around listening to Hamas *anashiid* for several hours, and I found that I was pleased and excited none the less.

As we arrived back at the house, the garden had been transformed into a festive area. Hundreds of people were sitting on chairs around an open space where some men were dancing Dabke, a traditional Arab folkdance, to loud Arabic music streaming out of enormous speakers. I was curious to get a closer look, but as the son did not really seem all that interested, I followed him back into the house. Part of the family was sitting quietly in the living room and the sheikh explained that two relatives were getting married. I asked if they were about to go out to celebrate with them and he answered instantly, 'No, I do not like these kinds of events.' I realized that the other family members in the room were of a similar opinion and I probably seemed confused as the sheikh politely said, 'Please go out to check it if you like.' All eyes turned to me and I decided just to sit down for a while. It was, after all, this particular family that I was visiting, and even if a foreigner usually gets away with making mistakes, I did not want to take the risk. Not yet. Many religious

Muslims cannot accept a wedding where men and women are mixed. The preferred setting is that the women celebrate separately, which will also allow them to remove the hijab (headscarf) and dance freely. Men are also expected to celebrate separately, but the groom is allowed to visit the bride among the women. The wedding that took place outside was all but such a setting. Men and women were present at the same celebration, pop music with sinful lyrics and messages − according to Islam − was played and people were dancing. For men and women to mix in such a setting might lead to immoral thoughts and acts, triggered by the music, which should be avoided by separating the sexes. Sinful messages, meaning lyrics of love that are not sung to your wife or husband but to any man or woman, are considered haram according to Islam. Any relationship or love between persons who are not married is forbidden among the religious Muslims, so gatherings where such feelings or actions could be stimulated (mainly known for including popular music) are seen as immoral. As the evening went by, I decided to have a look in the garden after all. The music continued to bawl and the local *shabab* (young men) were taking up most of the dance floor. The women who were watching the dancing men and whispering frenetically amongst themselves, illustrated the sheikh's words. Perhaps they were searching for the right husband for themselves or for a friend or relative. It became even clearer what was going on as a couple of women dared to enter the floor and hesitantly danced for a short time. All eyes turned to them and I heard later that this short 'performance' usually became the main topic of conversation in the village for months. It might even lead to huge family problems and even fights. I stayed for a couple of hours, but could hear the party lasting until the early morning hours from my bed.

During my return to Beirut, where I was residing at that time, in a similar minivan on a warm evening on the following day, it struck me that the music I had heard in the different settings, both during my time in Baalbek and previously, differed widely from one another. The main differences were the beat and the lyrics, which I only understood partly since my Arabic was not fluent at that time. My suspicions were soon confirmed. There were differences, major differences. As briefly mentioned before, I realized that religious hard-line Muslims, in general, do not listen to music containing any lyrics or elements opposing the religious traditions as it is considered forbidden (haram) by Islam. At the same time, I also learnt that religious Muslims, such as sheikhs, but also political parties, such as Hamas and Hezbollah, produce and use music existing within the frames of what is allowed (halal) according to Islam. The picture became clearer; however, I did wonder how it was all interlinked and how it all made sense.

Voices of a sheikh

Three years after my experiences in Baalbek I returned to Lebanon and my discussions with Islamic scholars and others continued, or, actually, really started. The meaning and content of *anashiid* turned out to have as many answers as discussions and I often wondered whether music as I knew it was always forbidden in Islam, or if it was rather the present circumstances that stretched such rules or if it was commands from God? I returned to the same family in Baalbek and during a three-hour talk on the roof of the house, overlooking the wide fields, the sheikh explained surprisingly that nothing in the holy Qur'an states that music is forbidden. 'Let me visualize the matter', the sheikh said. He narrated a story in the Qur'an when the Prophet Muhammad's wife went to a wedding. On her return the Prophet asked her, 'What did you do tonight at the wedding?' The wife answered, 'Nothing.' The Prophet asked, 'Why? Why did you not sing?' As this story, when Muhammad encouraged his wife to sing in public, is told in the Qur'an, Muslims cannot claim that music per se is forbidden according to the religion. The discussion about haram and halal in relation to music is in general a discussion about what the particular music contains and how it is being used. OK, but what about *anashiid* that his son spoke about in the car three years ago? What is that all about in such context? The sheikh must have noticed that I seemed confused. He explained that in order to differentiate between songs as a whole and halal music according to Islam, Muslims talk about *anashiid*. The distinction lies in the lyrics of the song and how these lyrics are used. I had heard, not only from this sheikh but also from several Muslims, that the main rationale to distinguish a haram song from halal concerns the issue of love. I was raised with the thought that love in any shape or form was something beautiful and desirable, a belief that was about to be questioned. Thankfully, the daughter of the family brought us some fruit and tea that helped the blood sugar rise as the time was approaching 2:00 a.m. and the discussion on the roof seemed to have just started. The sheikh rubbed his beard, looked out over the fields from the rooftop, and said that songs were basically not allowed to 'steal' people's emotions. But what if the singer is married, I wondered? Is it also forbidden that his/her wife's/husband's emotions are 'stolen'? No, such songs were considered halal if the intention, through the lyrics, was clear, he said calmly while offering me the sweetest orange I had ever tasted.

As I went to bed that night, on the floor in the living room where most activities took place during the day, I reflected upon our last conversation. I had begun to understand what it was all about, even though my questions were, if possible, more numerous than ever. I also remembered the drive with the son in Baalbek during the last visit some years ago. The Hamas *anashiid* we heard in the car did not include any instruments, something that I did not realize earlier. Was that a musical coincidence or a conscious religious choice? Did the haram/halal discussion also have something to do with instruments? I suddenly remembered that during my three years in Palestine a friend of mine who plays *darbakke* (Arabic drum) used to say that his profession was haram according to Islam. I eventually fell asleep, but as the sheikh was not present for breakfast in the garden the following morning, I called him as I could not wait to ask him more questions. I could somehow hear how he smiled about my enthusiasm and he explained with a soft paternalistic voice. The issue of instruments in songs is also related to the Qur'an. The Qur'an speaks of how instrumental music was used during battles in that time. It is mentioned, though, that two kinds of instruments were not used and are therefore considered forbidden in Hadith: *watariaat* (string instruments) and *darbakke* (Arabic drum). I then realized why my Palestinian friend claimed that his profession was forbidden according to Islam. However, some religious scholars and interpreters claim that the two types of instruments are allowed if they are used in halal songs, meaning *anashiid*, he said, something that I would discover soon in the political context of *anashiid*.

A few weeks later I met with the sheikh in his office in Beirut as I was asked to drive him to the bus leaving for Baalbek. As I started the engine the radio went on and the song 'Ya rabba la tushur samaa Lubnaan' (God don't leave the sky of Lebanon) by the Lebanese singer Wadia Assafi played. The sheikh fidgeted uncomfortably in the seat, but he tactfully explained that another reason that makes a song haram is if singers are using the elements of God for an atheistic purpose, as in this song where heaven is used in a patriotic manner. I reacted immediately by turning the volume down and he seemed at ease. Out of curiosity I asked if he ever listened to this kind of popular music in his car. No, he said, never! As we drove, and without asking, he told me that he was aware that some of his sons listened to other kinds of music than *anashiid* and that it was fine with him as long as they did not do it in his presence, and particularly not in his car. The one who is probably the strictest in his family regarding music is his wife; a large argument arose on the wedding day of one of his sons. The wedding was divided between men and women, so far so good. But as the men's party was supposed to take place in their house and the son planned to play all kinds of popular music on his big day, contradictions arose. The mother thought it was shameful to play such music in their house, or at all, and did not agree at all. But as the father, the sheikh, argued that it was the son's day and that it was therefore his choice, the music was played. But his wife never agreed and still did not agree to play music other than *anashiid* in their house. As many days and nights as I spent in their house, I have so far never heard any tunes other than Qur'an verses from a religious TV channel.

Anashiid *in the studio*

I recently travelled to Amman, the capital of Jordan. I had heard that Amman was one of the places where *anashiid* was produced in the Middle East and I wanted to see it for myself. One of the most famous *anashiid* bands, al Rawabi, is in Amman and I obtained the phone number of the manager of the band. I called him immediately upon arrival at the hotel. He did not speak English so

I switched to Arabic, which usually helps, but he did not seem to understand me, or did not want to understand me! We hung up and I asked a sweet lady beside me for help. She realized the problem and immediately called him back. I could understand that she explained who I was and what I wanted, but he was not interested and hung up again. Now what, I thought? He did, however, leave a number for the New Sound studio. Great, I thought, it was at least something, even though I did not really know what this particular studio did. I called and the man who answered spoke perfect English and seemed really enthusiastic about my plight. We decided that I would visit the studio the following day. 'Just let the taxi driver call me as you approach the sport stadium and I will guide him', Mutassem, as his name was, said.

The following day I did as I was told and, through guidance on the phone to the taxi driver, I managed to find the right entrance. However, I was unsure if it was the right place as the building seemed empty and like a shanty. But suddenly I heard loud male voices, as if they were having an argument, and I instinctively felt that it was the right place! When I knocked on the half-open door the five men inside turned silent, and one of them, Mutassem, said that he was surprised I found the place and that he expected a call from me first. They all seemed so modern. Normally dressed, no beards, and no external attributes that gave away that they were religious Muslims. 'Yalla, let us go inside the studio to talk', Mutassem said. The studio was as modern as the men with brand new equipment and prizes and awards covering the walls. It was only Mutassem, the sound technician, and me in the studio. But soon after we entered, another man joined us. It turned out that he was one of the founders of the al Rawabi band, and I got all excited. The grumpy man on the phone might have had a plan after all. As I had previously explained the aim of my visit, I hardly had to ask anything before Mutassem began explaining his view on music and religion, and of course information about the studio itself. The studio mainly recorded music related to Islamic topics, but may sometimes also produce music containing political issues. 'Our studio is a bit unique as we carefully select the topics, bands, and musicians we work with', he explained. 'We work with all types of topics except the ones that have a bad influence on people. We cannot record songs about love or sexual issues, for example, or songs using religion or God in a bad way.' Mutassem first said, 'It is according to religion.' But, then he changed his mind and said it was rather according to values. He repeated several times that he actually wished that people could go beyond religious labels when it came to music, or any topics. I wanted to stretch the discussion a bit further, so I asked about the usage of the music they record. As it had come to my knowledge that the problem was mainly the influence that the music had on the behaviour of people, I wanted to understand how they could be sure that the music they recorded was not used in a wrong way even if it was halal from the beginning. They all explained that they could never know because the music they produced was often very powerful and emotional. It often had a great beat, so it could actually be used in the nightclubs. If people get aroused and use the music we record in a wrong way there is not much we can do, even if that is of course not the purpose. I recalled again what the sheikh told me. He explained to me that it was very difficult to control such things, but that it was his personal duty, mediated from God, to prevent it by preaching about the correct ways of living. In addition, it was his duty to stop any contradicting acts that came to his attention, such as people listening to *anashiid* while drinking alcohol.

Mutassem explained that his life as a practising religious man is rather new. 'Some years ago I used to go to clubs and drink and enjoy my life, but I started to question what this kind of life was for and what purpose it filled. At that time everything circulated around what to do the coming weekend, what to wear, what to drink, etc. I began to question many things with my lifestyle and I had a turning point where I turned to religion to find the meaning.' He began listening to the Qur'an and praying regularly. This was also the time when *anashiid* entered his life. 'I used to listen to love songs, Scorpions, Creed, Amr Diab, etc., but then I stopped and began listening to Mishari al Afasi. He is a man who has inspired me a lot!' Mutassem told me that he was sitting in a café when it all happened. Al Afasi entered the stage on TV dressed in a traditional abaya. His message was that just because you believed in God and practised your religion, it did not mean that you should not enjoy life and interact with all kinds of people; on the contrary. You should support the century you live in and use its positive qualities. 'I call this period "the awakening" and it happened to me about 10 years ago. Nowadays when I think about the old music I used to listen to, it does not only disturb me regarding the religious aspect', he said, 'I really feel that the production quality is very low, the voices are usually really bad and it is cheaply made.' Mutassem explained that Amer Khaled was another person who had inspired him a lot during this new period in his life. Amer is not a sheikh as such but he is a religious preacher who has inspired many people, particularly youth of the twenty-first century, to acknowledge that Islam does not have to be boring and old fashioned. In the same regard, he mentioned a TV channel, called The Awakening Channel, that targets people who 'came out of the box', meaning that Islam can be suitable to people's lifestyle of today. The channel promotes *anashiid* singers who are still very religious, but not in the old-fashioned way. The channel also addresses the West by playing *anashiid* music translated into English, for example. 'I believe this is an extremely important issue. Since music is "talking" and Muslims are often misunderstood, it is important to translate our message into English or local languages and to not continue living in our small box.'

The discussion in the studio naturally moved on to the topic of *anashiid*, or *munshid*, the singers of *anashiid*. *Munshid* are spiritual people who sing together in order to deliver certain types of messages, or at least that is what it should be all about, Mutassem said. In Islam *anashiid* should be understood as an umbrella, part of the whole music industry, all three explained. Some topics under the umbrella of *anashiid* are, for example, nationality, religion, children, suffering, and parents. Within these issues there is nothing that has to do with Islam, like Islamic *anashiid*. It does exist but it is completely different and it is actually a fault of the West, which calls any topic of the ones mentioned Islamic *anashiid*. It derives from the West's difficulties to separate politics and religion, he explained. Okay, I thought, but I have also heard Muslims call all of these topics Islamic *anashiid*. The founder of the al Rawabi band wanted to clarify more and explained that one should separate traditional and modern *anashiid*. The traditional one stems from the days of Muhammad until approximately the 1970s. This era was permeated by *anashiid* that mainly concerned religious topics and is known through a famous singer named Abu Mazen. When the songs were political, they mainly stressed specific occasions like the massacre in Hama, the Ibrahimi massacre, and the song 'Burning the al Aqsa mosque', talking about when Zionists entered the mosque in Jerusalem in order to burn it down. During this time there were no studios or advanced recording systems. People brought recorders and recorded cassettes into their houses, where it spread from person to person and house to house. The music of this time did not reach many people, but it had a powerful effect on the ones that it did reach. It was a great challenge to produce and use Islamic songs during this time as the regimes in the Middle East were generally controlled by a secular system. The leaders in that time preferred songs of love by, for example, Om Kolthom and Fairuz and they opposed people who spread Islamic messages. People singing about Islam were not in the spotlight at that time, but they still had to be brave as they were constantly discouraged.

Anashiid *and Hamas*

Some years ago during an interview in the West Bank in the Palestinian territories, a man affiliated to the Palestinian resistance movement Hamas (Harakat al Mukawame il Islamiye, the Islamic resistance movement) told me a story that I will never forget. It stirred a curiosity in me about how music was used in political environments permeated by Islam and how it might affect the person listening to it. We met in a secluded building far away from people, as all Hamas-affiliated persons in the West Bank were scared to talk about their organization in public since the Fatah takeover in 2007. The man explained that he had been in and out of prison since the takeover for reasons like listening to Hamas *anashiid*. Sometimes the Fatah police or security would visit just to go through his computer. If it contained anything related to Hamas he was imprisoned on the spot. But he said he did not care any more. He had obvious problems with walking, as he was harshly tortured in prison. As we sat down he told me the story about his friend who, about a year before, attached explosives to his body in order to enter Israel and blow up himself and as many of the enemy as possible. As he was caught before he committed the act, he was sent to prison. When he was set free, my informant asked him what made him have the courage to do such a thing. He answered that he listened to Hamas music (*anashiid* created by Hamas bands). My informant explained that his own opinion is that music in general is used for fun, and *anashiid* to create a spiritual feeling. But both are also used to support people's humanitarian values, and since the Palestinian people are living under Israeli occupation the humanitarian values might be stretched to mean resistance for freedom as it did for his friend. 'It is a moral war for us to get our rights back and in this aspect music is important. Since the Palestinians have the right to resist against occupation, we cannot say that Hamas resistance music is bad, it is rather a helpful tool for encouraging and keeping the resistance alive. Sometimes we should use violence to show Israel that we are still here and ready and in such regards music/*anashiid* is a tool that fighters use', he explained. After the meeting, a friend helped me translate a few Hamas battle songs that the informant sent me from YouTube, and not only the beat and music (containing all sorts of instruments) but also the lyrics were very powerful. For example, they spoke about how rockets should be hit in the livers of the oppressors and that the occupiers should be obliterated. A similar vein runs through all halal topics as the Palestinian war on Israel is considered as a mission of jihad (religious duty/war) in accordance with Islam.

Hamas bands exist both in the Gaza Strip (no longer, at least officially, in the West Bank after the Fatah takeover) as well as in the diaspora countries. There are two famous Hamas bands in Lebanon, namely Amjad and al Waed, and I have spent some time with the members of Amjad. The band has 13 members and was established in 2007. Their studio is located in Saida in a narrow street and in the same building as a carpentry store. To reach the studio you have to pass through the dust of wood, climb a narrow staircase, and enter a thick, solid door. You really had to know there was a studio in order to find it. But once inside, the studio, as the one in Amman, was modern with new equipment. I was told that the studio was mainly built by donor money from supporting individuals. The group was not necessarily affiliated to Hamas, but Hamas supported their music and their resistance against Israel. All the members of the band have regular jobs and are working with the band in their free time. They have recorded three albums so far and the fourth is on its way. Four of the band members were present when I visited the first time and when they began to speak about *anashiid* it was very similar to what I had heard before, for example, from the sheikh. So I supposed that religious Muslims somehow had a similar understanding of what *anashiid* was and what it should be. I wondered what the difference between a mere *anashiid* band and a politically affiliated band was. Apparently, *anashiid* created by Hamas bands can be divided into four main categories: grief about leaders and martyrs (basically people killed in battle), tribute to the same, unification, and resistance purposes. But they do also produce songs for hajj (pilgrimage) and weddings according to Islamic values, of course, where religion has to be part of the songs to be accepted by the audience. The main differences between

Figure 11.1 Carin Berg and a band member of Amjad in their studio (Saida, Lebanon)

any *anashiid* band and the politically affiliated ones seem to be related to resistance or songs directly addressing the particular organization.

Other than recording CDs, they also perform at different festivals, mainly political ones for Hamas or Palestinian causes. Sometimes they are asked by, for example, Hamas to produce songs for specific occasions, such as for the last war in Gaza 2012. 'For our band it is important that we choose subjects for the *anashiid* that people will like and can connect to because their participation is related to our choice of subjects. For example, if we sing about jihad or if we produce wedding songs, we know that people will be eager to listen and engage. To our band in general, the most important subject permeating all the songs is although moral related to Islam,' one of the members explained. So does Hamas have certain rules as an organization of what kind of music is haram or halal? Not precisely, I was told. On some levels, Hamas will take a stance on music, but it is done more privately and perhaps more as Muslims than political representatives. There is no general open policy on the issue from the authority. There were, however, occasions when Hamas took action against the usage of music and the wrong usage of *anashiid*, mainly in Gaza, but again at a low level. It has happened that the Hamas police in Gaza took action against music, such as closing down concerts and CD shops, but these were rather acts against specific individuals than direct orders from the government of Hamas.

Anashiid *and Hezbollah*

It was in November last year and the last day of the biggest Shi'a Muslim commemoration, Ashura, was about to take place. Ashura is the final day of 10 days of mourning for the assassination of Ibn Ali Husseini, the grandson of Muhammad. I had participated in several of the daily events in Hezbollah's main meeting hall, Sayyed Shuhada, in Dahiye, the Shi'a area of Beirut. Each day a religious man told a part of the story of how Ibn Ali Hussein was about to be killed ending with the Ashura day as the actual day for his assassination. During the events the previous week, I spent my time in the huge hall together with thousands of black-clad Hezbollah women. The men were on the other side of a small fence in the same hall. All were occasionally crying out loud, hitting themselves in the head with the fist symbolizing the pain of the martyr. Nowadays, Hezbollah members are not allowed to hit themselves with any objects as they did before, so they only use their hands. But members of the second biggest Shi'a organization in Lebanon, Harakat Amal, are still cutting open their heads, which was also one of the first sights I saw that very morning of the last Ashura day. As I was in a taxi, a group of men came walking barefoot, covered in blood, singing loud in unison, while hitting themselves. The driver said, 'No, no this is wrong. Not Hezbollah, Amal area.' I had heard about it, but actually seeing it was rather bizarre. I was dropped off where I 'belonged' and I noticed that the security alert was high. Most of the roads were closed for cars, and as I had no idea where I was or where I was going I decided to follow a group of black-dressed women. Half an hour later we ended up outside the Sayyed Shuhada where I sat down in the street among thousands of waiting women. Loud *anashiid* streamed out of the speakers as some women mumbled Qur'an verses and others chatted with each other.

After about an hour of waiting, a man started singing with short breaks in between when all, both men and women, burst out in a loud voice of religious slogans in tribute to Ibn Ali.

The singing suddenly turned to storytelling and the week-long story was about to peak with the killing of Ibn Ali Hussein. People sat, stood up, cried, and hit their heads and hearts with their fists. Specific women were wandering around handing out tissues for the crying and others were making sure no one fainted, which was a rather common scenario that I had experienced throughout the week. I felt that I blended in pretty well, dressed in black and wearing a headscarf. But regardless I had many eyes on me and the ones who dared to ask what I was doing there thought I recently got married to a Shi'a Muslim. Suddenly *anashiid* streamed out of the speakers again and people stood up. But this time it was more powerful and accompanied with several instruments. People raised their fists and screamed slogans acknowledging Ibn Ali and Hezbollah but also slogans against Israel and America. The thousands of people began to walk on, what turned out to be, a three-hour walk through all of Dahiye, men separately from women. Speakers were placed along the road where men were screaming slogans, which the masses answered, or singing political *anashiid*-like songs. My friend had told me during that week that special CDs were recorded for the Ashura, mainly commemorating Ibn Ali, but also with messages of what Shi'a Islam is all about and why it should be understood as the right denomination within Islam (implying that Sunni is not).

After the Ashura week, I met with the manager of Hezbollah's military band in order to understand better what I had heard and seen. He was also a conductor of several *anashiid* bands within the organization. To me, Hamas and Hezbollah *anashiid* appeared to be rather similar, but it seemed to be important to make some differences clear, mainly in terms of the religious branches Shi'a and Sunni. He explained that the Shi'a *anashiid* is more restricted and the religious Shi'a always follow a role model regarding what is permitted and not. 'At the moment, for Hezbollah, our model is Imam Khomeini. And because Khomeini pushed children to learn about and to play music, Hezbollah now accepts the kind of music that we perform in this military band and what Hezbollah uses in general. Such means that Hezbollah do not permit any music contradicting Islam, but at the same time they use classical pieces or halal songs sung by, for example, Fairouz.' Even though he claimed that Hezbollah is stricter in the usage of music than the Sunni

Figure 11.2 Hezbollah march during the last day of Ashura, in Dahiye (Beirut, Lebanon)

Muslims, this particular point seemed more liberal than what I had previously heard. He further explained that the military band itself do not perform, or produce, battle songs as such, but that Hezbollah resisters/fighters still listen to their music to get support for their missions. Other Hezbollah-affiliated bands specifically produce and sing these type of songs, such as Wilayiy, Israh, Fajer, and al Ahed. He could not specify further what bands I had heard during the Ashura, but usually one of these bands performed specific songs for the different religious occasions.

Discussion

Music in general and as part of religious practice is a contested issue among Muslims and often misinterpreted in the West, where Islam is frequently understood as rather rigid and unable to synchronize with contemporary times. Music and Islam is a challenging topic as it exists in an era where traditional religions are in decline and postmodernity is challenging any system that purports to be all-defining. As I was initially conducting research on other topics when it came to my knowledge that the usage of and discussions around music filled a core function in Muslim societies, it took some years before I began my own full-time research on the matter. However, I conducted sporadic interviews and regular chats with people as often as I could, which is why I did not restrict myself to only focus on, for example, one band, one studio, or one organization in this chapter. Music and Islam is a motley subject, which I tried to illustrate by including different voices and scenes from the field. Hence, I found it more useful to move among a variety of cities, countries, and locations to receive several voices rather than selecting one or two. In addition, it was not always a matter of strategic selection, but rather related to opportunities where I suddenly found myself in situations, meeting people, beneficial for this project. The political usage of music (*anashiid*) could have functioned as a chapter on its own, but simply using the term *anashiid* without placing it within its correct framework and background will leave undesirable blanks for understanding its complexity. Further, my curiosity for trying to grasp what *anashiid* is all about continuously grew during my stay in the field, which is the reason why it finally came to outline most of the chapter.

Heaven and land

Most religious Muslims use the Qur'an for guidance and to explain why all kinds of music should not be permitted nor prohibited per se. However, the guidelines in the Qur'an do not fit a general understanding of, for example, pop music of today or music as most people know it, which is the main reason why religiously accepted music is termed *anashiid*. *Anashiid* covers pretty much any topic as long as it exists within the customs of Islam, meaning in terms of both lyrics and contextual factors. The prohibited customs vary according to whom you ask, but it mainly concerns issues of love between persons who are not married, whether it exists in the lyrics of the music itself or if it is played in any setting where the music could trigger such acts to happen. Alcohol is another issue raised within the discussion of music and Islam. Listening to music while drinking alcohol, whether *anashiid* or not, or listening to music containing words about alcohol is clearly forbidden and will bring negative consequences on doomsday. In addition, music that misuses religious matters, such as God or the prophets, is also against Islamic customs. Even if most Muslims seem to decide for themselves what to listen to in music, *anashiid* or not, it is mainly religious scholars who are in charge of, and have the authority for, maintaining religious order in Muslim societies. It appears though to be the usage of certain instruments that is the issue with most diverse opinions. Some reckon that the Qur'an is clear on the matter and that such should be respected, while others feel that as long as the previously mentioned issues are considered, the use of any kind of instrument should not be a religious cause. The main threat, to any Muslim, of acting against the will of God is the consequences it will have on doomsday, not only considering alcohol as mentioned above. It is said that if you have more negative than positive remarks in your protocol at the doomsday, you will not go to heaven but to hell. If those negative remarks include the misuse of music, hot metal will forever be placed in your ear.

Readings

So far, there are not a lot of readings on music and Islam as an organizational practice. However, a newly published special issue of the journal *Contemporary Islam* on 'Music and Islam' can provide an introduction to the subject as a whole (Springer, 2012, vol. 6, no. 3). Moreover, writings on the relationship of music and Islam can be found in Jonas Otterbeck's 'Battling over the public sphere: Islamic reactions to the music of today' (*Contemporary Islam* 2, no. 3 (2008): 211–28), and A. K. Rasmussen's 'Performing religious politics: Islamic musical arts in Indonesia', in John Morgan O'Connell and Salwa El-Shawan Castelo-Branco (Eds), *Music and Conflict* (Urbana: University of Illinois Press, 2010). Another reading, published by one of the leading writers on music in the Middle East today, is Mark LeVine's *Heavy Metal Islam* (New York: Three Rivers Press, 2008). LeVine's book concerns the specific topic of heavy metal music produced in the Muslim world, mainly by Muslims themselves. In addition, this book contains an index of further readings.

Author

Carin Berg is a PhD student of Peace and Development Studies at the School of Global Studies, University of Gothenburg, Sweden. As she was previously involved in several academic research projects concerning the Middle East and also having resided in the area for several years, she holds a unique ethnographic expertise of the region. Her publications on related topics include *Tunes of Religious Resistance? Understanding Hamas Music in a Conflict Context* (New York: Springer, 2012) and *Hamas and Music in the Palestinian Context: Production, Perception, and Usage* (Bloomington: Indiana University Press, 2013).

Chapter 12

Muslims and the art of interfaith post-9/11
American Muslim artists reach out to New Yorkers in the aftermath of September 11

Munir Jiwa

Preamble

On January 19, 2002, a spectacular event took place at the Cathedral of St John the Divine in New York City, called *Reflections at a Time of Transformation: American Muslim Artists Reach out to New Yorkers in the Aftermath of September 11.* An initiative of the American Society for Muslim Advancement (ASMA), this event was aimed at 'healing wounds' and 'building interfaith and intercultural bridges' and was to celebrate the diversity of Muslim communities in New York with and through its artists – visual artists, musicians, poets, and filmmakers among others. This event, a first of its kind, sparked numerous other events throughout the years, where Muslim communities have begun including their artists/cultural producers to become the 'voice and face' of representation to the wider public. My work with Muslim artists has been an attempt to think about Muslims in new ways that neither restricts them to theological belief nor locates them only at mosques. It has been an effort to rethink and remap the locations where we normally find Muslims, to question and make more complex secular/religious divides, and to think about aesthetic practices in different contexts: within the art worlds and in Muslim communities.

Narrative

Staging the Reflections event

On a calm and snowy afternoon on January 19, 2002, just months after the attacks on the World Trade Center and the Pentagon, Synod Hall of the Cathedral Church of St John the Divine, on the upper west side of Manhattan, was filled to capacity. If one had not heard or read about the event taking place and walked in off the street, one would have been met with a pleasant surprise – more Muslims than they had probably ever seen at a church. The event, Reflections at a Time of Transformation: American Muslim Artists Reach out to New Yorkers was put together by the ASMA

Society of New York, 'a not-for-profit religious, cultural, and educational organization dedicated to building bridges between the American public and American Muslims in a myriad of fields, including various media and the arts'. As guests entered, artistic works of different backgrounds and styles greeted them: Afghan children's drawings, Zarina Hashmi's wood block prints, Shahzia Sikander's PBS video installation on 'Art of the 21st Century', Michael Green's silkscreen of a woman kneeling in prayer, Shekaiba Wakili's photographs of Muslim women, Naziha Rashid's paintings of Iraqi village life, a Mumtaz Hussain sculptural piece of the twin towers with hands raised in supplication, and works by world renowned calligrapher Mohamed Zakariya, designer of the US postage stamp commemorating the Eid festivals, all brought together under the installation of more than 150 doves by artist Dolly Unithan. Further along, on either side of the artwork exhibition, were candle-lit tables filled with dates, figs, and apricots surrounded by palm trees. The attendees filled up all the seats and many stood along the sides of the hall facing the stage. The master of ceremonies, Brian Lehrer of WNYC and NPR Radio, New York, introduced himself and then each of the speakers that followed. To a gathering of more than 600, world famous Senegalese vocalist and musician of the Mouridiyya tariqa, Mor Dior Bamba, took the stage and recited the *adhaan*, the Islamic call to prayer. His echoes vibrated throughout the cathedral and accompanied the stillness and silence of those present who listened attentively, including imams, sheikhs, priests, rabbis, spiritual elders, UN ambassadors, the deputy mayor of New York, New York Fire and Police Department representatives, and many more from various ethnic and cultural backgrounds, mostly professionals, dressed in their finest. The *adhaan*, along with the church setting, the artwork, the poetry, the music, the palm trees, and the food, set the tone and mood for the evening, and reinforced the themes of gentleness, mildness, and peace, that were all part of the larger story.

Daisy Khan, executive director and co-founder of ASMA, who had the vision of such an event, followed Bamba's presentation: 'The death and destruction in New York City that was caused by a terrible, terrible act that has happened in the name of Islam has propelled the Muslim community in New York City to respond in many different ways and one of the ways that I want to respond is the way the Prophet would have responded – to just talk about the humanity we all belong to.' Further contextualizing the evening, Khan continued:

> Since September 11th, Muslims have gone to churches, to synagogues, to schools, to explain our faith. However, people still kept asking, 'Where are the Muslims and why aren't they doing anything about it?' So I started thinking about this and I said what is it that we are not doing right? Maybe we need to respond in a more gentle way. So I looked around for the mildest people in our community, the artists in our community. The person I called was Mohamed Zakariya.

In placing the Reflections exhibit both within the context of the events of 9/11 as well as calling on the prophetic tradition, Khan was linking together an Islamic past with the present in a tradition of dialogue, exchange, and outreach by stressing a 'common humanity'. But how to think about a 'common humanity' just months after the events of September 11, was no easy task. For Khan, the event was to be a 'time for reflection and healing', as well as for 'outreach and interfaith dialogue', in a way that was going to 'help others understand us'. But as she continued, it was also about 'understanding ourselves'. These efforts were further stressed as artist Mohamed Zakariya took to the stage: 'Catastrophes have brought us here, but not all is lost. Through our art we pick up these broken pieces and try to put them back together and make something that is going to work. Revenge, suicide bombing, things of that kind, they have no place in Islam. They must never have a place in Islam, never, never.' He continued,

> Islam is really a soft thing, not a hard thing and so we have to approach it with softness and be soft to each other, as the Prophet said. Make it easy and not difficult. So we should put away those angry words, the harsh and strident rhetoric that we have been dealing with for all these years and that we've suffered through this sweet religion with this beastly stuff. Come out into the light and be bright, be bright in America, and look in the mirror, that's what we have to do. As-salaamu alaikum.

Promoting 'softness' based on the Hadith and Sunna of the Prophet Muhammad was also a way of acknowledging and distinguishing the practice of an Islam different from the exclusive version promoted by Al-Qaeda or the Taliban. The authority gained from basing peace and dialogue in Islamic history was also an effort to mainstream this version of Islam in the American public. Using artists as a way of doing so recalled the importance of art in Islamic history. Its important role was made clear by Imam Feisal Abdul Rauf, founder of ASMA and arguably among the most prominent Muslim leaders in the United States at that time:

> We have invited you to sample some American Muslim expressions of art. This medium, a rarely used window, will open for you a glimpse into the House of Islam ... The greatest moments in Islamic history, those epochs when Islamic civilization peaked, were periods when the arts were highly prized.

Discussion

Romantic framings of artists' 'aura' was to add to the 'spirit' of the evening, but just as important was identifying artists as American Muslims, and connecting them to an Islamic art history. Although artists and art were used, in this context, to promote Muslims as 'gentle', 'spiritual', and 'beautiful', as the directors had put it, it did not escape the particular time and reason for such an event/exhibition at the Cathedral Church of St John the Divine just months after the events of 9/11. That Muslims felt 'compelled to do something' as Daisy Khan had said, was both because of the 'media depictions that are misrepresenting us' as well as based on being minorities in the West, and in the United States more specifically. Notions of artists as the 'conscience of the community' to promote a sense of a 'common humanity' was also caught up in the desire of the event organizers to draw on the 'cosmopolitanness' and cultural capital (Bourdieu 1993) of artists to promote an American Islam. This focus not only shows how artists' identity and art were being defined by the Reflections event, but how a specific understanding of artists had to be constructed in order to represent American Muslims.

The event coordinators were not art experts, but they did develop their own elaborate and sophisticated team of experts, including artists, to evaluate the works of art that were submitted via an online call for artwork, through email lists like the Muslim Students Associations at various colleges and universities, as well as drawing on artists' own networks. What is significant is not that they were not 'experts', but how various communities were brought together, through art, in order to learn about one another. After the exhibit, Khan had explained to me that at the level of iconography, they were looking for art that was 'not overtly political', and that 'fit the theme of peace, prayer, and reflection', and works that resonated with 'Islamic art'. Because 'coherence and unity' were the aim, as Afghan-born artist Shekaiba Wakili said, works that embodied the theme of promoting a 'common humanity', were also chosen. The exhibiting artists were selected on the grounds that their artwork would play all these parts. But, at the personal level, they also selected artists who would be willing to participate as American Muslims, knowing that their art would be related to an Islamic art history.

Though the selection process for the event was based on an emphasis of function over form, certain works such as those by calligrapher Mohamed Zakariya were featured to reinforce the Islamic art connections. As Daisy Khan had said, he was the first person she thought of when trying to reach out to artists. Not only was Zakariya someone with whom ASMA was in contact through other Islam- and interfaith-related events, but Zakariya had also come into the spotlight around 9/11, when the United States postage stamp commemorating the Eid holidays that he had designed, was launched just days before. By displaying the Islamic calligraphic works of Zakariya side by side with works of other artists that could not necessarily be tied visually to Islamic art, the works came together in their own fragmented ways, to tell a story of American Muslims. This relational aspect of the works of art to each other, was yet another way that the coordinators tried to achieve thematic unity. What is remarkable is that in doing so, they even went further than most museums, first in their privileging of contemporary/living artists, which museums often have a difficult time in doing, but also in being open to the different possibilities of works such as Shekaiba's photographs, or Afghan children's drawings, being seen as 'Islamic'.

At the Reflections exhibit, invoking the 'universal' was used in the service of localizing Muslims, localizing the function or 'social life' of art, as well as localizing the way meaning was produced. The works displayed and performed could be brought into an Islamic fold because of the place and time in which they were being exhibited and used. The efforts in relating contemporary Muslim artists to Islamic art by the coordinators must also be seen as part of the self-representation process of a Muslim community as a minority in the West, even though artists themselves may have had more formal aesthetic reasons for doing so. In this light, the 'universal' that Khan was emphasizing was not based on formal art properties, such as line, color, depth, or perspective, resonating with the concerns of Islamic art. Rather, they produced a notion of the 'universal' through the thematic content of the artwork, read in and by the context of the overall event. When asking Daisy Khan about the notion of the 'universal', she pointed to the diversity of artists, as well as their various ethnic backgrounds, and the fact that many of them were women. But she also highlighted that each of the artists, in her or his own way, came together to see the unity of the works, as well as the unity of the works in the effort of trying to emphasize a 'common humanity'.

Beardsley and Livingston in the 1991 work by Karp and Lavine, *Exhibiting Cultures: The Poetics and Politics of Museum Display*, likened museum exhibits to a photograph, suggesting that much depends on 'who is holding the camera', and the 'choice of subject, the type of lens, the angle of vision, the moment chosen for looking – all determine the character of the image' (105). Like museum exhibits, the Reflections event could be seen as a snapshot, a particular version of a community's story, built by various actors, where the struggle for 'coherence and aesthetic will' (105) of the event would have to be balanced with the particulars of the art itself. Also important were the 'hypothetical' curators or coordinators, a team convened by ASMA, behind the lens, as they imagined and then put into practice the event where the 'subject (theme) is as large and complex as the art of ... an entire group of cultures' (105) even if the theme of the event might be the same. Convening Muslims was tricky since the artists and their work could not come to represent or privilege any one culture or geography, but this worry was given relief by the many different works on display.

While Beardsley and Livingston's notion of an exhibit as photograph is useful, likening the Reflections event to a festival seems to better capture its temporal and 'living dimensions', and its 'special purpose' (Karp and Lavine 1991: 280). In addition, in doing so, the experience of the event moves from the individual artist and her work, to the way works related and added to the event. What might be gained in the breadth of representing a community might be lost in the depth of each particular artist or their work (Beardsley and Livingston 1991: 105). Similarly in the same volume, as Crew and Sims (1991) have put it, 'It is the event that is primary, not the things or even our directed thoughts about them. And it is in the place/time of the event that the audience takes part, becoming co-creators of social meaning. Authenticity is located in the event' (174). At the Reflections event, authenticity was not necessarily to be located in individual works of art, but rather in the experience of the event itself. As we will see through the artists' narratives below, claiming to be American Muslim artists was not being discussed, at least at this event, in relation to iconography that visually reflected being both American and Muslim. Rather, art and a specific identity were taken up to add voice to the overall event.

Artists' Reflections

Looking for tensions or exclusions, which would help me understand the political process of the Reflections event, the relationship between individual artists (many of whom I had known prior to the event), and their collective relationship to the event, seemed to be a particularly telling juncture. In most of my work with these and other artists, I presented artists in relation to their art and in the context of spaces that one normally associates with the art world: museums, galleries, and biennials. I also looked specifically at artists' narratives about their work because I was relating to artists as individuals, exhibiting as Muslims, but more so showing their works under other cate-gories: as women, Arabs, Asian Americans, Africans, to name a few, or by art-historical categories. Their narratives were important since many artists claimed that discourse was, in addition to the art itself, a way of constituting oneself as an artist, and that debating art and art worlds was very much a part of what it meant to be an artist. Entering exhibits as individuals or in small group shows, the spotlight was on the artist and her work and not on the site itself. Focusing on an event like Reflections, however, posed a tension between the relationship of an individual artist and her work to the larger exhibit itself: a tension between individual artist and community representa-tion. Concerned that a focus on the event's overarching theme and outreach efforts might detract from the individuality and creativity of the artist and their own multiple identities, I asked various artists about this as much as I could at the event itself, observed their responses to other event attendees and also met with them later, individually and in the context of other exhibits.

Many artists claimed that the Reflections event was among the first times they were exhibiting their works under the category 'Muslim', and in a way quite different from the way Islamic art is usually exhibited – in terms of particular traditions, genres, and formal properties of art. They believed that the reception of their works differed when they were exhibiting their works as individuals in mostly non-Muslim settings versus in settings where Muslims were exhibiting their works as a group, or in Muslim-majority settings. After 9/11, many artists were worried about being in the spotlight as Muslims, having to answer somehow for the Taliban or Al-Qaeda's interpretation of Islam. 'As individuals, our voices are hardly heard', said artist Naziha Rashid, an Iraqi-born painter. 'Once they know I am Iraqi or Muslim, it all becomes so political. There has to be more beauty. I want my work to be beautiful. It is hard when you feel like you are an artist working all alone. That is why it is also important to work in community. The exhibit at the cathedral showed the strength and creativity of our community.' In the same vein, artist Shekaiba Wakili, a photographer, said, 'After 9/11 people were looking for responses by Muslims as Muslims. It was hard because many of us are active in education, social activism, dialogue groups, but we don't always do so as Muslims. We usually think about these things in terms of gender or ethnicity or just being a minority or just as humans.' Shekaiba continued, 'It is important to educate one by one, but it is also important to do so as a community coming together with a common voice. But when we talk about community, what community is that? At least through this event, ASMA Society has helped create a Muslim community, and make Muslims and even non-Muslims feel like they belong to an Islamic community without being so judgmental of how much we know about Islamic theology.'

Artist Reem Hussein, the only artist in my study to have been born and raised in the United States, made similar comments, but she also spoke about being veiled: 'I consider my art to be Islamic art, but that is not so much a concern as is the way I get taken up in mainstream art worlds. Because I wear the veil, people can't get past talking about that, which means all the stereotypes about Muslim women's so-called oppression. It is nice to be at gatherings where you can talk about identity and realize that even if you are veiled you are capable of talking about other things. For me, highlighting art is not only about turning discussions away from the hijab back to my work, and the history of Western art, or Islamic art, but that is the place I am really coming from.' As she claimed that Muslims need to do much more to educate, she was also aware that because Islam had become so visible and public since the events of 9/11, it would mean having to educate others on the themes that were being taken up at the national level. 'The New York art scene generally makes no room for religion or religious experience. They are pretty secular and it is mostly about markets. Even when you talk about being Muslim in the art world, it means that you have to talk about the relevant themes the news has decided for us. There is definitely an advantage to working with a community where you can discuss the formal properties of calligraphy or issues of identity that are not always linked to the veil.'

Artist Zarina also talked about the power of working in a community that 'gets it', that is, that understands you. 'Sometimes you get tired of all the explaining in the art worlds. That is why I like working with academic communities as well. The conversations are different.' But Zarina also cautioned against the liberal Muslim thinking that was positing an Islam about peace and pluralism. She continued, 'The difficulty with much of Muslim identity politics, even in academic worlds, is that by identifying as the good Muslim from America, you know, the ones who are all for peace, means running the risk of all the non-American Muslims being the bad ones.' This tension is something we return to below, as we look at some of the politics of representation. As the artists spoke to me about the event, it seemed that their narratives focused more on the identity politics of being American Muslim than on their specific works. Their relationship to the event was, like the event itself, concerned with issues of the way Islam and Muslims were being portrayed in the mass media. In addition they also reflected on what it meant for them to think more about identifying as American Muslims as a community. As Zarina had said, 'Freedom is not just about looking at the individual artist's freedom and creativity, but the way that art might work to mobilize communities.'

In addition to debating the category 'American Muslim', artists also spoke about their relationship to Islamic art, which they did not see as determining the kind of art they produced. 'On the one hand just because you are Muslim it doesn't mean that you make Islamic art, whatever that means. On the other hand, there are artists who would like to expand Islamic art boundaries so that it will include contemporary works', remarked Shekaiba. In addition to Reem, who saw her work as Islamic art, the work of Zarina and Tunisian-born visual artist Emna Zghal, was very much influenced by Islamic art and their work was certainly narrated in the context of being Muslim. As Emna reminded us, sometimes you can look at a work and think, 'What is so Islamic or Muslim about this, especially when you identify or are identified as a Muslim artist? But some artists use Islamic themes or have been influenced by a certain pattern that does not always come across visually as Islamic.' She continued,

> Many of us also use the platform of being Muslim to talk about the issues that the art worlds don't want to talk about. The minute you say you are a Muslim artist, you subject yourself and your work to some relationship to Islam, but unfortunately, the things that you are supposed to talk about have already been decided by the American media. The problem is that the history of Orientalism and racism already overshadows what you say and do, but we have to continue being activists and educating, and find different connections and ways of talking about Islam and being Muslim.

For Emna as for many other artists, the topic of Islamic art today was linked to the politics of Muslim identity, because it was, as she said, 'a problem of classification and categories in the West', which themselves 'need to be questioned'. She further stated, 'In the West, we try to expand art world boundaries to see the contribution Islamic art history has made to the Western art history, but at the same time, as contemporary Muslim artists, we are also questioning what Islamic art is. We highlight more or less depending on the context, where we are exhibiting, and who our audiences are.'

The connections that Imam Feisal had made between American Muslims and Islamic art was as Zarina explained, 'a way of reclaiming an art history (Islamic) that contributed much to the West'. Asking Zarina about the specific works she exhibited at the Reflections event, Asmaan, Zameen, Suraj, Chaand (Sky, Earth, Sun, Moon) she said, 'I didn't submit them thinking these are the most Islamic of my works, or how American they were. I wanted my works to be seen with many other works of art and performances and I thought Muslims and non-Muslims should be able to see this diversity.' Relating these works to Islamic art did not seem to be a concern since the works in relation to one another would disprove any essentialist notion of the questions that Emna had asked, 'What is Islamic art and what kind of art do Muslims make?' In addition, artists recognized that the achieved coherence and thematic unity of 'peace' and a 'common humanity' outweighed the particular concerns of each of the artists and their works.

In response to Khan's framing of artists as 'gentle', and the 'conscience and spirit of our community', Malaysian-born artist Dolly Unithan said, 'There is something deeply touching and human about this. If artists can help create a spiritual experience and common humanity through their art then this is some small way we can touch the human soul.' Having spoken to Dolly several times after the event and then meeting with her over the next couple of years during research, I began to understand her approach to art as something embodied and something to experience with multiple senses, especially as she narrated it through the example of the Reflections event. Dolly, who referred to herself as a 'spiritual' person and as someone 'belonging to humanity', said that she did not like to really be identified as an American or Muslim, or having her works seen as Islamic art. 'I want my work to be able to speak to everyone and sometimes you wonder why there are all these labels.' Dolly continued, 'I install my Doves in places where there are many people. They are supposed to be experienced together in communion. They are supposed to remind people of our common yearning to be free. The cathedral, where I have exhibited before, provides a wonderful place for my work to achieve what I want it to do.' For Dolly, it did not matter that she had been identified as an American Muslim for this particular event, as she said – for her, the larger issue was that her art installation 'might bring hope to a community in need', and to a community that wanted to 'offer itself and the world a different view of Islam as one of peace and common humanity'.

Dolly Unithan's Doves installation serves as an example of how the Reflections event, rather than glossing over the particular works of the exhibiting artists, provided the 'perfect environment', as she said, for her art to be installed. The materiality of each dove – the fact that they were made of papier-mâché – seemed to be less of a focus, than the fact that there were a 150 doves suspended on a canopy through the middle of Synod Hall soaring over the crowd throughout the evening. This particular arrangement played a 'significant role' Dolly said, in the 'aesthetic experience' the doves were supposed to 'effect and be affected by'. In addition, Dolly pointed out that even though the dove is a 'transcendent, universal symbol of peace', her Doves need to be installed in particular settings and in particular ways for them to have meaning. 'As an artist, I want to be able to show that art can have many different roles and art should be shown in different places, not just museums or typical places', and repeated, 'I want art to be an experience that touches the inner chord of life.'

Measures of success: new networks, alliances, and building bridges

Despite the various backgrounds of people convened at the Reflections event, the overall representation aimed to be one of coherence, unity, and common purpose. 'Making Muslim space' was as much about expanding art world boundaries as it was about thinking about the different ways an Islamic community brought together different people. The overall event, rather than each specific artwork and performance, brought artist and art into a different configuration: one that privileged community over the individual. But to look at the specific works of art, or to hear specific musical pieces, or poetry recitations, was to be reminded again of the particular artist and her individual creativity, so important for the New York commercial art scene.

When asking artists why they participated, especially since many had told me previously that they always worried about emphasizing one identity over another, I was met with a host of responses, which showed not only the diversity of reasons for their participation, but also how empowering it was for artists to take representation in their own hands. Working side by side with the event coordinators, artists talked about the different backgrounds they came from, the theme for the event, and the way in which the works should be physically mounted for the best 'effect'. Decorating Synod Hall, the choice of food, and the agenda and order of the evening were all a joint affair, as most exhibitions are. The difference here was that Muslim artists among other Muslims, themselves had initiated the event and decided how they wanted to be represented.

Seeing their role as advocates for a representation of Islam and Muslims different from mainstream media, as many of the artists said, they were also interested in learning about other Muslims, and more specifically the work of Muslim artists. As Shekaiba said, 'So much of this is also about networking and pooling our resources together as Muslim artists.' She also said that educating others about Islam and being Muslim means that 'we also have so much to learn about ourselves and the internal differences within different Muslim communities'. In referring to the Reflections event, she said, 'I have learned so much more about the Senegalese Mouridiyya and also about the growing Latino/a Muslim population. We also have to think more about the relationships between African American Muslims and immigrant Muslims as well as the different kinds of Muslims there are.' Shekaiba also talked about the need to learn more about the different theological practices of various Muslims, as well as being inclusive of 'secular' or 'non-practicing' Muslims because 'they all have a relationship to Islam, especially after 9/11', and that 'they might have something to teach the community, and help expand its resources. Strengthening ourselves here means sharing our privileges abroad.'

The Reflections event was referred to more in terms of 'achievement and potential' than 'success or failure'. It was not measured by how well the artwork sold, and in fact, the artists and the organizers were mostly silent on the selling and buying of art in their discussions with me. Nor was success based on how well a poetry recital or a musical piece was done. It was on how well the overall message was conveyed, how well people walked away thinking more positively about Muslims, and the new partnerships and networks formed, including those among artists. For ASMA, covering all the areas of their organization's objectives – religious outreach, interfaith and intercultural dialogue, pluralism and education, and the promotion of culture and the arts – as evident in the artists' narratives and the new connections forged, served as a measure of how well they had done as an organization. But as Imam Feisal said, 'Our work is never enough. We always have a lot more to do.' Although intended as a 'balm' as Daisy Khan put it in the scroll that greeted guests as they entered the cathedral, the most tangible measure of the event was the convergence of religion and art in a collaborative process.

Futures

The Reflections event belonged to many people, including the audiences. What can be argued from the observations I made, and from the coordinators' and artists' own narratives, is that the event was both that of ASMA's efforts in convening Muslims through artists in order to think more about the representation of an American Muslim identity in an intrafaith, interfaith, and intercultural setting, as well as the story of artists who in their efforts of expanding art world boundaries, were thinking more about the spaces and sites of exhibition, and in thinking more about issues of Muslim identity, found themselves together at this intersection. The interweaving narratives running throughout the Reflections event – one of the story of an American Muslim community, and the other the story of individual artists and works of art that helped create and shape it – is most certainly an achievement worth celebrating. The gathering of a community in order to represent itself through artists while keeping faithful to its own organizational mission as well as the artists' creativity and their work, is a story worth retelling.

This chapter has been particularly challenging to think through especially in the context of the efforts in building the Park 51 Islamic community center near Ground Zero in New York City. This project became controversial in May 2010 due to the efforts and financial backing of Islamophobic groups attempting to use the project as a political wedge for the midterm elections, raising national fear by calling it 'the Ground Zero Mosque'. Although Imam Feisal Abdul Rauf is no longer part of that project, he is the visionary behind it and has become well known in the United States for his tremendous efforts in interfaith dialogue and civic engagement. This chapter has tried to show how his efforts, along with the efforts of Daisy Khan and ASMA, despite all the personal and professional politics they are mired in currently, were among the first to bring a wide range of Muslims together after 9/11, through art, to engage with each other and with those from different traditions. To write about the Reflections event more than a decade later, has especially been a lesson for me as I often question the kind of pluralism and diversity Muslims are supposed to parade and perform to prove their loyalties in America, and to appease the non-Muslim American public. What these artists help us understand is a particular way in which Islam and Muslims were being framed in America at a particular historical moment in the years just before and after 9/11. So much has changed in the world, and yet more than a decade after the events of 9/11, in so many ways, the national frames through which Muslims are identified and represented remain very much the same today, perhaps even intensified. Islam and Muslims are still framed through what I have been calling the five 'media pillars' of Islam, namely: 9/11 as a temporal frame, terrorism/violence, Muslim women and veiling, Islam and the West, and the Middle East as the spatial/geographic frame.

Returning to my ethnographic research with a particular focus on the Reflections event raises another concern. I spent a great deal of my time tracking the various exhibits in the New York art scene where many of these artists showed their works, and my interest was to study their artistic practices in various art world sites where the identity 'Muslim' was made public. To identify these artists as Muslim, and to present them in this chapter in a particularly Muslim context runs the risk of isolating this identity and context over the art galleries, museums, and mostly non-Muslim spaces where they exhibit their works, not forgetting the numerous exhibits of their works since then. Nonetheless, I think the Reflections event helps us think through the diverse sites where artists do their work, the various relationships they forge, and the many uses and purposes of art-making, including for intrafaith and interfaith/intercultural dialogue. The enduring success is that more than a decade later, countless more events have followed that first post-9/11 Reflections event, and it has left us inspired by the positive contributions Muslims are making in the United States, as evident through its artists.

Readings

One of the great challenges of studying Muslim artists has been the academic literature within which they might be understood. Studying Muslim artists in the United States has been even more difficult, given that my own discipline of anthropology rarely studies the West, and when it does, it is usually through ethnic and cultural categories, and rarely through the category

'Muslim'. The following works in anthropology, art history, and religious and area studies have been useful for me in terms of thinking about Muslim artists in the United States. In the area of the anthropology and sociology of art, I would suggest the following important works for their theoretical and methodological frames as well as for their discussions on culture and museums: Howard Becker, *Art Worlds* (Berkeley: University of California Press, 1982), Pierre Bourdieu, *The Field of Cultural Production: Essays on Art and Literature* (New York: Columbia University Press, 1993), James Clifford, *The Predicament of Culture: Twentieth-Century Ethnography, Literature, and Art* (Cambridge, MA: Harvard University Press, 1988), Ivan Karp and Steven Lavine (Eds), *Exhibiting Cultures: The Poetics and Politics of Museum Display* (Washington: Smithsonian Institute Press, 1991), Ivan Karp *et al.* (Eds), *Museums and Communities: The Politics of Public Culture* (Washington: Smithsonian Institute Press, 1992), and Vera Zolberg, *Constructing a Sociology of the Arts* (Cambridge: Cambridge University Press, 1990). The two outstanding ethnographies of art, one on Indonesia and one on Egypt, that my own work draws on are: Kenneth George, *Picturing Islam: Art and Ethics in a Muslim Lifeworld* (Malden, MA: Wiley-Blackwell, 2010) and Jessica Winegar, *Creative Reckonings: The Politics of Art and Culture in Contemporary Egypt* (Stanford, CA: Stanford University Press, 2006). A very useful work that is more time specific to art and aesthetics after 9/11 is Jill Bennett, *Practical Aesthetics: Events, Affects and Art after 9/11* (London: I. B. Tauris, 2012). A critique of how Muslim artists and art by Muslims has been mobilized in the United States, including by the state, is Jessica Winegar, 'The humanity game: art, Islam and the war on terror' *Anthropology Quarterly* 81, no. 3 (2008): 651–81. Works on contemporary Islamic art, including discussions on the term 'Islamic art' can be found in Wijdan Ali, *Modern Islamic Art: Development and Continuity* (Gainesville: University Press of Florida, 1997) and David Bailey *et al.* (Eds), *Veiling, Representation and Contemporary Art* (Cambridge, MA: MIT Press, 2003). A work on bridging the art worlds and religious worlds is discussed by Robert Wuthnow, 'Art leaders and religious leaders: mutual perceptions', pp. 31–70, in Alberta Arthurs *et al.* (Eds), *Crossroads: Art and Religion in American Life* (New York: The New Press, 2001). A widely read edited volume on the varieties of global Muslim networks across time and space is by Bruce Lawrence and miriam cooke (Eds), *Muslim Networks from Hajj to Hip Hop* (Chapel Hill: University of North Carolina Press, 2005). A book on some of the major themes involving Islam and Muslims in the post-9/11 American public sphere by a non-academic Muslim religious leader discussed throughout this chapter is Feisal Abdul Rauf's *Moving the Mountain: Beyond Ground Zero to a New Vision of Islam in America* (New York: Free Press, 2012).

Author

Munir Jiwa is the Founding Director of the Center for Islamic Studies and Associate Professor of Islamic Studies at the Graduate Theological Union, and a visiting scholar at the Institutions and Governance Program at UC Berkeley. He holds a PhD in Anthropology from Columbia University and an MA in World Religions from Harvard Divinity School. His research interests include Islam and Muslims in the West, media, aesthetics, critical theory and decolonization, secularism, and religious formation. He is the recipient of prestigious grants from the Carnegie Corporation of New York, Ford Foundation, Henry Luce Foundation, and the Social Science Research Council. Since 1995 he has worked with Religions for Peace on interfaith programs around the world. Currently, he is serving on the Islamic Studies Advisory Group for Public Education at Stanford University, on the Steering Committee for the Contemporary Islam group at the AAR, and an advisor to the Islamophobia Documentation and Research Project at the Center for Race and Gender at UC Berkeley. He has a manuscript under review, titled, *Exhibiting Muslims: Art, Politics and Identity in New York City*.

Chapter 13

Global Muslim markets in London

Johan Fischer

Preamble

Halal is an Arabic word that literally means 'permissible' or 'lawful'. Conventionally, halal signifies 'pure food' with regard to meat in particular by proper Islamic practice such as ritual slaughter and pork avoidance. In the modern world, halal is no longer an expression of esoteric forms of production, trade, and consumption but part of a huge and expanding globalized market. In the modern food industry around the world, a number of Muslim requirements have taken effect, such as an injunction to avoid any substances that may be contaminated with porcine residues or alcohol, such as gelatine, glycerine, emulsifiers, enzymes, flavours, and flavourings. My narrative explores modern forms of halal understanding and practice among Malay Muslims in London, that is, the halal consumption of middle-class Malays in the diaspora. The state in Malaysia has systematically regulated halal production, trade, and consumption since the early 1980s. Malaysian state bodies such as Jabatan Kemajuan Islam Malaysia (JAKIM), or the Islamic Development Department of Malaysia (in English), regulates halal in the interfaces between Islamic revivalism, the state, and consumer culture. The Malaysian state's halal logo issued by JAKIM displays in Arabic the word 'halal' at the centre and 'Malaysia' at the bottom. In shops around the world, consumers can find state halal-certified products from Malaysia. The main motive for focusing on Malays in multi-ethnic London is that the Malaysian state's vision of and commitment to promoting halal specifically identifies London as a centre for halal production, trade, and consumption. The fieldwork for this study is based on extended periods of fieldwork in Kuala Lumpur and London between 1996 and 2010. During fieldwork in London, I spent a great deal of time in halal restaurants, in butchers' shops, grocery stores, supermarkets, and hypermarkets selling halal products.

Narrative

Halal landscapes in London

During my fieldwork it was obvious that London is in many ways a focal point for Muslims in the United Kingdom, and Edgware Road in the city centre and Whitechapel Road in the East End, for example, are good examples of major changes and developments in the business and entrepreneurial environment in the city over the past decade or so. Most of the shops, kiosks, restaurants, cafés, money transfer agencies, barbers, and estate agencies in these areas are businesses with Muslim ethnic backgrounds. In these areas halal is a distinctive presence on signs and in butchers' shops and restaurants.

Around 2005 halal-certified products in large numbers were appearing in super/hypermarket chains such as Tesco, Asda, Sainsbury's, and Morrisons. In effect, the novel ubiquity of halal in some parts of London can be seen as a form of urban space making. These super/hypermarkets are marketing their halal meat as 100 per cent halal authorized by recognizable Muslim halal certification bodies such as the Halal Food Authority (HFA), an organization set up in 1994 to certify halal meat. More generally, super/hypermarkets require meat that is halal certified by locally recognized bodies such as HFA. In this way, halal is being lifted out of its traditional base in halal butchers' shops to become part of 'world food' ranges in major supermarkets.

In June 2006, Tesco announced that it would be sourcing one billion Malaysian Ringgit (RM), about US$285,000,000, of certified halal products over the next five years to service selected UK stores.

The huge Tesco Extra hypermarket in Slough outside London boasts of having the widest 'world foods' and Asian world foods ranges including halal in Britain. Downstairs there is a more traditional halal butcher operating as a concession selling fresh meat. In November 2006 in Tesco Extra, I found Maggi chilli sauce produced and certified in Malaysia, and a halal 'Curry Special' butter chicken with no certification/logo on it. In August 2009 when I returned to this fieldwork site to explore recent developments, I found the following certified halal products in this same store: Malaysian Lingham's chilli sauce and a range of similar products from Malaysia certified by JAKIM; Koka Oriental Style Instant Noodles produced in Singapore and certified by Majlis Ugama Islam Singapura or the Islamic Religious Council of Singapore; Mae Ploy Green Curry Paste produced in Thailand and certified by the Islamic Committee Office of Thailand; Knorr Mushroom and Chicken Flavoured Soup Mix produced in India and certified by International Food and Nutrition Council of America (IFANCA), one of the world's major certification bodies; Great Food Falafel produced in the United Kingdom and certified by HFA (this product was also kosher certified by two different Jewish certification bodies); Tahira Turkey Nuggets produced in the United Kingdom and

Figure 13.1 The JAKIM halal logo

certified by World Islamic Foundation, a UK-based certifying body; and Chicken Pakora produced in the United Kingdom by Gazebo and certified by HFA.

In that same store, I found the following uncertified halal products: Chicken Goujons produced in the United Kingdom by Aisha's Original Recipe; Chicken Spring Rolls produced in the United Kingdom by Maysum; Chicken Korma and Pilau Rice produced in the United Kingdom by Mumtaz; Easy Chef Doner Kebabs produced in the United Kingdom; Maggi/Nestlé Coconut Milk Powder Mix produced in Sri Lanka; Strawberry Jelly Crystals produced by Ahmed Foods in Pakistan; and Achar Gosht Curry Mix produced by Shan in Pakistan.

Anecdotal evidence from my fieldwork in this area suggests that Tesco, by using this store in Slough as an entry into the halal market, has reduced sales among halal butchers in the surrounding area. Around the same time, in the Asda supermarket in north London, I found HFA-certified chilled chicken and mutton.

In the Oriental City Shopping Mall in Colindale, a suburban area of north London, there is an Asian supermarket that also sells fresh halal meat and a whole range of other halal products. This supermarket is designed to accommodate the tastes of various Asian groups that live in the area. Another Malaysian halal-certified product in this supermarket is canned mackerel in tomato sauce produced by Ayam Brand in Malaysia.

This development testifies to the proliferation of halal as a globalized religious market. It also shows that Southeast Asian countries such as Malaysia,

Thailand, and Singapore dominate halal certification followed by IFANCA and local certifying bodies in the United Kingdom, whereas the Middle East and South Asia are not really involved in institutionalized certification by Islamic organizations or state bodies.

The dominance of these Southeast Asian countries also reflects another important point for my London ethnography, namely, that it is in Southeast Asian countries such as Malaysia, Singapore, and Indonesia that halal most of all extends into food other than meat and even into non-food products.

Hence, as most smaller halal shops and butcheries in London are run by Muslims that are not of Southeast Asian descent, it is most common to find halal meat as the primary commodity here, whereas the halal products found in a Tesco hypermarket, discussed above, are more rare.

Unlike halal meat in butchers' shops, halal products in supermarkets are packaged, so customers can look for recognizable and proper logos on packaging among the expanding world food ranges.

Before entering into how middle-class Malays in London navigate the halal landscapes of butchers, convenience or grocery stores, as well as supermarkets/ hypermarkets, I discuss these in their own rights. Halal is highly visible in signs and logos in the urban landscape. There are hundreds of halal butchers in London, that is, shops that mainly sell meat. First, these butchers can be classified according to ethnicity. Some butchers are run by Pakistani, Indian, Bangladeshi, Mediterranean, or Afro-Caribbean Muslims, for example.

Another classification of halal butchers pertains to certification. Only a fragment of the numerous halal butchers in London are certified by the Halal Monitoring Committee (HMC) or the Halal Food Authority (HFA), the two major certifying bodies in Britain that are competitors in the UK market for halal certification.

Much of the halal meat sold in London comes from convenience stores or grocery stores that also sell a wide variety of groceries and sometimes Islamic paraphernalia such as stickers, rugs, holiday cards, and plaques with Islamic calligraphy among other things.

As we shall see in the case of Malay middle-class Muslims in London below, shopping for halal cannot be divorced from the context in which it is bought. Hence, the spatial context (atmosphere/feel/ambience) of food consumption as practice may be just as significant as the intrinsic qualities of the food and its ingredients. Halal is shaped not merely by religious self-understanding but also by much more mundane understandings and practices.

Halal in Malaysia

I have conducted fieldwork in urban Malaysia and its capital Kuala Lumpur for extended periods of time since 1996. Fieldwork in Kuala Lumpur and London have generated a variety of materials allowing me to explore the

Figure 13.2 Ayam Brand mackerel in tomato sauce

proliferation of halal from an anthropological perspective at different levels of the social scale: in the everyday lives of consumers and as a phenomenon inseparable from expanding markets, state certification, Islamic revivalism, and capitalist transformations. My informants migrated from Kuala Lumpur to London and I discuss their migration narratives with special emphasis on understandings and practices of halal in these two locations. Of the Malaysian population of around 28 million in 2010, about 67 per cent are indigenous Malays (virtually all Muslims) and tribal groups, also labelled *bumiputera* (literally, sons of the soil); 25 per cent are Chinese; and 7 per cent are Indians.

To pre-empt Islamic revivalist groups (*dakwah*) the state started to 'nationalize' Islam. In fact, today Malaysian Islam may be the most monolithic and most state regulated in the Muslim world. Thus, the state's attempt at moulding a modern form of Malayness is intimately linked to challenging Islamic discourses or *dakwah*, each with particular ideas and standards of how to combine consumption and Islamic practice.

Over the past three decades, the Malaysian state has effectively certified, standardized, and bureaucratized halal production, trade, and consumption. The reasons for this are many, but the proliferation of halal in a country such as Malaysia cannot be divorced from the fact that the country over the past three decades has witnessed steady economic growth, the emergence of large groups of Malay Muslim middle-class consumers as well as centralized state incentives to strengthen halal production, trade, and consumption.

Before super/hypermarkets became dominant in Kuala Lumpur, as is the case today, halal was mainly about trusting the authority of the local halal butcher's shop, older Malay middle-class informants told me. Since I started doing research in Malaysian shops in the mid-1990s this tendency has become much more clear. Non-halal (*tidak* halal) products such as pork are for the most part either stored in a small, secluded room away from the main shopping area in both super/hypermarkets. Wine and other alcoholic drinks (*wain*) are stored in another room in hypermarkets and non-halal products can also be located at a specific counter. This trend is also noticeable in contemporary Malaysian convenience stores.

Store managers in these shops told me that 'normally' JAKIM does unannounced inspections twice a year. A store manager in a supermarket in central Kuala Lumpur explained that 'We have to make sure that the standard of handling the halal counter meets requirements and city hall will do the same,' that is, city hall will check on the freshness, expiration, or damaged products as well as the halal certificate. Hence, halal is inseparable from wider concerns about cleanliness and proper handling of products in super/hypermarkets. In all these stores it is essential that management have a valid halal certificate to show customers. Halal logos are ubiquitous and they signify a transition towards impersonal, regulated, and standardized ways on shopping in the relationship between seller, certifier, and buyer.

Eating in London

The question I will now turn to is how my Malay informants in London understand and practise 'eating in', that is, how halal products such as meat and the public spaces in which they are bought are conceptualized. My survey data from London show that most Malays prefer to 'eat in' compared with 'eating out' in restaurants. What is more, these survey data indicate that Malays in London mostly shop for groceries in either hypermarkets or supermarkets, as it is also the case in urban Malaysia. These Malays, however, most often buy halal products in local grocery stores or halal butchers' shops. These practices are different from those of the Malay middle class in Malaysia, who mostly shop for halal in supermarkets and hypermarkets. In my conversations with food authorities and Islamic groups, I learned that rumours of fraud and falsely certified halal meat are common. The halal market in London is fragmented and unregulated, and the question is how this point conditions Malays' everyday shopping for halal in various forms of halal spaces.

Mascud is a Malay imam in his thirties who moved from Kuala Lumpur to London in 2002 where he works as a religious counsellor at Malaysia Hall, a facility that provides accommodation for Malaysian students who have just arrived in London. At Malaysia Hall, there is also a canteen where Malaysian halal dishes are served. Mascud lives with his family in Cricklewood, north London. He would normally shop for halal in a grocery store near his house, as this is the most convenient place in terms of location, price, and quality. Often he would also go to the Shepherd's Bush Market, a historic market that caters to a variety of ethnic groups selling both non-food and food items. When shopping for halal, he pays particular attention to the hygiene of establishments. My impression during fieldwork was that most of these halal butchers' shops actually seemed to be clean. He explains to me that it is not enough to make sure that meat, for instance, is properly slaughtered; he should also be sure if it is treated in an unhygienic manner or if the earnings are used for haram purposes such as gambling. Mascud, like nearly all my informants, agrees that even though it is not an Islamic injunction that halal be produced, sold, or handled by Muslims, he prefers to shop for halal from Muslims. Mascud can be seen as a kind of Islamic bureaucrat in a diasporic context. In his view, Malays living with non-Muslim Chinese in Malaysia may sharpen Malay alertness to contamination from non-fatal sources. To Mascud, this apprehension about the food habits of the other was also significant in a British context where general indifference about food clearly contrasted with Malay particularity. Mascud explained that several Chinese had told him that the Chinese are compelled to eat pork every day, even in 'vegetarian food'.

The range of dishes my Malay informants would cook at home reflected a complex mix of Western and Asian food. In the eyes of most informants, a proper home-cooked meal consisted of meat (poultry, beef, or lamb mostly), rice, and vegetables. Hence, these elements were essential to their home cooking. Chicken and a variety of chicken curries in particular were favourites with my informants, that is, chicken was considered healthy and affordable at the same time. Meat was eaten on a daily basis and included in a variety of curry dishes as well as quintessentially 'national' dishes such as rich coconut beef (*rendang daging*). Another favourite dish cooked at home was fried rice (*nasi goreng*). Informants would also cook seafood at home. The inclination towards Asian foods did not exclude Western dishes.

Zurina is a single woman who came to London in 2005. She lives with three flatmates in south London. Zurina loved to invite her friends to an 'English-style' breakfast that included halal sausage or roasted chicken. Interestingly, Western food is often considered 'exotic' because of its 'lack' of flavour compared with Asian cuisines of Malaysia and Thailand, for example.

These middle-class Malays are accustomed to a highly globalized, multi-ethnic, and cosmopolitan food market in urban Malaysia, and this is clearly reflected in their food choices when they 'eat in'. As long as the food is considered halal, they would cook a wide variety of dishes in their homes. Besides meat, which most of all is subjected to halal/haram judgements, alcohol and gelatine are often also sources of concern.

Another issue among some middle-class Malays in London is the limited availability of ingredients used in Malaysian cuisine. Often Malays will shop for these in Chinese supermarkets such as Loon Fung in Chinatown or elsewhere, or in Thai grocery stores. Some of these Malays bring back spices from Malaysia, or they ask friends and family to do so.

Many Muslim groups with divergent understandings and practices of halal compete in this expanding market in Britain and globally. However, my Malay informants do not like to buy halal from certain ethnic groups or avoid others. In other words, ethnicized space does not significantly condition halal consumption. Instead, as Mascud, for one, argues, appearance, piety, and devotion – being a 'practising Muslim' – are essential markers of trustworthiness when shopping for halal. Thus, the spatial context for shopping for halal conditions understanding and practice. For instance, if a butcher is wearing gold rings or necklaces, considered to be haram, Mascud reasons that the butcher is probably not sufficiently knowledgeable about halal either.

However, as discussed above, Mascud represents a particular and authoritative halal discourse, and I will now explore how my informants went about shopping for halal in their everyday lives.

Nazli is a single man who came to London in 2001 to study, and he is also a student councillor with an Islamic student organization. He lives with 15 other students in a hall of residence in central London. He was fastidious about proper certification. Consequently, halal space making hinges on certification above anything else. Like Nazli, most informants observe the atmosphere and appearance of the halal butcher or shop assistant to judge the halalness of the meat or other types of products. Local halal butchers were favourites among Malay consumers in London, because the meat is affordable compared with halal meat in supermarkets. Conversely, halal in supermarkets is normally certified by an Islamic organization. Nazli contends that in London, most Malays would prefer to cook at home. As many of my informants are students like Nazli, it is obvious that the aspect of thrift, as Nazli notes, is central to Malay food consumption. However, even informants high in economic capital prefer to cook at home, and they feel that eating out is in many cases a pragmatic necessity in connection with a busy lifestyle of work and travels. Nazli acknowledges that eating at home was also a preference that was related to the familiarity of certain types of dishes such as chicken curry that could be personalized in the home. He even asserts that most Malays would try to find a house near a halal butcher or grocery store selling halal products. Data from my respondents and informants indicate that most Malays in London shop for halal because of thrift, convenience, and familiarity with a local shop rather than going to a supermarket or hypermarket as a primary preference.

Informants would tell me that 'best deals' are often discussed among Malays in London. When I was out shopping for halal food with informants, we frequented butchers' shops that were said to have the 'best deals' in halal meat.

Murni is a man in his twenties. He is married to Altaf who is about the same age. The couple moved to London in 1998 to study and they now both work in the financial sector. The couple lives in a house in Walthamstow in northeast London. In Murni and Altaf's local halal butcher's shop there are 'extra services' compared to supermarkets. Still, informants are often not quite sure about halal meat at these butchers' shops, and they negotiate the afford-able prices and high levels of service against the more expensive and reliable types of certification to be found in supermarkets. Comparing their local halal butcher's shop with Tesco, both Murni and Altaf would agree that Tesco is cleaner, and this is a point generally held by informants.

Fatimah is a single woman who had lived in London since 2005. Besides studying, she works for a phone company. Fatimah shares a flat with two friends in north London. Unlike the majority of my informants, normally Fatimah shops for groceries in supermarkets such as Tesco Express (it was open 24 hours), Sainsbury's and Waitrose (a UK supermarket that is often con-sidered upmarket) that are situated close to her home, and Green Valley (a delicatessen with a good halal selection and fresh meat certified by trustworthy authorities). Consequently, halal is to a large extent premised on the context in which it is displayed and sold and not simply halalness as an intrinsic and abstract quality that complies with a particular religious injunction.

Alina moved to London in 2005 together with her husband Hasan. They live in a small flat in south London. She is fairly fastidious about eating out and is surprisingly relaxed about shopping for halal in butchers' shops and supermarkets in London. She uses Muslim websites (e.g. the website www. salaam.co.uk that features discussion forums, news updates, and a database on halal restaurants) to access information about halal and haram products, and she does not think that the current availability of halal products in London is satisfactory. However, above anything else, her shopping for halal is condi-tioned by thrift and convenience, meaning that local halal butchers' shops and grocery stores are Alina's favourites. Alina's husband, Hasan, does much of the couple's shopping for halal in halal butchers' shops, convenience stores, supermarkets, and hypermarkets. Hasan finds the current availability of halal products in London satisfactory. To Hasan, the issue of thrift dominates, that is, he goes to Tesco on weekends because it sells not only clearly certified but also costly halal food, and on weekdays, he buys halal food in a halal butcher's shop near the couple's home or at the supermarket, Lidl, because the prices are low.

Like several other informants, Hasan's primary concern over halal in shops is cleanliness. Again, supermarkets are seen to be not only more hygienic but also more expensive. In the eyes of Hasan, it is comforting to see that in some halal butchers' shops, a copy of the Qur'an or a plaque with Islamic calligraphy is displayed, as this testifies to the devotion of the owner and employees.

Zurina discussed above, much like Alina, is surprisingly relaxed about shopping for halal in local butchers' shops compared with her understanding of halal restaurants. The central point here is that despite the fact that Zurina critiques many of these butchers for lacking proper or visible certification, the halal butchers' shops embody a certain 'Islamic' authority and expertise Malays rarely question per se even if these customers are not quite sure about the halalness of products.

Halal bought outside can become imbued with the values of kinship and unity associated with the house and above all with the kitchen. These kitchens of informants were comparable with those of the Malay middle class in Malaysia discussed above, that is, they were modern and equipped with kitchen appliances that helped inhabitants going about everyday cooking. My informants consume a wide variety of Western and Asian types of food available in London. Compared with Malaysia, where halal has become a kind of a naturalized standard, in London, middle-class Malays are more careful about the halalness of food. None of my informants lived alone, and rituals of sharing in privacy seemingly purified and legitimized the understanding of otherwise doubtful halal practices in the complex and ambiguous halal market. In other words, the import of halal into homes may translate ambiguous or malevolent (uncertified or improperly certified) commodities into something benevolent that can be shared and enjoyed within families or with friends or flatmates. When meat in particular becomes a mere ingredient among others in a range of well-known and craved dishes and cuisines cooked at home, its potential malevolence is mitigated.

'Anyone could have put up that halal sign'

The empirical material suggests two registers of understanding and practice of halal certification among Malays in London. The first group is relatively strict or purist about halal certification, whereas the second group tends towards a more pragmatic approach to these contested questions. Selected informants in each group represent diverse approaches to halal certification. In other words, these informants are exemplars of the scale of strategies involved in everyday halal consumption.

The heading to this section, a quotation from Nazli, illustrates the sentiments towards halal certification among the first group of informants. When we discussed the state of halal certification in London, Nazli complained that, as a general tendency, shops and butchers' shops simply put up a sign displaying the word 'halal' in Arabic and/or English. In the eyes of these Muslims, marking such products and premises lacks proper certification by a trustworthy certifying body that can be held accountable for the 'halalness' of products. Nazli also argues that anyone could put up a sign in Arabic that indicates halal: 'I worry about local halal certification sometimes because you can see people we don't even know creating their own halal signs and putting them up.' Conversely, Nazli finds that halal certification by HMC or HFA, the two main certifying bodies in Britain, is more reliable and trustworthy. As we saw in the previous chapter, he acknowledges that halal in the United Kingdom and elsewhere is increasingly about politics, power, and business – and not so much about religious beliefs and injunctions. Nazli hopes to see more shops and restaurants selling 'properly' certified halal products; as long as the certification process is ensured by a dependable certifier, he does not take the trouble to look at labels that could reveal if products contain alcohol or gelatine. To Nazli, proper halal certification with a convincing logo is sufficient proof that the products are fit for Muslim consumption. As in the case of most other informants, Nazli patronizes a local halal butcher's shop for meat; this requires trust in the Muslim butcher because, in most cases, there is no visible certification in such facilities.

Many Malay consumers in London favour local halal butchers, because the meat is affordable compared with halal meat in supermarkets. Conversely, halal in supermarkets is normally certified by HFA, HMC, or another Islamic organization. Consequently, to consumers, the proper 'branding' of halal commodities may represent a luxury that is not always affordable. Modern consumers are accustomed to a wide range of logos on products. Unlike halal meat in butchers' shops, halal products in supermarkets are packaged, so customers can look for recognizable and proper logos on packaging among the expanding world food ranges. To most informants, asking about certification in a halal butcher's shop in London means questioning the authority of the butchers. Most of my informants share this reluctance to enquire about certification and thus question the authority of halal butchers even though they are well aware that fraud occurs frequently.

Fatimah looks for two things when buying food in London: proper halal certification by a reliable certifier and 'vegetarian food', even though she is not a vegetarian. None of my respondents or informants are vegetarians, despite the fact that becoming a vegetarian would solve many problems for Muslims who are fastidious about halal certification. Fatimah only accepts certification by a local imam or food expert if this person is familiar to her. Thus, she often uses websites as consumer guides for halal in London:

> I usually refer to the London Central Mosque website. Because when I came to London to study it was on this website I learned about where to get halal food. So, if I'm familiar with a local Mosque or Imam I trust it's halal.

This sentiment shows that trust and personal relationships are essential in the understanding and practice of halal certification. Normally, however, Fatimah would go to Green Valley supermarket, a delicatessen, because she feels that it sells halal meat certified by trustworthy authorities, the meat is fresh, and, in general, the quality standard is high. What is more, this supermarket has a range of ethnic specialties from the Middle East, for example.

Alina, for one, is outraged that, in London, she can find false halal signs in Arabic that pretend to represent proper certification. Alina describes this as 'private' or 'shop' certification. Alina linked Malay fastidiousness about halal to the Shafi'i school of jurisprudence, that is, the Islamic school of thought in

Sunni Malaysia. With regard to the everyday understanding and practice of halal certification in London, she tends to see other groups of Muslims as 'others', whether they are very pragmatic, individualistic, and relaxed ('bad Malays' as it were) about their religion or very strict and dogmatic. Similarly, for instance, several informants see Brunei and Bruneians as being extremely purist about halal. Thus, when certification is an important question for one's own shopping for halal, it can also become an important marker of ethnicity and gender distinctions, for example.

When discussing halal with Hasan, the issue of thrift dominates:

> On weekends I go to Tesco. On weekdays, normally I buy halal food in a halal butcher shop near my place and I go to Lidl because it's cheap. They also have halal meat in Lidl, but in terms of certification I'm not so sure about this meat. I have never seen a logo. That is why I go to the proper halal butcher shop in Asda, for example. I think they have a HFA logo stamped on it.

The price level of properly certified halal conditions a range of shopping practices in everyday life. Hasan explains that, as a Malay in London, he is used to the reliability of Malaysian state certification, and that all other types of certification would be second to that. As a consequence, halal certification and logos are important for everyday shopping, during which he compares these types of certification with the unachievable state standards.

Zurina is aware that, although McDonald's and Kentucky Fried Chicken are not halal certified, more and more proper alternatives for Muslims in London are emerging. She reasons:

> The thing in London is that McDonald's and Kentucky Fried Chicken are not halal, so if I like to go to a halal fast-food place I go to the Chicken Cottage or any other fast-food place that is halal certified, halal logos at their doors.

Zurina had chosen Chicken Cottage after checking on the Internet and noticing the halal logo on the facade of a Chicken Cottage outlet. In general, she acknowledges all the authorities 'as long as it is a body, a well known and big organization that has undergone certain processes of the law'.

When I was out shopping for halal with Zurina and her flatmate in halal butchers' shops near their home in south London one day, I noticed that logos of certification were rare and not overtly displayed in these outlets. Zurina reasons that even though she feels that enquiring about certification in some of the butchers' shops is embarrassing, she would do it anyway, as many of these establishments simply put a sign on the door when they do not have a certificate. In other butchers' shops, the certificate is put up so far away that Zurina cannot see whether it is HFA or another body.

The point here is that proper halal is conditioned by visible certification, as a logo that inscribes institutional relations into material objects. Hence, the surface of these products represents a frontier surface that can be 'civilized' by proper certification. In other smaller stores catering for a Muslim audience in Zurina's neighbourhood in south London, halal meat is the primary commodity, whereas it is more difficult to find halal-certified non-meat products.

This point draws attention to the fact that certification of non-halal food to a large extent is a Southeast Asian trend. During my fieldwork, I found the most halal-certified non-meat products in large supermarkets as we saw it above, in the Chinese supermarket Wing Yip, and in Chinese stores in London's Chinatown. These products were either certified by authorities in Malaysia, Thailand, or Singapore. These halal non-meat products were hard to come by in smaller shops in Edgware Road or Whitechapel Road, for instance, which in most cases are run by Middle Eastern or South Asian Muslims.

The last informants in this register are Usmirah and Henny, who are flat-mates. They arrived in London in 2005 to study at University College and share a flat in central London close to the university. When I discussed halal with these two women in a café near University College, it was clear that they were uncertain about the state of halal certification in London. In fact, when Usmirah and Henny go about their daily shopping, they explore the labelling of products for any haram substances such as alcohol or gelatine. They scruti-nize the ingredients of halal-certified products as well, because they perceive that the certifying bodies in Britain lack credibility and authority and are only involved in certification for financial gain. As Usmirah notes, 'We look at logos, signs, labelling, ingredients, and then we decide. It's just that we are more familiar with the JAKIM logo.' Because Usmirah and Henny often look at labels on food, they are not really familiar with the wide range of halal logos in the London market.

This group of middle-class Malays is relatively strict about the halal/haram binary that requires proper certification. They are often interested in the certification of not only meat but also a whole range of other products. In this way, they support the current proliferation of halal. Furthermore, among this register of modern Muslim consumers, halal is not an individualized choice in everyday life but a religious injunction that should inspire a particular form of Muslim lifestyle.

'In our belief if someone says it's halal, we just take it'

The heading to this section is a quotation from Binsar that transpired during our discussion of halal in a Malaysian halal restaurant in Edgware Road. Binsar is a single man in his thirties and has lived in London since 1995. He moved there to study and now works as an architect. He lives with a friend in a flat in central London. Compared with the more purist Malays in the first group,

Binsar and the other Malay informants in this second group are more pragmatic and relaxed about their understanding and practice of halal certification. As an expression of this type of sentiment, Binsar explains to me that he basically trusts producers and sellers to live up to halal requirements, and that it is not his responsibility as a Muslim consumer to mistrust their intentions. Pragmatically, he also argues that there are no significant differences between various types of certification, such as JAKIM and local certification in London: 'I would take both, JAKIM and local certification in London, there's not too much of a difference anyway.' Binsar trusts the signs in Arabic stating that a product, in a butcher's shop or restaurant, is halal. He concludes that 'in our belief if someone says it's halal, we just take it. So if anything is wrong, we just blame the producer or trader.' To Binsar, certification by an imam or food expert would be at the 'bottom of the list', but he 'wouldn't say I wouldn't take it'.

Binsar's friend Abdul was also present in the Malaysian halal restaurant in Edgware Road during the interview and he had similar sentiments. Abdul is a 29-year-old man, and he lives with his wife and their child in a house in Colindale in north London. He moved to Britain in 1996 to study accountancy, and he now works as an accountant. Abdul puts it plainly that, in terms of halal and halal certification in London, 'I'm just not too concerned. I couldn't be bothered. I am a bit ignorant, so if I see a halal sign I wouldn't do more research.' Abdul is involved with United Malays National Organization (UMNO) work in London, but the Malaysian state's halal vision seems to be relatively insignificant and distant in his everyday life with his wife and child in north London. He feels that 'when you live outside Malaysia and can't really get what you need you just have to shut one eye'. Some of my informants indicate that everyday pragmatism in many cases becomes the order of the day when living abroad and without the imagined safety of state-certified products. Moreover, this informant pinpoints a feeling present with a number of my informants – the multiplicity and ambiguity involved in everyday halal consumption:

> I actually find it a bit confusing when I see halal products such as biscuits and sardines. I am sure that there are different interpretations in our religion, but the way that I have been taught at school is that halal only applies to meat. So these new products are confusing.

However, Abdul recognizes that the Malaysian state discourse on halal overwhelmingly is about business and profit and not to the same extent Islamic devotion: 'There is a lot of profit to be made on halal. Personally, I'm more liberal about eating non-halal, but the market is still very untapped. Even if I'm not very strict I would support halal as business.' As one of the few informants, he indirectly criticizes the massive commercialization of Islam that figures so prominently in the state discourse as well as the halal hype in

London. As a consequence, financial or patriotic support for Malaysia through halal consumption becomes the driving force behind practice rather than halal as an expression of personal religious devotion.

My study shows that although halal is important as an identity marker for all informants, it also requires a constant and shifting engagement of many Muslim consumers. At the same time, trust in halal is inseparable from visible certification and logos by some kind of trustworthy authority, be it a halal butcher who embodies this authority and trust or packaging with logos on them in a convenience store, supermarket, or hypermarket.

Unlike these young Malay men, Kamaruddin has not been widely exposed to Malaysian state halal certification. Kamaruddin is a single man in his fifties who left Malaysia in the 1970s to study engineering in Singapore. Since then, he has travelled extensively in many parts of Asia and Europe, and now he lives permanently in London where he works for engineering companies. He lives in a flat in Earl's Court, central London. Kamaruddin is the only informant not familiar with Malaysian state certification, which had not been institutionalized at the time he left Malaysia. In terms of halal reliability, Kamaruddin prefers local authorities such as HFA or HMC. More pragmatically inclined informants such as Kamaruddin simply trust the authority of these butchers' shops, which for the most part are not certified by any organization. Kamaruddin made clear to me that 'there are times when you don't know whether it's halal or not, so you just say a Muslim prayer before you eat'. He describes himself as a 'flexible Muslim' who is not overly subjected to religious injunctions, as was clearly demonstrated by his attitude towards halal and halal certification. I could not help speculate that in the eyes of some *dakwah* Malays, Kamaruddin could be considered a 'bad Malay'.

While Alina and Hasan are fastidious about proper halal certification in London, another Malay couple, Murni and Altaf, are more pragmatic. I first met Murni and Altaf at the Malaysia Day Carnival, and the points below transpired during a discussion of halal in a Starbucks outlet in Edgware Road. Murni admits that the couple is not very particular in terms of halal. They are only particular about pork.

However, Murni and Altaf are concerned when buying gifts for visiting other people's places: 'Then we do pay particular attention to it and go to a supermarket and select proper halal certification.' This point reflects the social significance of halal certification among some Muslim groups and individuals.

As we saw above, when asked why some Muslims are more fastidious about the understanding of halal and its practice, most informants indicate that a preoccupation with halal depends on the forceful impact of schooling, and thus the state, which provided information about halal as part of the Malaysian education system. As might be expected, halal knowledge and practice is also generated within families.

Although most informants are equally exposed to this type of knowledge in the Malaysian school system, everybody also acknowledges that individuals and groups have divergent understandings and practices of halal. Therefore, bringing food to other people's homes or as gifts is a sensitive issue, and the best thing to do, as a Muslim, is to ensure that what they bring is as properly certified as possible, as in the case of Murni and Altaf. With regard to the couple's personal halal food consumption, they are fairly pragmatic, although for non-food products such as shoes, Altaf contends that she, for example, will never buy a pair of shoes without enquiring whether they are made out of pigskin. She emphasizes that Muslims cannot touch pigs, and if they do, they have to wash in a certain way. Thus, Altaf would prefer more certification of leather products. Despite the fact that consumers see themselves as relaxed with regard to halal food, they may be more fastidious about non-food products that are not traditionally part of halal.

This second group of Malay consumers either reluctantly accepts the importance of halal and its certification or simply rejects it as a material, and therefore shallow, display of belief that is unnecessary in their everyday lives. However, the understanding and practice of halal among these more pragmatic Muslims cannot be separated from the fact that halal production, trade, and consumption are undergoing drastic changes, and that halal is part of powerful discourses and practices globally.

Discussion

Most informants would agree that, over the past few years, halal availability has improved greatly in Britain and London in particular. However, many Muslim consumers are uncertain about the moral implications of an expanding halal market and the pluralization of shopping choices and, thus, spaces, involved in halal. Even the most relaxed middle-class Malays in London experience con-fusion as halal spreads into new types of commodities and marks spaces in supermarkets, hypermarkets, and advertising. Belief, piety, quality, certifica-tion, cleanliness, thrift, patriotism, and convenience were all keywords to describe everyday halal shopping among Malays in London. Ultimately, the contradictory responses of informants underscore a central theme, that is, halal certification authorized by the Malaysian state as well as other authorities does not necessarily inspire confidence outside one's own kitchen. Contradiction and ambivalence are to a large extent generated by the sentiment that outside the control of one's home, there are few clear answers. Thus, consumers often have to figure things out for themselves and work out everyday shopping strategies.

This empirical exploration of halal demonstrates that proper certification is a question that even the most pragmatic Muslims are aware of and must negotiate in their everyday lives. In my discussion, I have not included other ethnic or Muslim groups, because this research effort is based mainly on Malays who embody a particular trajectory of halal. However, research I have done with other Muslim groups, such as Pakistanis, Bangladeshis, and Indians, suggests that, between and within these groups, purism and pragmatism represent powerful distinctions. In other words, distinctions between the self and the other are often manifested in being fastidious versus relaxed about halal and its certification as a moral register or category. Informants explained to me that visible halal certification and logos on products are probably the most reliable markers of halalness that Muslim consumers can observe in their everyday consumption.

Informants preferred state-certified products by far if they were readily available. State-certified halal in Malaysia was described as 'familiar', 'trustworthy', 'reliable', and 'convincing'. The way in which halal has developed in a country such as Malaysia will probably affect future tendencies in the global halal market with particular respect to certification and standardization. Thus, the Malay Muslim consumers can be seen as representative of trends that may prove significant in this global religious market.

Consuming halal among my informants suggested a religious and ethnic identity that to a large extent is impersonal and technological in nature, as halal has been lifted out of not only local halal butchers' shops, but also the domain of traditional religious authority. Hence, from trusting the authority of the local halal butcher, consumers now rely on the authority involved in proper Islamic branding through marking commodities with logos or accompanying certificates.

Readings

Modern and globalized halal is a relatively new field of study. The present chapter is to a large extent based on my book *The Halal Frontier: Muslim Consumers in a Globalized Market* (Basingstoke, UK: Palgrave Macmillan, 2011). For a study of halal in Malaysia and broader issues of 'proper Islamic consumption' see my book *Proper Islamic Consumption: Shopping among the Malays in Modern Malaysia* (Copenhagen: NIAS Press, 2008).

Author

Johan Fischer is an Associate Professor in the Department of Society and Globalization, Roskilde University, Denmark. His work focuses on modern Islam and consumer culture in Southeast Asia and Europe. More specifically, Johan explores the interfaces between class, consumption, market relations, Islam, and the state in a globalized world. A central focus in this research is the theoretical and empirical focus on the proliferation of halal commodities on a global scale. He is the author of two books as well as numerous articles in journals and edited volumes. Johan is currently working on a book with the provisional title *Global Halal Zones: Islam, States and Markets*.

Chapter 14

Researching Muslim converts

Islamic teachings, political context and the researcher's personality

Leon Moosavi

Preamble

The events in New York on 11 September 2001 changed the world in all sorts of ways. In academia, it led to a sudden rise in the amount of research being conducted on Muslims living in 'Western' societies. Researchers began to ask questions about how Muslim communities understood their role in non-Muslim societies, how they behaved in these societies, how non-Muslims saw them, and how non-Muslims treated them. My own PhD research followed this trend but in a fairly unique manner. I was initially interested in the meanings attached to hijab and responses to veiling, but after immersing myself in the literature in 2007, I realized that much had already been said about this topic. Rather than covering ground that others were covering already, I wanted to explore something that had been neglected so as to further understanding and make a significant contribution. I was fortunate in that I stumbled across an area about which little research had been conducted, and even better, which I found really interesting. This area was about the experiences of those people who were choosing to become Muslim from non-Muslim backgrounds. The topic seemed counterintuitive to some who were not convinced that many were choosing to convert to Islam at a time when Islam was associated with so much negativity. Yet, they were wrong, as I knew that there were many people converting to Islam in Britain, and that their everyday experiences in the post-9/11 context had not been sufficiently explored. In this chapter, I reflect on some of my experiences of organizing and conducting in-depth interviews with a range of Muslim converts. Ultimately, I hope to demonstrate that when conducting research on Muslims, several factors can shape the trajectory of the research, and in turn, the conclusions that can be drawn. These factors primarily relate to Islamic teachings, the socio-political context and one's own personality and identity.

Narrative

I decided from the outset that in order to gain an insight into the views and experiences of Muslim converts in Britain, I would need to have lengthy conversations with converts, asking them a range of questions to explore different facets of their lives. In methodological terms, this meant conducting in-depth interviews with those who were prepared to share personal information that in many cases may be sensitive and evoke emotional responses. My first task was therefore to identify converts who I could invite to be interviewed and hope that a suitable number of them were willing to cooperate. But how to find these converts? This was not easy because Muslim converts are dispersed and do not live in enclaves like other Muslims in Britain. Therefore, I turned my attention to the Internet as a novel solution. In 2008, when I was embarking on the interviews, Facebook was still relatively new in terms of being a popular way for people to interact. It was certainly not as popular or mainstream as it has become today. It was in this relatively new platform that I decided there might be a unique opportunity for locating interviewees. I began trawling through pages and groups dedicated to celebrating and supporting Muslim converts. Some of these were geographically categorized which meant that I was able to target UK-based converts. Facebook was of great benefit for me as it meant that I was able to locate hundreds of Muslim converts from around the UK with ease. All it took was a simple 'friend request' or message to explain to the convert what I was seeking to achieve and I could get the process of recruiting interviewees underway.

Anyone conducting research on a particular community needs to be mindful of some of the popular perceptions and attitudes that exist amongst that community. One of the most significant beliefs that is widespread amongst Muslims is that because of 9/11, non-Muslims dislike and are suspicious of Muslims. This extends to Muslims often believing that non-Muslims are Islamophobic, which can result in Muslims being particularly paranoid that people are seeking to spy on them in case they are involved in extremism or terrorism. In fact, it may be unfair to use the word 'paranoid' because studies have documented widespread Islamophobia and, furthermore, there have been numerous examples of Muslims being surveilled, detained, and interrogated by various agencies, which suggests that there are some justifications for Muslims being concerned about being spied on. For example, during the time I was conducting my research, Channel 4 aired two programmes entitled *Undercover Mosque* and *Undercover Mosque: The Return*, which carried out secret filming within mosques, accusing them of preaching hatred. Such examples, along with many others, encourage Muslims to believe they're frequently being covertly watched in order that they can be reprimanded. Regardless of how common it is for Muslims to be spied on, the perception that it is common is relevant for researchers because it means when one approaches Muslims and asks if they will speak candidly about their religious, political, and social beliefs, they can be suspicious of what the researcher's intentions are, whether they are trying to dupe or entrap them, and whether they really are who they say they are. I certainly faced this attitude on numerous occasions when trying to engage with Muslim converts on Facebook. It was common for the potential interviewees to seek thorough reassurance and even references when deciding whether to participate in the research, and even though I attempted to provide this, numerous potential interviewees either avoided responding to me or told me frankly that they were unwilling to participate. Some of this could be explained by them being too busy, not being enthusiastic about my project, and having had bad experiences of research in the past, all of which could be the case for any cohort, but for a significant portion, it seemed that the primary reason for their reluctance was that they were concerned how the research might be used against them and what difficulties it may generate for them. This caused me discomfort because I knew that my goal was not to harm them or even misrepresent them, but to empower them.

Not only are many Muslims concerned about being spied on, but, also in the post-9/11 context, it has become popular to research Muslims, leading many to experience 'research-fatigue' as a result of being inundated with requests to participate in research projects. Such an attitude was made clear to me when I was invited to talk on a panel at the New Muslim Project at the Islamic Foundation in April 2011 that was titled: 'Is the Muslim convert community being researched to death … ?' Now the existence of a tired as well as fairly paranoid, or rightfully suspicious, cohort of research subjects need not mean the end of one's research recruitment. The researcher can – as I did – make efforts to convince the potential interviewees that one is genuine, does not have a sinister agenda, and that the research may even be beneficial to the participants by revealing issues that are thus far not understood. Trying to generate this trust online can be fruitless though because there are pervasive cultural fears about meeting people in real life that one has first interacted with online. This is related to a social anxiety that dubious people deceptively lure victims to dangerous encounters via the Internet, which encourages caution when interacting in cyberspace. On some occasions, I sensed that the person I was contacting was uncomfortable with my contact. For instance, some of them prevented me from sending them further messages after initial contact, some replied with a string of questions about who I was and how I found them, and others responded with very brief messages and were reluctant to make firm commitments to meet me. Thus, gaining the trust of potential inter-viewees may be harder to achieve when interacting on the Internet than it would be in person. Having said that, the Internet, or specifically Facebook, offered me a unique opportunity to gain the confidence of potential interviewees. In some sense, it facilitated trust by allowing the potential interviewees to access a wide range of information about myself including being able to see my photos, the way I interacted with my friends, the messages my profile contained, the causes I supported and other personal information about myself. Thus, the potential interviewees were able to discern much about my character due to the transparency that Facebook offers. I believe that this led to some feeling as though they could trust me as someone who was a genuine researcher who cared about understanding the experiences of Muslim converts.

Eventually, almost half of my interviewees were first contacted via Facebook proving it to be a helpful tool. Facebook allowed me to publicize the research to people that I otherwise would not have reached. It also allowed direct access to converts without having to mediate with any gatekeepers. It was so helpful that I even found myself eventually in a position where I had to turn people away and tell them I could no longer conduct interviews as I had already significantly surpassed my target of 25 interviews. I found then, that rather than struggling to locate interviewees as many researchers worry about, I was inundated with offers of help. I believe this to be partly related to the fact that converts have a story to tell which is often neglected within public and academic discussions, but I also believe this is where it is crucial to mention Islamic beliefs. Regardless of the many popular misconceptions about Islamic teachings, at the heart of this religion is a strong emphasis on compassion, kindness, and being proactive in helping others. These traits meant that several of the converts were encouraged to help me by a resolute belief that they were doing something religiously good, by helping someone and/or by furthering knowledge. This may have been amplified by their desire to help a fellow Muslim, yet, this is not to say that the same Islamic-inspired generosity would not be extended to non-Muslims. In fact, some Muslims may be even keener to participate in research with non-Muslims, driven by a belief that it is the Islamic imperative to give a good example to non-Muslims so that they acquire a positive impression of Islam. So researching Muslims, especially those who are practising the faith, will often involve being the recipient of much hospitality. For me, this meant that I was often enthusiastically welcomed into the converts' homes and treated with great respect. On one occasion, the interviewee had arranged for a restaurant to deliver lavish food for me to eat with her family after the interview. This was particularly touching because this family was relatively poor and such a treat would only be indulged in on rare occasions. Many of the converts also made efforts to work around my schedule in ways that were convenient to me based on their desire to maintain polite Islamic manners.

There are other ways in which I found Islamic teachings influenced my research experience, specifically in relation to Islamic teachings on gender. Researchers may encounter difficulties in researching Muslims of a different gender to them because of the gender segregation that is encouraged by Islam. As a man seeking to carry out interviews with Muslim women as well as Muslim men, I found that some of the convert women were reluctant to be alone with me in an enclosed space since Islam discourages this as a strict way of preventing any possible *fitna* (public immorality). One solution that I considered to overcome this issue was through using online or telephone interviewing. However, I did not resort to this as I was able to offer all the potential women interviewees the option of having a friend or relative present during the interview. This led to 11 of the 22 women taking up the offer, none of which may have participated if the option was not available to them. Having a third party present in the interview is not ideal though. In practical terms, it makes it even harder to find a time to conduct the interview. In some cases, I found that this delayed arranging an interview for several weeks. Perhaps more crucially though, having another person present during the interview will have influenced what the interviewees said as they would consciously or subconsciously tailor their accounts to satisfy all people present in the conversation. For instance, in some of the interviews there were instances when the interviewee would seek out her husband's approval along the lines of: 'Can I tell him about that?' before disclosing certain information. Another manner in which the presence of a third person influenced the interview was when they interrupted. I found it rude to ask them not to talk and therefore, there were times when the husband began answering the questions or interrupting which caused considerable distraction. In one parti- cularly challenging example of this, the interviewee's husband dominated the whole interview and actually said more than the interviewee herself, often answering on her behalf. This seemed to be amplified by his Arab cultural background in which it is not customary for a non-related man to speak directly to another man's wife. There were also some interviews where young children were present, which also disrupted the interview. So, the Islamic teachings relating to gender created a difficulty in conducting the research. It did not prevent me from doing the research, but was a unique dimension that I had to navigate around.

It is religious sensibilities like these that a researcher who examines Muslim communities must be familiar with and sensitive towards. I found this true in other aspects too. For example, since some of the interviewees suggested conducting the interview in a mosque – perhaps a space they saw as safe and neutral – it was convenient that I knew how to behave in a mosque, from taking off my shoes when entering to remaining silent during the *athaan* (call to prayer). On more than one occasion in the mosque, one of the five daily prayers was due to be performed, and my ability and desire to participate would have shown the interviewee that we had commonalities. Again, this is not to say that non–Muslims would not be welcomed into mosques, but that it is important to familiarize oneself with the appropriate customs when entering into this setting. Other Islamic teachings, which I believe shaped the interview interactions, relate to Islamic teachings about avoiding talking negatively about others, making excuses for those who appear to have mis- behaved, and concealing one's misdeeds. All of these teachings may have shaped what the interviewee chose to reveal. My knowledge of these traits led me to strive to create a trusting environment and adequately probe issues to best reveal the interviewees' experiences. Ultimately, being aware of these Islamic preferences enabled me to consider when someone may have wanted to say something but their desire to be a good Muslim prevented them from doing so. However, Islam also stresses the need to always speak truthfully, meaning that the interviewees I dealt with may have been even more forthcoming than other cohorts of interviewees. Interestingly, talking to Muslims about being Muslim therefore means Islam is very present during the interview.

Discussion

My experiences of conducting research with Muslim converts taught me that when researching Muslims, the encounter will be shaped by Islamic teachings, the political context, and also the researcher's personality. These factors create both challenges and opportunities, which may make the research difficult to undertake but may also facilitate it. These factors also have a bearing on the findings that emerge. This does not mean that research is pointless because there are intervening factors which influence the findings though. Rather, one finds that through exploring the lives of multiple individuals who do not know each other but have commonalities in their identities, backgrounds, and lifestyles, one begins to gain a clearer picture after hearing consistent narrations. In other words, even though people don't always describe their lives perfectly, and even though they may not want to talk to you out of fear of reprisals, after asking several people the exact same question, one starts to see patterns emerging. These then flourish into research findings that can be analysed alongside existing literature using careful analysis.

A good researcher is candid about their own political biases, and although I did not have any zealous agenda to attend to during my research, I did openly acknowledge that, perhaps inevitably, I am sympathetic towards Muslims and hostile towards Islamophobia and racism. While traditional positivists would be critical of this admission, it is more common today for researchers to accept that it is legitimate to want to defend those who are disadvantaged and marginalized rather than just benefit from them. Aside from this, I felt as though I had a duty to convey fairly and accurately the converts' lives, especially since they had assisted me in completing the research, but also because much commentary has bypassed Muslims, theorizing about them without engaging with them. A history of Orientalism where 'we' spoke about and represented 'them' means allowing Muslims to represent themselves is a priority, and it is this that I tried to promote in my research.

Using the Internet to recruit interviewees can be a rewarding process. It is true that it may be an environment where distrust is the default, but it can still be helpful, as it was for me. I did not solely recruit interviewees from the Internet, but without it I'm sure my research would have looked markedly different and would not have involved as diverse a cohort as it did. I would therefore suggest that the Internet should be used as one part of a recruitment strategy, rather than the sole method. One must consider that users of the Internet are more likely to be young, educated, and relatively wealthy, which means there's an implicit bias with allowing it to determine your sampling frame. One should also recognize that as soon as one begins interacting online with potential participants, one's discovering begins. For example, I was immediately intrigued by the fact that it appeared as if many Muslim converts were networking with other Muslim converts on Facebook even though they hadn't met each other in real life and didn't seem to plan to meet. I was witnessing a new form of friendship that the Internet, and Facebook in particular, had facilitated. Through interacting with and observing converts online, I was already participating in a 'cyber-ethnography'. I was witnessing expressions and behaviours that would later influence my research findings. While the substantive part of my research material was gathered later in the in-depth interviews, I have to credit these early interactions as being instrumental in shaping the direction in which the research progressed. Thus, I was forced to think of how I was engaged in an informal ethnography online. More than my online encounters with converts, I realized that I was approaching the topic in a way that was shaped by my own experiences of living as a Muslim in a Muslim community, in other words, as someone who was living in 'the field' they were studying. Thus, the many impromptu but relevant conversations with non-Muslims, lifelong Muslims, and Muslim converts I'd had throughout my life relating to the topic, as well as the numerous observations I'd made of various incidents and media items that related to the topics I was interested in, all seemed to play some role in shaping my approach to the research.

One of the key questions left open for discussion is how being a Muslim studying Muslims may differ from being a non-Muslim studying Muslims. Some have claimed that for a researcher to understand the researched, one needs to be an insider, especially when it comes to researching minorities. As a Muslim researching Muslims, I did benefit from having relevant knowledge and perhaps I found it easier to acquire the converts' trust as a fellow believer, which is crucial with Muslims who, as explained earlier, often feel a sense of distrust towards non-Muslims who come asking questions. But there could just as well be unique advantages for non-Muslims studying Muslims. They may be offered more frank accounts because their status as an outsider may suggest that they are less likely to judge the interviewee by the community's standards. For instance, some of the interviewees I spoke to may have hesitated when providing answers to my questions bearing in mind that I may have had mutual friends or may attend the same places and events as them. It therefore seems a reasonable conclusion to state that neither insider research nor outsider research is better than the other, but rather, they are complementary in generating accounts of the same phenomenon from different vantage points.

Yet, perhaps the paradigm of insider versus outsider is a flawed model. In some cases, it is not clear as to whether interviewees will consider the researcher an insider or an outsider, even if the researcher considers him- or herself as one or the other. For example, would a British man conducting research on British women be considered an insider on account of his nationality or would his gender make him an outsider? How would all the other facets of his identity implicate his status as an insider or outsider? Both interviewers and interviewees have multiple facets of identity that intersect in complex ways, which means one's commonalities with the interviewee can be ambiguous and may even shift within one interview. I certainly seemed to face this ambiguity concerning my status since interviewees were not clear if I was Muslim because of my non-Muslim first name, and even when they discovered I was a Muslim, they were then confused as to whether I was a convert like them or not. It may even be too simplistic to assume that interviewees look at interviewers through insider versus outsider lenses. It may simply be that interviewees want to feel as though they can trust the researcher and strike up a rapport with them as an individual. Overall, I found that the interviewees were generally friendly and willing to help regardless of what they knew about me, and by implication regardless of whether they thought I was 'one of them' or not. Perhaps the insider/outsider debate over-theorizes a problem that is not such a problem in reality. Perhaps friendly and sincere interaction is enough to gain a valid insight into the lives of those that one is interviewing, as people generally want to welcome others, look for common ground, and cooperate in assisting them. Thus, it is not whether one is a Muslim or not that matters when researching Muslims, but that one approaches Muslims with a clear purpose and shows that they are trustworthy.

Researching the lives of others can be nothing short of fascinating and also educating. While interviews are contextual interactions where knowledge is co-produced by both the interviewer and the interviewee, they still leave the interviewer with original insights into the lives of the people being studied. The cooperation of the interviewees is precious; I found the converts to be very generous in their hospitality and their desire to answer my questions. It was a pleasurable experience for me and I truly understand why many researchers find meeting participants to be the highlight of the whole research process. I endeavoured to minimize forms of bias where possible, in order that I could capture the converts' experiences in their own terms as well as can be expected. Overall, I was pleased with the depth of insight provided by the research process. I managed to complete numerous unique interviews that were extremely valuable for their rarity and expediency. Although there were struggles in completing the research, none were insurmountable. The success of the interviews was reflected in that the analysis of the interviews led to numerous observations and understandings that I had not conceptualized before the interviews. The interviews were therefore pivotal and formed the foundations of the arguments that I went on to make in my PhD thesis, some of which were rather unexpected, but the unexpected is exactly what good research should produce.

Readings

One of the most comprehensive resources that explores the dynamics of Muslim communities in Britain can be found in Sophie Gilliat-Ray's *Muslims in Britain: An Introduction* (Cambridge: Cambridge University Press, 2010). Alongside this, I would recommend Ron Geaves's older but still relevant *Sectarian Influences within Islam in Britain: With Reference to the Concepts of 'Ummah' and 'Community'* (Leeds: University of Leeds, 1996), which offers readers an illuminating insight into the diversity and tensions that exist amongst Muslims in Britain. For a more specific but still general overview of Muslim converts' experiences, readers will enjoy Kate Zebiri's *British Muslim Converts: Choosing Alternative Lives* (Oxford: Oneworld, 2008). An inspiring resource that provokes many intriguing questions for those undertaking field-work can be found in *Taking Sides: Ethics, Politics and Fieldwork in Anthropology* by Heidi Armbruster and Anna Laerke (New York: Berghahn Books, 2008). Those interested in a groundbreaking paper relating to the insider/outsider debate can consult Ann Oakley's 'Interviewing women: a contradiction in terms', in Alan Bryman's and Robert G. Burgess (Eds), *Qualitative Research* (London: Sage, 1999). These are initial recommendations that may generate better understanding of some of the issues touched on in this chapter. There are of course many other relevant and stimulating resources to be found.

Author

Dr Leon Moosavi is a lecturer in Sociology at the University of Liverpool, UK. He specializes in the sociology of race and religion and is an expert on topics relating to Islamophobia, conversion to Islam, and Muslims in Britain. Originally from Manchester, he completed his PhD at Lancaster University in 2011. His PhD thesis was entitled: *Islamophobia, Belonging and Race in the Experiences of Muslim Converts in Britain.* He has travelled to several countries to talk about his research and has contributed to topical debates in mainstream media on numerous occasions. Aside from engaging in sociological enquiry, Leon enjoys supporting Manchester City FC.

Chapter 15

Studying Muslims and cyberspace

Gary R. Bunt

Preamble

This chapter explores changing approaches to analysing and researching Islam and Muslims in cyberspace, based on substantial personal experience 'in the field'. The field is virtual, but has a real-world impact at many levels, with increasing implications for Muslims in local and global contexts. As such, it has become an important subject for academic study. Specific and innovative methodological approaches are required, and these continue to evolve in response to changing issues and technological shifts. The following narrative seeks to reflect on experience to date, and considers ways in which digital content can be integrated into academic discourse. The approach is multidisciplinary and interdisciplinary in nature.

Narrative

Studying Muslims and cyberspace – a personal perspective

I have been researching Islam and the Internet for 20 years. The nature of this exploration has changed considerably. Initially, my research was undertaken on what would be seen now as very primitive technology. USENET groups and FTP platforms, together with e-mail, were the only research tools available to me. Initially, in the 1990s, I became interested in this subject in order to record the discourse taking place between scholars and activists in relation to Islam and Muslim issues. These were increasingly taking place electronically. A substantial amount of data was appearing, in pre-browser contexts, which meant that this information was simply raw text. Nevertheless, it was providing a fascinating resource that was over and above the traditional avenues for academic exploration.

At the time, I had to print off reams and reams of articles and materials for later discussion. This was not structured. I had not realized at the time that this would become a key research interest for me, as I was working on my PhD in relation to Islam and decision-making processes. While this was not a thesis about electronic media, it was clear that digital discourse in the mid-1990s was beginning to impact on ideas of religious authority online. This could mean that scholars were simply exchanging views in various online groups, or e-mailing information to one another to discuss approaches to shared issues. A traditionally insular world was slowly opening up to new ideas and influences, albeit in selected contexts. Some locations were more wired than others. In some cases, the files that were circulating was simply copies of the Qur'an in digital format, or copies of other significant texts. There were no digital media files at that time.

With the emergence of browsers such as Netscape Navigator and Mosaic in the mid-1990s, changes in interface meant firstly an expansion of interest in the Internet as a medium, and also the emergence of prototype Islamic websites. When I was lecturing, I became aware that students were starting to cite these materials within their essays, often without considering the provenance of the data that they were using or its implications. Searching using early search engines (pre-dating the ubiquitous Google) was also having an impact.

There was a tendency to cut and paste information into essays, a phenomenon that has not really changed in the ensuing years. Students were presenting themselves as more web literate, albeit on desk-based machines that will be seen as primitive today. The levels of digital literacy were often way above those of academics who were seeking to teach them, and I recognized the gulf of knowledge and also of an awareness of source materials. In order to try and deal with that, I established a listing of recommended sites entitled Islamic Studies Pathways. This was initially intended for local student use only and it featured 20 significant sites that I had determined as appropriate for study use. I noticed immediately that many people from outside of my institution were starting to access the list, even though it wasn't the only listing on the Internet that recommended resources to do with Islam. I was writing the sites in terms of academic utility on my own listing. The initial 20 sites quickly became more than a hundred, as there was an exponential growth in Islamic Internet resources in the late 1990s.

It was at this time that I determined that there needed to be some analysis of the impact of these resources on readers, in terms of their influence and circulation. This was particularly important in relation to the translation of the Qur'an, where numerous English-language versions were starting to appear online. Students were bringing these to class, without considering who had generated them or whether they were 100 per cent accurate. There was also content being generated from a variety of political and religious perspectives, some of which were more digitally literate than others; I noticed that groups without traditional affiliations to mosques or government organizations were effectively developing an online following through their Internet sites. These would present as a 'one-stop shop' for Qur'anic resources, practical information, and opportunities to network with like-minded individuals; in some cases, these were also attempts to engage non-Muslims in dialogue and encourage conversion to Islam. Questions emerged on how one identified a website or resource as 'Islamic', requiring a breakdown of attributes relating to symbolism, language, design, and motivation of site developers.

I started observing these phenomena, and recognized the need to record what I was viewing. This required the development of methodological skills that were way beyond those that I had developed in other areas of academic research. This meant a process of trial and (often) error, as I determined the most appropriate ways in which to record and analyse material in a frequently shifting cyber landscape. I tried to draw on ideas from other academic disciplines, which were perhaps more digitally literate than those of theology and religious studies, which is where I was operating. This, together with discussions at conferences, helped me to establish a rudimentary approach to online discourse.

Determining the context in which information is presented online was of great importance. There are different notions of data capture, fieldwork, and the need to respond to evolving cyber environments which are not always logical, rigid, or scientific in their development. Research techniques in this field require the knowledge of how search engines operate, for examples through the ways in which deep searching can acquire information, and how alternative interfaces using different algorithms provide different types of results.

It has also been necessary to develop an understanding of the way in which sites are designed, and how different levels of readership may be attracted to different areas of the web. There are particularly nuanced models of readers and content. In some cases, there can be barriers such as pay walls, users' IT knowledge, and the requirement of membership in order to access specific areas of online activity.

I decided that I would present a phenomenological approach to Islam on the Internet, in which I surveyed and commented on the impact of this nascent digital culture through concepts such as sacred space, activism, and ideas of religious identity. My initial analysis emerged in my book, *Virtually Islamic* (Cardiff: University of Wales Press, 2000). Over the years, I have (hopefully) refined my approach in subsequent research, which has emerged in a variety of books and chapters.

There was a considerable spike in interest in online discourse in relation to Islam after the events of 9/11 and the aftermath, particularly in Iraq and Afghanistan. This opened up a relatively obscure area of academic discourse to scrutiny from numerous other disciplines, and from interested parties outside of academia. I increasingly had to record online activities and keep records, which went way beyond my initial approach of printing out pages and storing them on my hard drive. The sheer bulk of discourse in relation to jihad, which was emerging not just in textual form but also through an increase in multimedia approaches, not only put a strain on my hard drives but required specific skills of time management and data control. I had to learn about hacking, cracking and other forms of digital disruption that were taking place in the name of various religiously inspired movements. Again, this was a set of skills that I had to acquire 'on the hoof'. I had to learn how to track down the origins of various sites as well, through DNS and other methods. These are not typical skills for Islamic studies. I was drawn into website development, learning HTML, CSS, and a variety of approaches to page construction.

I was logging key developments online in relation to Islam. I was doing this through my website. The original Pathways site continued, but I opened up a listing of key resources and articles on Islam online at virtuallyislamic.com. In 2003, in an effort to manage all of this information, I started recording on a daily basis the key activities taking place online in relation to Islam: this became the Virtually Islamic blog. I have maintained this through thousands of postings ever since, logging and occasionally commenting on critical developments. I have found that this has provided a useful adjunct to more time-bound publications and research that I have presented elsewhere, and have recommended blogging as an academic tool for others in the field.

I now also use Facebook, Twitter, and Tumblr in order to keep on top of the numerous developments that take place in relation to the subject area. This has exposed me to a variety of new materials and influences, and the online resources that are generated have become a clearinghouse for others to send in links and comments. This has been in addition to my traditional academic activities, such as lecturing and marking! This subject is 'always on'.

I have had to respond to changes in technology as well, given that we are now increasingly within a mobile digital framework, in which we are used to accessing the Internet through a multiplicity of devices. Whereas in the past access to the Internet and the World Wide Web required deskbound computers, now a variety of portable devices mean that their materials can be accessed wherever there is a good phone signal or Wi-Fi point. The sheer volume of material that has emerged also means that we are in the position of a digital overload, and it is not possible to observe and record every activity in relation to Islam and the Internet, especially given that this is presented in a multiplicity of languages. Initially, the majority of the discourse was in English language and other Latin scripts. The development of coding in other languages, away from the Latin script, not only reduced the digital divide but it increased the amount of materials that one had to research and reference.

Whilst this has been an area of academic interest from a variety of perspectives, there is still a great deal of work to be done in this area necessitating intensive analysis. A great deal of my own research has been undertaken in close proximity to events, and there is scope to go back and look at developments with the benefit of hindsight. Unfortunately, the absence of archives during the formative period in relation to the Internet means that this can be a problematic activity. Existing resources such as Internet Wayback Machine only provide a snapshot of materials; much has been lost, including significant pages associated with major world events. This makes it difficult for researchers on a number of levels, given the often abstract and ephemeral nature of digital content. Some sites and pages only appear very briefly on the radar, before they are taken down, hacked, or edited. This has been particularly true in relation to online materials associated with jihad.

One dominant theme has been that of al-Qaeda and militaristic 'jihad'. Al-Qaeda had an online presence prior to 9/11. However, this did not attract substantial interest. Naturally, that changed after the attacks and their aftermath. The presence of statements justifying the attacks, images commemorating the 'martyrs', and statements from key leaders such as Osama bin Laden, emerged online. This was in conjunction with materials appearing in chat rooms supporting the attacks, and considering future strategies.

I had been quickly informed of the attacks on 11 September 2011. At that time, in my office, I had a very low speed Internet connection, so on the day was acquiring information through chat rooms and basic news channels. Servers where data relating to the attacks was being circulated were overloaded, so it was very difficult to get an accurate impression online of what was happening. There was a great deal of conjecture, including the origins of the attacks.

Within the period following the attacks and their implications, academic research did not necessarily top my agenda. However, I started to gather news information and other material that were posted online. I also archived key statements and materials from al-Qaeda. In the intervening months, I built up a substantial online archive through data capture. This included screenshots of key pages. I also downloaded websites in their entirety. This is a somewhat laborious process, and not one that was easily facilitated by the poor quality of hardware and software I had at the time.

For each page, I had to track back and find where it had been published and by whom. This required looking at Whois resource sites which unpacked ownership of pages, locations of servers, registration details of URLs, and related material. On occasion, I also received e-mails which required a similar process. This was all very rudimentary, and as I only work within the public domain, I did not access closed secured-access sites.

Since 9/11, I have been continuing to collect data in relation to jihad. It forms one small sector of my overall study of what I described as cyber Islamic environments. The same processes that I used in the post-9/11 context have now been refined. I am downloading any video that I see relevant, through using KeepVid and commercial video downloading packages (I use iSkysoft iTube Studio and others). Downloading videos became important as the jihad-related material became more sophisticated and prevalent, in a variety of languages: the emergence of specially edited videos included those in a newscast format, which assembled materials from diverse sources which were then narrated by a 'newsreader'. In one example, on his desk lay a Kalashnikov and the Qur'an.

These items did not always stay on the Internet for very long, so it was essential to make copies. The technical quality of videos has improved in line with changes in technology, so that they have become a natural part of jihad-oriented discourse. It has also been necessary to download a variety of online publications: these are often in PDF format, and have become increasingly sophisticated, presenting editorials, reportage, religious interpretation, and statements from leaders seeking to motivate potential jihad operations and recruits.

These were put into sharp focus with the development of an English-language magazine by Anwar al-Awlaki and Samir Khan entitled 'Inspire'. This publication achieved a great deal of publicity through its use of a magazine format, encouraging people to build bombs in their kitchen, and offering practical advice for would-be jihad fighters in domestic and international contexts. The inspirational statements from al-Awlaki in the English language had been deemed significant influences on a number of jihad operations in Western contexts. Al-Awlaki was assisted by Samir Khan, who had previously been proactive in blogging on jihad-related activities from the USA; he moved to Yemen to be with al-Awlaki, and both were killed in a drone attack in 2011.

As a researcher, I have had to read a number of these magazines; sometimes their content has been controversial, with a strong line in rhetoric. There were also attempts at 'humour' and engaging a variety of audiences. At all times, I have attempted to archive this stream of invective and conjecture, although I have chosen not to engage with the authors of these and other online materials. There are some researchers who have chosen to go online and discuss the intricacies of the dialogue with the authors of jihad magazines and websites. While this might have validity, I feel that there has to be a degree of separation between the researcher and the subject area.

This is particularly true within such a security-linked area as jihad. I advise students only to go to specific sites where there are safe downloads of jihad materials; I tell them not to put the magazines or related content onto data sticks or their laptop, especially if they intend to travel abroad. This is essential, especially for Muslim students or those whose profile might suggest a Muslim identity. There are also contexts in which students should not download such materials: public libraries, shared computers, and other systems may have filtering technology to establish the identities of surfers, or simply to block access to such materials. If an individual is in a public place observing a jihad video, that could bring that individual to unwanted attention. I can recall using Internet cafés in Muslim contexts whilst researching on jihad, and trying to make sure that people were not looking over my shoulder.

Within the current climate, and because of legislation in various countries, it can be illegal to access some of this material. Naturally, this makes it a very difficult subject to research on a practical level. There have been cases where students have been targeted by their institutions for downloading and printing out such content, and this might lead to police action. These are considerations where there is acute sensitivity within the Islamic studies context that do not necessarily apply within other subjects areas.

When I was lecturing during the aftermath of 9/11, I happened to be running a course on Islam in the contemporary world. The agenda changed completely given the developments, and seminars became a place where news and views could be exchanged. The profile of the students included several with Muslim identities. During the classes, we were bringing in links to a variety of online materials for discussion. There was a level of analysis when 'live' news came into the lecture, for example, during the period where US and other forces entered Afghanistan. The material was not in the textbooks, but really had to be discussed. There was a reliance on online material, including news broadcasts and articles. We also used the websites generated by the Taliban and their supporters, together with al-Qaeda websites and those of other supporters. This provided a perspective on events that demonstrated to the students how online media was having an impact on the discourse associated with post-9/11 contexts.

By the time of the invasion of Iraq, digital media was becoming more prevalent. Bloggers inside Iraq had been recording their experiences of Saddam Hussain's regime. Discourse was emerging not just in English, but also in Arabic as the digital tools improved. This meant that I was downloading pages, recording videos, and having to deal with a wider range of media from all sides. This included the main protagonists in Iraq. The jihad organizations utilized the web to film executions of the hostages and other victims. They also made statements outlining their policies, and recorded military action. Extensive statements were archived through a variety of chat rooms. I found that I had to use passwords in order to enter some of these.

There were areas of the web that were increasingly becoming closed to researchers. There was suspicion about the motivations for anyone visiting a site, with fear of being monitored by security organizations. All sides were increasingly uploading video footage, even at the height of conflict; news broadcasters, to augment their own footage, would often use this. The role of Internet media as actuality was increasing. Saddam Hussein's capture and subsequent execution were also recorded and circulated online – being surreptitiously recorded together with images of his corpse. This is not the last time the death of an Arab dictator would be recorded and circulated; the death of Colonel Gadhafi was also captured on mobile phone, but was circulated much more rapidly online through social media sites.

I subsequently drew on such experiences to discuss approaches towards the source materials with academic colleagues in the UK. This was through the Learning and Teaching Support Network, a UK-based network of subject centres relating to a variety of academic disciplines; I was involved as a coordinator for religious studies, but found myself increasingly drawn into activities associated with Islamic studies and the post-9/11 context. I organized a workshop for academics in 2002, in which we exchanged experiences about teaching Islam and how that had changed following 9/11. The subject was viewed with suspicion among some, whilst there was also an increase in interest in studying it from students. Naturally, we had to respond to both areas. Subsequently, in 2005, I organized a national conference on teaching Islamic studies in which this subject also was a dominant one.

In part, this led to the development by the Higher Education Academy's Islamic Studies Network, in which I was also involved. Approaches to online materials became an important area within the discipline, especially as Islamic studies had become the subject of strategic importance, recognized by the UK government. Responses to digital discourse were starting to enter mainstream academic discussion, especially in relation to Islam and the Internet.

By the time of the 7/7 bombings in London, digital media was becoming more integrated into the story. The bombers had filmed themselves making statements associated with their intended actions. Film in the immediate aftermath of the bombings was taken on mobile phones. Blogs responded to the events, exchanging responses.

Key events and episodes in relation to Islam and Muslims have played out online in the intervening period. The so-called 'Green Revolution' in Iran in 2009 demonstrated the potential power of social media, as a means of coordinating and organizing protests. Again, this was something that required responses in terms of monitoring, recording, and archiving. What made this particular sequence of events important was the growing impact of Facebook and Twitter, together with the utilization of YouTube in order to record what was going on in the streets of Tehran and elsewhere.

The significance of social media in relation to academic discourse and understanding intensified in the events of the so-called Arab Spring, which commenced in December 2010. Whilst this was not an 'Islamic' revolution, and in fact was inspired by a number of factors such as economic deprivation and oppressive political circumstances in diverse countries and contexts, one element that was particularly highlighted during events was the use of the Internet.

Facebook, YouTube, and Twitter were three significant channels through which a variety of activists and organizations mobilized during the events of the Arab Spring. Early cell phone footage of protests in Sidi Bouzid rapidly spread online and influenced demonstrations throughout Tunisia, and later in other nations. The footage was picked up by broadcasters such as Al Jazeera, and quickly circulated internationally. Although the technical quality of this material was poor, the emotional response was great and it inspired many activists and organizations. It put the regimes under the spotlight too, and they did not necessarily know how to counter the influence of this social media.

I became aware of the impact of these events through online chat rooms and Twitter. I started to monitor key events. I downloaded film clips, and Twitter materials. I also re-tweeted posts that were being generated through Twitter channels. What was initially a movement based in a small town in Tunisia quickly became an international event. As a researcher, I found myself monitoring events minute by minute through social media. Every time I saw a webpage or Facebook page that I felt had some relevance, I would take a screenshot of it and archive it. There is no formal archive of Twitter, so I was also recording material. Additionally, I was using my blog pages to repost, then keep track of materials.

Once the protests had reached Tahrir Square in Egypt, it was necessary to monitor events on several fronts simultaneously. I was using mobile media as well as portable devices in order to do this during my day-to-day activities. Occasionally, I was in direct contact with people who were posting at the heart of events, even though I was sitting in West Wales at the time. I was conscious that material being gathered would be relevant to my future research.

Religious authority issues have been another long-term concern in relation to the study of Islam and Muslims on the Internet. This again has required development of specific methodological approaches. I became particularly interested in the development of fatwa-oriented question-and-answer websites, in which people would send in questions for an online response. This was an extension of similar print media services, but with the benefit of broader international audiences and a high degree of searchability for their developers.

I found myself increasingly drawn to online responses to a variety of issues, and this would require making copies of the so-called fatwas or religious opinions. I did not send in my own questions, as I felt that this would be ethically inappropriate. There were times when it was feasible through some sites to determine the identity of the petitioner, which meant that issues of confidentiality could have been damaged. It was possible for readers to 'shop around' for opinions using a variety of databases and services. This in itself is having an impact on ideas of religious authority, where traditionally oriented religious leaders were being usurped through digital channels that offered anonymity and different perspectives.

Some scholars complained that they were spending a lot of time answering questions, which were simply for 'entertainment' rather than having any particular transferability or authority. As a measure of analysing attitudes to key concerns, fatwa databases and services have been useful. I archived a substantial amount of materials prior to analysing them on several issues, exploring them from diverse perspectives. There is potential further research in terms of looking at types of subjects covered and ignored, which are an indicator of the ideological religious values of platforms. Some more traditionally oriented organizations have deemed it necessary to go online to present their own worldviews, including similar question-and-answer sessions. Those platforms that have developed extensive services, such as Islam Online, generated a substantial profile; one issue with Islam Online was that the substantial archive of opinions and advice was compromised when several key people within the organization left after a dispute. Some of these key players emerged on another website, OnIslam. However, researchers looking into Islam Online today would have to use other channels to access materials that are now generally unavailable. In order to research in this area, one might apply Internet Archive in order to look at materials that are now lost. The case of Islam Online is one indicator of the necessity for substantial archives to be available for researchers and other interested parties.

It is difficult to measure the impact of sites such as this in general terms. They can be found in a number of contexts and have certainly been the subject of labour and material investment in order to develop and maintain user-friendly services. They can be found in Iran as part of a myriad of Islamic resources emanating from centres of authority such as Qom and elsewhere. In Egypt, al-Azhar introduced a telephone hotline for questions, some of which were also posted online (this was a service that necessitated payment). In Singapore, a long-standing service provided by the country's Muslim organization included an archive of religious opinions that were searchable. In Saudi Arabia, a number of scholars have gone online to provide archives of the authoritative declarations and opinions.

Given that these materials are now accessible through a multiplicity of devices, the opportunities for people to get advice and information very quickly have been extended and it is suggested that their influence has increased. In some ways this has become an authority industry or 'fatwa machine'. As such, recording and analysing such output is very important. I tend to check these services and databases quite regularly; some of the advice is clearly linked to issues of serious personal concern to the affected parties, and there is a high degree of emotional resonance in the questions and situations that are presented on these pages. In other cases, it could be suggested that there is an overemphasis on fatwas and opinions for every occasion, certainly within the types of unusual bizarre questions that appear on some databases. Of course, there are differences in approaches to these ideas of religious authority, not just between Sunni and Shi'a spheres of influence, but within them. These are useful in presenting diversity of opinion on shared issues. Religious authority is now also presented through social media; scholars and others will place their thoughts on Twitter. Perhaps there is an immediacy here that was not found within traditional and considered scholarship, and one wonders whether in the heat of the moment some opinions presented would be best left to the personal sphere.

Within shifting media landscapes, I have found it important to integrate these types of materials, even though they might lack academic references and context. They have been useful within teaching, to bring in practical examples of authority issues which can affect people at grassroots level, especially those who are consulting 'Sheikh Google' for an opinion. They demonstrate how there are differences in approach towards religious authority issues, and provide information on popular and trending topics.

Discussion

Academic approaches towards studying Muslims in cyberspace

Within the study of Islam, there is the need to integrate non-traditional skills with more conventional academic approaches. For the generations of digital natives who had been brought up using Internet-related media, this can be easier. As with other areas of research, there are also significant time management concerns, especially in relation to the fact that there is a constant flow of information coming into social media channels associated with the subject areas. I often use the Twitter manager package TweetDeck, which alerts its user every time a new tweet emerges through a bleep or chime. This is constant when a hot topic is emerging online.

The best advice (which I occasionally follow) is to draw a line in relation to events, and try not to research after a certain date point. This is easier said than done at some time; the net result is that there is a lot of research obtained as raw material, but when deadlines approach there is limited time to write it up.

This is particularly true for those students undertaking research on Internet materials, especially when they have to deal with the other distractions of digital media: checking Facebook, shopping, chatting with friends, and googling for pictures of trending subjects and memes are all distracting elements that can interfere with academic pursuits. Having said that, the Internet does offer a chance for more lateral thinking on different subject areas. It does open up a broader range of resources, but these will need to be appropriately referenced and verified. There are dangers of cut-and-paste culture. Plagiarism has become an increasing concern with the emergence of substantial online content.

A number of my students now write and research on digital matters, either for undergraduate essays or for dissertations. I am developing research with PhD students in associated fields. This means that a more nuanced approach towards digital content is being developed personally. I am conscious of others working in the fields of religious studies who are undertaking a variety of research projects on aspects of digital media. This all contributes to enhancing our views in relation to cyberspace, and there is a great deal of transferability between these projects and those specific to the study of Islam. I am also conscious of projects that have been undertaken from other disciplinary focuses. The interdisciplinary element of these subject areas has made my academic pursuits more interesting and exposed me to a variety of areas in which to write, research, and present that I would not have anticipated when I started looking in this field. In part, this is because of the changing religious and political climates in association with Islam and Muslims.

It has also been important to look at the ways in which the Internet has made an impact on Muslims in minority context. I have undertaken research in relation to UK issues. I have monitored the websites of various organizations, both at national and local level; it has been interesting to observe the ways in which social media have been applied in these contexts. There has been increasing recognition of the need for mosques, for example, to put their activities and services online. This opens them up to community and wider public scrutiny. It can be a public relations exercise. You can provide a hub for discussion, as well as more practical information on daily prayer and other ritual expectations. Some mosques extended their social media activities onto Facebook, YouTube, and other areas.

In relation to religious authority, the emergence of sermons online has also been significant. I have talked to people in Abu Dhabi recently who discussed how sermons are going to be put online for a variety of audiences, and how this has been integrated into the development of mosques. There is a long-standing history of sermons appearing online, both from recognized religious leaders and from others; the sermons being downloadable. In some contexts, they have been copied and circulated on CD in audiovisual format.

There have been attempts to present more youth-oriented advice and materials; the Egyptian context shows how individuals (and their organizations) such as Amr Khaled has developed online resources to present their worldviews integrating YouTube, Facebook, and Twitter. Some channels have presented a youth-oriented approach to this activity in order to develop a 'streetwise' ethic in their religious pronouncements and to make their message more attractive to younger people.

The extent to which this material is a significant part of overall surfing patterns is perhaps open to conjecture. The numerous distractions of content presented through hardware such as Xbox and PlayStation, which are fully capable of viewing Internet materials, are unlikely to be used often for looking at Islamic content online. Web TV and other interfaces simply make the media landscape more competitive, as well as offering alternative approaches and channels for accessing cyber Islamic environments.

As a researcher, I find that the area of Islam and the Internet is one that has required considerable adaptation of approach over the years. There are moments when it has been an immersive activity, requiring or indeed demanding full attention. I have permanently crashed and burned a number of hard drives, simply through the sheer bulk of material with which I have had to deal. I have at times had several devices running simultaneously in order to gather materials. There is need for constant backup of data in order that research is not lost, and so that materials are stored and recorded appropriately (and made 'future proof', especially given the lack of archives in other contexts).

It is suggested that issues associated with researching Islam and the contemporary world also apply to specialist researchers on Islam and cyberspace. They are important for anybody working on issues to do with contemporary Muslim expression in practice. As such, developing generic skills associated with, for example, storing page sites and content, keeping archives, developing galleries of screenshots and site archives, and monitoring and recording social media, are relevant and useful for everybody engaged in Islamic studies.

This is in addition to the fact that many significant resources associated with the field can be found online, and there are opportunities to network and acquire new information in ways that were unthinkable 20 years ago. This does not mean that traditional skills and knowledge should be lost, rather that approaches should be adjusted and skills developed within appropriate academic frameworks. The learning environment has shifted in response to online developments. In the future, one would anticipate greater integration of digital content within overall analyses of contemporary Islamic concerns.

This has been reflected in the post–Arab Spring context, where discussions on events in a variety of contexts have naturally incorporated digital media. For example, in Syria, since 2011, the events surrounding the battle between the Assad regime and 'revolutionary' forces has played out through Facebook, YouTube, Twitter, and other channels. All sides have used the media to make statements. At times the regime has attempted to shut down various Internet channels, but there are creative ways around them.

Religious expression has form part of the overall discussions, for example, when specific authorities have placed the opinions online in relation to events. All the while, the outside world has been observing these pronouncements, which are frequently re-broadcast and re-transmitted through conventional media and online media. The blurring between the traditional journalist and other citizen bloggers and journalists continues.

As students and academics working in the study of Islam, having an awareness of these developments and tuning in to the changes in the ways in which religious concerns are expressed through the Internet is increasingly important. As the digital divide is reduced, more people have access through portable devices, the threading of Islamic digital discourse into the wider fabric of Muslim society continues.

Readings

Research on Islam, Muslims, and the Internet is a developing field. There are some gaps in relation to the available literature, and it is often under-represented in general studies on contemporary Islam. My own writing has sought to chronicle developments in cyber Islamic environments, including *Virtually Islamic: Computer-mediated Communication and Cyber Islamic Environments* (Cardiff: University of Wales Press, 2000), *Islam in the Digital Age: E-jihad, Online Fatwas and Cyber Islamic Environments* (London: Pluto Press, 2003) and *iMuslims: Rewiring the House of Islam* (London: University of North Carolina Press/ C. Hurst & Co., 2009). Key early works from diverse disciplinary perspectives include Bruce B. Lawrence's chapter 'Allah on-line: the practice of global Islam in the information age', in Stewart M. Hoover and Lynn Schofield Clark (Eds), *Practicing Religion in the Age of the Media: Explorations in Media, Religion, and Culture* (New York: Columbia University Press, 2002), Peter Mandaville's chapter 'Transnational public spheres: information and communication technologies in the Muslim world', in *Transnational Muslim Politics: Reimagining the Umma* (London: Routledge, 2001), and aspects of Dale F. Eickelman and Jon Anderson's edited book *New Media in the Muslim World*, 2nd edition (Bloomington: Indiana University Press, 2003). miriam cooke and Bruce B. Lawrence's edited volume *Muslim Networks from Hajj to Hip Hop* (Chapel Hill: University of North Carolina Press, 2005) contains chapters relating to Islam and Muslims in cyberspace, including by Carl Ernst, Jon Anderson, and myself. Göran Larsson's edited book *Religious Communities on the Internet* (Stockholm:

Swedish Science Press, 2006) features chapters on aspects of Islam and the Internet. A useful study relating to religious authority online is contained in Mohammed A. El-Nawawy and Sahar Khamis, *Islam Dot Com* (New York: Palgrave Macmillan, 2009). Philip N. Howard's *The Digital Origins of Dictatorship and Democracy: Information Technology and Political Islam* (Oxford: Oxford University Press, 2010) includes analysis relating to digital and political identities in Muslim contexts. Rüdiger Lohlker's edited book *New Approaches to the Analysis of Jihadism: Online and Offline* (Vienna: Vienna University Press, 2012) explores approaches towards studying expressions of 'jihad' in diverse contexts. The journals *Arab Media and Society* (www.arabmediasociety.com), *Contemporary Islam: Dynamics of Muslim Life* (Springer Press), and *CyberOrient: Online Journal of the Virtual Middle East* (www.cyberorient.net) publish articles on aspects of Islam and online expression. Websites tracking aspects of Internet media and Islam include Digital Islam (www.digitalislam.eu) and my own Virtually Islamic: research about Islam in the digital age (www.virtuallyislamic.com).

Author

I work at the University of Wales Trinity Saint David, on campuses in Carmarthen, Lampeter, and Swansea. I'm a Reader in Islamic Studies. When I can drag myself away from my digital devices, my interests include exploring the beautiful countryside here in Wales (open space rather than cyber space), and listening to a variety of music – especially rock, blues, and reggae.

Chapter 16

Women studying for the afterlife

Mareike J. Winkelmann

I promise that I shall observe the rules and regulations and that I shall study with great dedication and that I shall stay away from those things that are a waste of time and that I shall never display any immoral behaviour. I promise that I shall dedicate twenty four hours a day to studies in accordance with the timetable of the Jamia and that I shall obey the command of those in charge of the Jamia and accept any punishment if I break any of the rules and regulations.

(Students' pledge, from the brochure of the madrasa)

Preamble

Owing to my interest in comparative religious studies, along with topics related to gender, from my first visit to India, which was in 1997, the idea was beginning to take shape that I wanted to find out whether, apart from the male *ulama*, or Islamic religious scholars, there would be female equivalents. During an MPhil programme (1999–2000), this idea became more concrete under the supervision of Khalid Masud, who encouraged me to find out about madrasas for girls in India, as this would be the place to start from, if one were to find out about any such thing as female religious authority in the making.

Narrative

Thus I returned to India in late 2000, planning to carry out a pilot study, prior to commencing my PhD in 2001. In Hyderabad and in Delhi it was relatively easy for me at the time to gain access to various such madrasas for girls, which, however, changed rather drastically in the aftermath of 9/11, barely one year later, by which time I wanted to start doing fieldwork and depended on having the same kind of access to the madrasas. Instead, I literally spent weeks drinking tea with the men in charge of running one particular madrasa in New Delhi, which thanks to the help of a colleague was willing to allow me inside their premises. With my then scanty understanding of Urdu, I simply persevered, biding my time until one day the young alim in charge of running the madrasa on behalf of his father allowed me past the ominous door in the front room, where the men used to sit together, listening to the Qur'an recitations from inside and talking about personal matters.

The young alim's wife was one of the key figures inside this madrasa for girls between twelve and seventeen years of age. The young women hailed from all over India, as the men in charge were part of the Islamic lay-preachers' movement known as the Tablighi Jamaat. The girls seemed to find it curious to have me there – they were quite used to the idea of surveys and census-like procedures, but for me to sit in on their classes was rather odd, unless, of course, I wanted to convert to Islam, which became a sport among them over time, as they were eager to see who would manage to convert me in the end.

To provide an impression of what the madrasa looked like: there I was in the middle of an area known as *basti* Nizamuddin, known otherwise for its railway station in the other part of the colony and for the famous *dargah*, or Sufi shrine, which was close to the madrasa. To get there, I would usually get down from my auto-rickshaw, which drove me from my south Delhi home in Gulmohar Park, where Amitabh Bachchan used to stay earlier, right up to where the ill, the disabled, and the infirm would line up on a daily basis in order to beg, as the *dargah* would distribute free food and was known to be frequented by pious visitors handing out alms to those in need. On my way I would pass various bookshops selling Islamic books, as well as the so-called Tablighi Markaz, the 'headquarters' of the Tablighi Jamaat. From there I used to walk down narrow, winding lanes, lined with tea stalls, food shops, perfume sellers, and, above all, butchers. Those who have not yet visited India, this is a country marked by crass contradictions. While it is commonly known that Hindus consider the cow sacred and hence would generally abstain from slaughtering or eating the same, this does not hold true for the large Muslim populace in India. Apart from occasionally giving rise to communal tensions, especially on occasions such as the annual Muslim Eid festivals when lots of cattle are slaughtered, this Muslim *basti* in New Delhi is known for its eateries, such as Karim's in the Old City, as well as numerous small kebab-stalls where people like to go for a snack at night.

As a result, my daily route was often marked by large kettles, placed over gas stoves or open fire, in which cow legs would simmer away, or carts with cow heads stacked up – quite a ghastly sight! An equally important daily negotiation for me was how to dress. Since my very first stay in India I was quite used to and rather fond of wearing traditional Indian clothes, however, due to my height I was advised by my Indian friends *never* to wear a burqa, as one would surely mistake me for being a cross-dressing male in that case, which could have landed me in trouble. Instead, I wore the usual salwaar kameez, generally avoiding bright colours, short sleeves, tight fits, and ensuring I always had the obligatory *dupatta* or scarf, or even a shawl at hand in winter. Now, taking the above as a given, the actual problem was not just what to wear, but how to wear it and where to wear what. In other words, whenever I would walk around the *basti* wearing a tightly wound headscarf, the non-Muslim shopkeepers or youths would shoot me angry glances or comment on how I was a despicable convert in their eyes. On the other hand, if for once I decided to leave my head uncovered while walking around the neighbourhood, the Muslim shopkeepers would often call out that I would surely go to hell for my lack of decency. So, fieldwork was a daily negotiation between promises of either heaven or hell, between trying to project myself as a virtuous, pious woman, and still trying to be myself in the process. Needless to say, this didn't always work out very gracefully.

The ambiguity regarding my social roles, presence, and behaviour in this environment did give rise to conflicts. As an unmarried woman, I should not have been walking around alone, and certainly I should not have interacted so freely with the men in charge of running the girls' madrasa. Interestingly enough, when wearing a headscarf I seemed to adopt the 'habitus' of a pious young woman involuntarily, unconsciously, almost automatically. I would make sure that 'nothing was showing', that is, while sitting down on the floor, my salwaar should loosely cover the features of my lower extremities, especially making sure my ankles would remain covered at all times, while the kurta or kameez would hide the features of my upper body, forearms, and chest, the last being additionally covered by my *dupatta* or scarf, which was tightly wrapped around my head, then falling loosely around my shoulders and chest. Keeping everything in place was often quite an exercise, which certainly became easier over time.

Much easier to interpret, on the other hand, was my role as a soon-to-be bride, as I was going to get married to a Punjabi Hindu and live within the structure of the typical extended family from the second year of my fieldwork onwards. These events were often discussed, thus giving rise to related topics, such as birth control, for example. Although they believed that it was religiously prohibited for them to use contraceptive devices, the young women were nevertheless very much aware of the fact that it would be difficult for them to raise more than a certain number of children. Hence, they argued in favour of some 'creativity' with regard to spacing pregnancies and childbirth, which basically came down to methods of natural family planning. Unlike some other women I interviewed in the Old City, these women were not in favour of trying to outnumber the Hindu majority in order to regain political power, thus procreating with a political agenda.

As for the potential for conflict, one day a friend of the young alim called me over to his perfume shop in the vicinity of the madrasa. The girls giggled away at the request, leaving me clueless as to what to do. Knowing that such a private meeting would hardly be deemed appropriate, on the one hand I shied away from it, while on the other hand, not wanting to risk my standing with regard to the men in this community, I complied. In other words, I was afraid that if I didn't accept the invitation, maybe I would be barred the next day from entering the madrasa, which I had come to depend on for my fieldwork. It is worth noting that I did manage to identify and visit other girls' madrasas in and around Delhi as well, but for the purpose of my study, this madrasa was the most ambitious one in terms of its curriculum. In the end, as I didn't want to risk anything, I went to meet the young perfumer and still got myself into trouble. When I entered his shop, he asked me to accompany him to a house on the other side of the road, closing his shop for the time being, as he wanted to engage in an intimate get-together. There was a lot of explaining to do and this was not the first time I was confronted with numerous clichés about 'foreign' women, but the situation was delicate, as I wasn't sure whether he was alone. Thankfully he was, nor was he inclined toward violence, and eventually I simply managed to talk him out of his endeavour, by ranting endlessly about any trivia that came to mind, thus diverting his attention from his initial intention. After some time I managed to leave politely, my heart racing, and drenched with sweat – I had been afraid and realized that I should have been much more careful.

The above incident touches upon a number of issues that a lot of researchers are confronted with in their daily work. One aspect is that as a researcher one has to be open toward informants, respondents, and the environment one has chosen to work in, while at the same time, this openness is almost forced upon the researcher, as one is highly dependent on one's field and thus vulnerable to unwanted advances on the part of others, who may simply misinterpret the role of the researcher in this context. The problem for me was that I couldn't have asked any of the girls to just accompany me, as they live under very strict rules pertaining to the concept of purdah, or female seclusion. For example, the girls were hardly ever allowed to leave the madrasa, except for paying a visit to the doctor, to attend lectures in another building, or if they were due to go home for a visit or during a vacation, at which time they would always be picked up from the madrasa by a desig-nated guardian, that is, a male *mahrem*. Otherwise the girls were studying and living together in this small school. The school comprised of a front room, behind which was an assembly area with adjacent bathrooms, and upstairs were a number of smaller rooms used as classrooms during the day and where the girls would sleep at night. I have to add that since that time, the madrasa has shifted to Okhla, where now they have a proper compound and a lot more space. The small building at the time made such a crammed impression, with the girls' belongings and mattresses being kept to the sides of the respective rooms, while all of the free space was used for studies. The girls would sit on the floor, which was covered with rugs or small mats, and books would be the only prop they used. In other words, no desks, chairs, or blackboards were utilized. The students had their books, along with their exercise books, especially for learning to write Arabic, which was very important to the students.

Many of the girls, especially those belonging to what I refer to in my thesis as the 'core families' in charge of initially establishing and later on running the madrasa, were competing with regard to being the most pious. Markers for such piety were wearing long socks, even during the scorching Delhi summer heat, along with wearing black gloves, apart from the commonly worn burqa and face veil or *niqab*, and generally avoiding going out. While many of the young women hailed from families with Tablighi affiliations, for some girls acquiring a pious lifestyle was with a view to their marriage prospects. Most of the girls were from relatively poor families and were hoping to marry some-one from the Gulf states. Of course, these men would only want a very pious young girl and hence the students cultivated the above virtues in an attempt to also become fluent in Arabic and dreaming already about their wealthy lives in another country. Such were the dreams of the young women, whose lives were otherwise marked by austerity. No TV or radio was allowed inside the school or even in general, though while in conversation with them, I some-times realized that their lives were not that black and white either, as they seemed quite aware of, for example, recent TV commercials. But officially, they were not allowed to waste time on such worldly trivia.

In terms of what the girls studied, reference can be made to the madrasa curriculum known as the *dars-e-nizami*. With slight modifications, this was also the basis for the girls' studies. Besides, they learned subjects such as home sci-ence, computer skills, and spoken English, which I taught later on. With regard to how the young women assessed their type of education compared with secular education, it deserves mention that by and large even the most vocal young women in the madrasa were rather unaware of alternative options. This was an important point for them, especially when it came to choosing the right school for their children. Some of the teachers, after all, were married already and had children, many of whom went to the Hindi-medium after-noon session of public schools nearby. But upon reaching the age of purdah, the girls would be likely to withdraw from the public schools in favour of beginning to attend a madrasa as well. Generally speaking, the young women were not very well oriented when it came to their immediate surroundings; that is, they knew the area they were staying in, along with some other landmarks in and around Delhi, but other than that they often appeared to be more familiar with what was going on in other 'Arab' countries, like Iran, Iraq, or Palestine, rather than being involved in what was happening in local Delhi politics, which at the time was actually quite favourably inclined toward the Muslim communities under Sheila Dixit and the Congress Party.

Discussion

Driven by the desire to find out more about the dissemination of Islamic knowledge through girls' madrasas, I focused on madrasas at the secondary level, that is, for girls between roughly twelve and seventeen years of age, as puberty appeared to form a major divide between girls staying at home to prepare for marriage and those who (were allowed to) continue their education. While school attendance of any kind did not seem to be problematic for Muslim girls prior to puberty, for girls between twelve and seventeen years of age the prospects of marriage and staying at home form an alternative for those practising purdah.

During the initial stages of fieldwork, my findings indicated that there were different types of girls' madrasas at the secondary level. Attempting to do justice to their diversity, I came up with the following distinction: to begin with, there appeared to be girls' madrasas whose curriculum was not based on the standardized *dars-e-nizami*. In such cases the term madrasa mostly stands synonymous for an Urdu-medium school with some Islamic content. Herein, generally (modest) Islamic dress is compulsory, the basic tenets of Islam are taught along with some Arabic, and 'advice' literature for young women like the late nineteenth-century *Bihishti Zewar* (Heavenly ornaments), or the *Ladkion ka Islami* course (The girls' Islamic course) are prescribed for reading. Second, there were girls' madrasas combining the respective state curriculum for secondary education with Islamic teaching. Here, the extent to which Islamic subjects are taught varies. While some schools may merely prescribe modest dress for girls and teach some form of religious knowledge (*dini talim*), others may incorporate subjects like Arabic and the history of Islam, apart from observing fixed prayer timings. I refer to these schools as 'dual type' madrasas. Finally, there are girls' madrasas whose curriculum is rooted in the *dars-e-nizami*, offering more or less exclusively religious education for girls at the secondary level, along with a number of worldly subjects. With a view to my main research question regarding the link between girls' madrasas and claims to female authority in Islamic matters, I chose to do fieldwork in a girls' madrasa of the third type, because this seemed to be the place where such claims to religious authority were highlighted most.

The girls' madrasa I did fieldwork in was founded under the patronage of the Nadwatul Ulama (known for their attempt to bring about reconciliation between the different Islamic schools of thought (*madhhaib*) in matters of jurisprudence, apart from being favourably inclined toward the independent application of reason in matters of jurisprudence (*ijtihad*) and promoting an inclusive concept of Islam), another important piece of information being that the Nadwatul Ulama's former director of education, Saiyid Abul Hasan Ali Nadwi (1914–2000), was also influential in the Tablighi Jamaat (Malik 1997: 471), the very same movement in which the 'men in charge' of the madrasa were active. In Nadwi's biography, the Muslim 'minority psychology' is mentioned as the main reason for the coming into being of *makatib* and madrasas in India. With regard to minority rights, the Indian constitution grants the 'right to freedom of religion' and 'cultural and educational rights for minorities', as subsumed under the heading 'fundamental rights'. Nadwi claims that Muslims established institutions of Islamic learning to ensure the preservation of Islam at a basic level in secular India and to counter their fear of cultural domination at the hands of the Hindu majority.

In this regard, Salamatullah notes in *Hindustan mein Musalmano ki Talim* (Muslim Education in India) that in post-partition India, Muslims feared the manipulation of secularism on the part of the non-Muslim majority. In line with the commonly held view that, following partition, Muslims became more conscious of their religion, such forms of cultural domination had the potential of causing damage to the construct known as the 'cultural' Muslim identity. As a result, Muslims struggled to preserve their institutions of religious learning in an attempt to put a halt to the perceived deterioration of religious and moral values. In line with the above, morality is perceived as something that is not merely confined to a textbook or set of principles, because society at large is responsible for moral education. In other words, value-oriented education begins at home, extends to the neighbourhood, and should be continued in school, where ideally the environment is conducive to good actions. Thus, teachers should function as role models, not through command and punishment, but through precautions and through creating a 'healthy' atmosphere. The above suggests that moral education is defined as a subject that cannot be limited to a fixed timetable, nor is it merely part of the curriculum, as it represents a process permeating all academic activities.

With the development of Islamic education in all its diversity, the gap between non-Islamic education and madrasa education widened. The following examples illustrate the extent to which both education systems coexist without allowing for too many points of contact. In the madrasa I came across a host of stereotypes regarding non-Islamic education, though neither the teachers nor the students were familiar with alternative forms of education. The young women's concerns centred on the 'free mingling of the sexes' and the disastrous consequences of 'immodest' behaviour, which according to them stood in a causal relation with teenage pregnancies and sexually transmitted diseases. Similar ideas were expressed by the president of the Islamic Centre with regard to the flaws of non-Islamic education. In Khan's opinion, Islam is entirely scientific and all-encompassing; thus 'modern' knowledge does not add anything new to what is written in the Qur'an. A second point of criticism is that 'secular schools' merely provide labour-market oriented education, while madrasa education is oriented toward God. Moreover, while secular schools teach the possession of worldly things to be the main aim in life, Islamic education teaches that material things are merely means required for making life easier, rather than representing ends in themselves.

Despite their reservations with regard to non-Islamic education, many nevertheless argue that the aim of educational reform should be the integration of Islamic and secular knowledge. Such reforms could take the shape of allowing for a Western 'hardware', that is, Muslims should appropriate the technology of the West, combined with Islamic 'software', designed to preserve Islamic values. Underlying this reformist model is the idea that in Islam there is no distinction between theology and science, as man's task has been laid down in the Qur'an as observing nature. This injunction in turn is interpreted in such a way that the 'Islamic sciences' originally combined theology and science, and it was only in the course of history that this inclusive view of the 'Islamic sciences' was reduced to theology, thus marking the onset of what many perceive as the decline of Islamic education.

Regarding the extent to which the contentious *duniyavi* or 'worldly' subjects were implemented in the madrasa, the official curriculum included maths, Hindi, science, and English. However, my observations suggested that apart from English, none of the above-mentioned subjects were actually taught. When I asked the teachers, the Principal badi appa replied that as of now they lacked sufficiently trained staff for these subjects. As many of the madrasa teachers have had little to no exposure to non-Islamic forms of education and training, the above-mentioned problem is of common concern. In the madrasa, the students were expected to have attended government schools up to class VII, which also served as a justification why there was no need to teach more non-Islamic subjects. After all, the students should have been exposed to non-Islamic learning before starting their religious education, and by a similar token they were encouraged to pursue their studies after graduation, for example, in government colleges and universities. However, my observations indicated that most of the students and teachers did not have much or even any exposure to non-Islamic forms of education prior to enrolment in the madrasa.

When I asked badi appa and some of the other teachers why they wanted their daughters to receive English-medium education and why they preferred them to attend the Delhi Public School, they unanimously said that these days 'we think that it is good for girls to get as much education as possible, prior to reaching the age of purdah', which is to say prior to puberty. While girls below that age should get as much exposure to non-Islamic or *duniyavi* subjects as possible, from puberty onwards they 'have time enough' to dedicate themselves exclusively to religious studies. The suggested educational trajectory represents an alternative to the 'dual type' madrasa, wherein the state curriculum is taught alongside Islamic subjects. What the teachers suggested was education in *duniyavi* or 'worldly' subjects and *din* or faith in stages, divided by the marker of puberty.

While it seemed to be a common stereotype that children are generally 'lured' into attending a madrasa, my findings suggest that in the case of the madrasa this may hold only for students who are the first to receive any kind of formal education in their families. As children of illiterate parents in rural areas, it is possible that they would not be able to understand the content of the madrasa's advertising brochure, as it is written in Arabic, mixed with Arabized Urdu. Rather than luring children into attending a madrasa, my data suggest that the main reason for seeking admission in the madrasa is the free education provided, combined with lodging, food, medical care, and above all the religious merit for the family of a girl who studies in a madrasa. Apart from the last mentioned, the quality of education provided may also convince parents to seek admission for their daughters. According to the men in charge, who were both religious scholars, the madrasa had turned out to be a success so far, because even though the madrasa was merely promoted by word of mouth, parents come to the madrasa 'like customers come to a shop'. In their opinion, it is the quality of education that makes the madrasa so popular. The manager explained that the curriculum is based on the *dars-e-nizami*, albeit in an adjusted form to fit the shorter duration of the girls' studies. Due to the extensive language classes in Urdu and Arabic, the course initially was designed to take six years, but, according to the manager, 'clever' girls could complete the course in five years.

One of my interlocutors in the Old City suggested I keep my eyes open with regard to issues pertaining to female labour migration to the Gulf States. He pointed out that some teachers may not teach primarily out of choice, but with a view to 'qualifying' for a husband working or studying in the Gulf States. The same interlocutor was particularly interested in the ensuing legal concerns, explaining that single parenting had become an issue with a substantial bearing on the local Muslim communities. As a result, the All India Muslim Personal Law Board was under pressure to find solutions to the 'problem' of controlling women's sexuality and with regard to women who wished to remarry once their husbands settled abroad. In this regard, one particular story was brought to my attention in the madrasa.

Roughly one year after she graduated from the madrasa, a young teacher from one of the 'core families' got married in August 2002. As she was only fifteen years old, she was considered too young to live with her husband, who was an Indian student in a madrasa for boys in Medina. Initially, the young woman continued to live with her parents in Nizamuddin for a few months, and this arrangement was supposed to go on for about a year. During that year she intended to carry on teaching the Mansurat and the Qirat-ur-Rashida to the second- and third-year students in the madrasa. Following this interim period, she was meant to join her husband in Medina. When I asked her what she was planning to do there, she said that she would not teach in Medina, because she wanted to continue her studies. She also told me that there was a well-known girls' madrasa in Medina, for which her in-laws had already sought enrolment on her behalf.

The bride's cousin, who was also a teacher in the madrasa, reported in detail how the wedding had been, because following the simple ceremony her cousin stayed in Okhla with her new in-laws for about a month. Once her in-laws had left for Riyadh and her husband for Medina, she temporarily returned to her parents' house. She also took up teaching again for the time being. In our conversations, the bride emphasized the value of the gold jewellery, which her husband and in-laws had given her, and she proudly displayed her ornamental gold rings. But above all, she appeared saddened by the fact that her husband had left her behind, and with both happiness and pain reflected on her face, she appeared more mature than before.

Instead of staying with her family for another year, it was soon decided that the bride would join her husband in Medina after bakr-e-eid in early February

2003, because the family deemed it better for her to be reunited with her husband as soon as possible. The young woman was visibly delighted at the prospect of seeing her husband again that soon. Prior to her relatively sudden departure, she took leave from her teaching activities to bid her grandparents farewell in their village. The bride's cousin explained that once her cousin's husband completed his education in the madrasa in Medina, she was supposed to return to Delhi after one or two years. Upon her return from her grandparents' place, the bride added that as her in-laws lived in Riyadh, she and her husband, who by then had come to India to 'fetch her' (*us ko lene ke liye*), would live by themselves. She was also happy to recount that her husband had already found an apartment for them, and that he had bought furniture especially for her, because as a student he used to live in a single room. The above story suggests that for the young bride, who hailed from the same lower-caste Ansari background as the founder and manager of the madrasa, her education and accomplishment in leading a pious life facilitated what most would consider a good marriage, as she was to settle abroad with the son of a relatively well-to-do family.

During fieldwork, conversations with the founder, manager, and the Principal badi appa, brought to the fore that they were part of a network that linked them with a number of other families in *basti* Nizamuddin through common areas of origin, caste, and their active involvement in the Tablighi Jamaat. To begin with, it struck me that two of the fourteen teachers were maternal cousins, whose respective female siblings above the age of purdah were studying in the madrasa as well. Moreover, the cousins' fathers hailed from the same Barabanki district, in the vicinity of Lucknow, as the founder. Like the manager, the two fathers had studied in the Kashful Ulum madrasa for boys in Nizamuddin, a madrasa established by Maulana Muhammad Ilyas, the founder of the Tablighi Jamaat. In short, the three families appeared to form the backbone for many activities in the girls' madrasa, such as taking turns looking after daily affairs and taking decisions with regard to matters pertaining to the curriculum. In addition, all the men were actively involved in doing Tablighi work, and the cousins' fathers and the founder also taught in the Kashful Ulum madrasa for boys. Apart from kinship, the shared worldview influenced by their affiliation with the Tablighi Jamaat had brought together this group of men, and bonds were maintained, reinforced, and extended through arranged marriages between children of the 'core families'.

Furthermore, teachers and students were mainly recruited through family ties and Tablighi work, and similarly international contacts too were maintained through the Tablighi work of the founder and manager. Both used to travel all over the country and beyond on a regular basis, also to raise funds for the madrasa. Many students from places outside Delhi told me that they had come to know about the madrasa through the travelling men associated with it. Conversations with students and teachers in the madrasa suggested that many of their male family members, such as husbands, fathers, brothers, cousins, or uncles were active in the Tablighi Jamaat or taught in the Kashful Ulum madrasa for boys in the nearby Tablighi Markaz. Whenever the students and teachers spoke about their male relatives' Tablighi activities, such as the regular travelling 'in the path of God', they did so with admiration. At times, their admiration was paired with a tinge of envy, as their male relatives' lives appeared to symbolize the mobility, freedom, and excitement they were missing. In addition, the young women greatly valorized their relatives' Tablighi activities, and on many occasions they expressed regret that owing to their observance of a very strict form of purdah activities such as 'travelling in the path of God' were beyond their possibilities. Still, the madrasa's curriculum prescribed the Tablighi Jamaat's core piece of literature or 'manual', namely the Fazail-e-Amal (Virtues of everyday actions), for daily reading throughout the five-year course.

The madrasa and the Tablighi Jamaat both seek to create a milieu marked by deep piety. In the case of the latter, this becomes explicit in the Fazail-e-Amal, in which the processes of sanctifying everyday life and its actions are laid out in minute detail. The manual's basic teaching is that certain virtues displayed in daily behaviour are valuable for the accumulation of religious merit (*sawab*) for the Hereafter. One of the Fazail's main teachings, namely that one should abstain from futile things, also appeared to play an important role for everyday life in the madrasa. As a result, the students and teachers were rarely ever found with idle hands, because everyone seemed to be occupied doing something or the other, such as studying, reading, handiwork, or chores, at all times.

Despite all efforts at creating an environment shared by equals, inequalities nevertheless continued to surface. In the madrasa, I observed inequalities based on caste, class, as well as on rural and urban backgrounds respectively. Language, for example, represented a divider cutting across all sections: while badi appa and the young women belonging to the 'core families' were apt speakers of Arabic and used 'elaborate' Urdu with confidence, others required Hindi translations in order to understand their Urdu textbooks. Many girls hailed from non-Urdu speaking families, or their spoken Urdu did not contain the same Persian and Arabic influences, as either their primary education had been in Hindi, or, as we saw earlier, they were the first (female) family members to receive any kind of formal education.

In an attempt to gain a better understanding of the Tablighi Jamaat's position regarding women and education, I found a publication titled *Women in the Field of Education* in one of the bookshops opposite the Tablighi Markaz. Tabligh (preaching) is defined herein as an action based on the Prophet's call to faith (*dawah*) and the efforts adopted by the Companions (*Sahaba*), carried out with the aim of reviving faith (*din*) and Prophet's practice (*sunnah*) among the believers, out of a perceived need for self-reformation. Reminded of similar arguments made by late nineteenth-century reformers, women in particular are thought to be in need of self-reformation, as they are found guilty of perpetuating un-Islamic customs associated with household rituals, while simultaneously being burdened with the responsibility of acting as the source of guidance for the future generation.

One means of effecting women's self-reformation are the recommended weekly religious (*dini*) programmes for women, which ought to include the following elements: educational content (*talim*), reminders to perform prayers (*salat*), reminders regarding punctuality in counting rosaries (*tasbihat*), encouragement to study books on virtues (*fazail*), a constructive approach toward raising children, and encouragement to make an effort to send men out in the path of God. In line with the above, on Thursdays, weekly meetings or *jamaats* were organized in the madrasa for the students, their female family members, and for women from the neighbourhood. This so-called 'Thursday Program' generally comprised of recitations from the Qur'an, traditions of the Prophet (*ahadith*), prayer (*namaz*), religious poetry in Urdu (*naat*), exegesis (*tafsir*), Islamic law (*fiqh*), value-oriented literature (*adab*), and finally also the students' own poems (*naat*) and anthems (*taranas*) in praise of the madrasa. As the programme was held in Urdu and Arabic, the latter was translated into Urdu for those 'outsiders' who did not speak the language. While for the young women belonging to the 'core families', knowledge of 'true Islam' was directly linked with mastery of Arabic, for the majority of lower-caste rural students, Arabic merely represented but another tough subject they had to master.

The poems and songs, referred to as *naat* and *taranas* respectively, appeared to constitute one of the few socially accepted means for emotional expression in the madrasa, apart from representing the only forms of music allowed inside the madrasa. When I asked the teachers how the students learned to sing the anthems, they replied that tapes were readily available in the nearby Tablighi Markaz. The students also showed me their notebooks, in which they had written down the poems and anthems. I observed that sometimes the Urdu and Arabic words were written in beautiful calligraphy, while other poems appeared to be merely scribbled down. When I tried to find out more about the difference, the young women told me that apart from reproducing lyrics and tunes from tapes, they also liked to copy tunes for lyrics they had written in praise of Islam, the Prophet, and the madrasa. The students either learned to sing the anthems from the tapes directly or one of the teachers sat down with the students in the staff room, adjusting each student's composition to fit the tune. The student in turn repeated each line while writing down the words, sometimes adding marks that indicated the correct intonation and the rhythmical rise and fall of the voice. Apart from the well-known Urdu poems and the readily available anthems, some of the melodies I heard the students sing during the Thursday Program definitely reminded of popular Hindi film tunes. Even though, in line with the worldview of this particular Muslim community, watching movies was forbidden, but not being exposed to the latest Bollywood songs at all seems almost impossible in any Indian setting.

Decisions with regard to what is taught in a girls' madrasa are often informed by a particular understanding of Islamic womanhood on the part of the men involved in running the madrasa. This underlying ideal of Islamic womanhood is closely linked with the madrasa's educational aim of bringing about a sense of values and manners (*adab*) in the students. Even though lessons in *adab* may only take up a relatively small portion of the official timetable, a sense of *adab* permeates much of the everyday interactions in the girls' madrasa. Introducing the students to and grooming them in the rules laid out by the community's understanding of *adab* appears to be pivotal for the madrasa's educational aim of bringing about the reform (*islah*) of morality (*ikhlaq*) and actions (*amal*). The students, on the other hand, may nurture hopes for upward social mobility through cultivating a visibly pious female self.

For the sixteen girls studying in the final year in 2002, who were roughly between sixteen and seventeen years of age at the time, marriage ranked above anything else. When asked what they wanted to do after graduation, they answered in the following order: (1) get married; (2) teach in the madrasa in case they needed more teachers, teach elsewhere in similar girls' madrasas, or establish other girls' madrasas; (3) do *tabligh*; and (4) organize *jamaat*, which they defined as preaching and leading women's meetings on Islamic topics in their respective communities.

The majority of the madrasa graduates hail from a lower- to lower middle-class background, while the founder, manager, 'core families', and most of the students also have a low-caste background. This may easily undermine the graduates' standing among high-caste Muslim communities or vis-à-vis those 'in authority' who claim high descent. Simultaneously, however, purdah provides lower castes with a strategy facilitating upward social mobility, as a sense of modesty, patience, and obedience are instilled in the young women through socialization. In other words, the extent to which women can afford to live in purdah may set them apart from women of a lower social standing.

In order to appreciate why pedagogical innovation may sit uncomfortably with those in charge of setting the curriculum in the madrasa, we should keep in mind that for the founders, teachers, and students, their identity as Muslims in a minority situation appeared to be central to their self-definitions. For the teachers in the madrasa, being a good Muslim stood synonymously with social capital, because their daily income depended on their piety.

My fieldwork experience suggests that being 'in purdah' (albeit temporary in my case) actually starts from within. Being a student in a madrasa for girls changed me: the girls witnessed my soon-to-be marriage into a Hindu family, the stages of pregnancy and subsequent birth of my daughter – so from representing a more or less alien concept of being a researcher, my biography intertwined with theirs for some years, and I am sure the encounter left its marks on both sides.

Readings

It is hard if not impossible to find books specifically dealing with madrasa education for young women in India. However, there are numerous authoritative works on gender-related issues, including education, for the Indian context along with Urdu books shedding light on (male) madrasa education from both a contemporary as well as a historical angle. A wonderful introduction to the Indian context from a gender perspective is Patricia Jeffery's *Frogs in a Well: Indian Women in Purdah*, 2nd edition (Delhi: Manohar, 2000), along with Gail Minault's *Secluded Scholars: Women's Education and Muslim Social Reform in Colonial India* (Delhi: Oxford University Press, 1998). As far as the male perspective regarding madrasa education is concerned, see Jamal Malik, *Islamische Gelehrtenkultur in Nordindien: Entwicklungsgeschichte Tendenzen am Beispiel von Lucknow* (Leiden: Brill, 1997) and for a more contemporary account, see Yoginder Sikand, *Bastions of the Believers: Madrasas and Islamic Education in India* (New Delhi: Penguin, 2005). With regard to the emergence of the lay-preachers' movement called Tablighi Jamaat, see Khalid Masud (Ed.), *Travellers in Faith: Studies of the Tablighi Jama'at as a Transnational Islamic Movement for Faith Renewal* (Leiden: Brill, 2000). Some of the Urdu materials on Indian madrasa education mentioned in this contribution include Maulana Wahi-duddin Khan's *Din wa shariat: Din-e-islam ka ek fikri mutala* (New Delhi: The Islamic Centre, 2002) and Salamatullah's, *Hindustan mein musalmanon ki talim* (New Delhi: Maktaba Jamia Ltd, 1990).

Author

Mareike J. Winkelmann no longer works as a full-time researcher, though two years ago she was involved in a project on intercultural understanding among students of secondary schools in Germany (KWI), but earlier on she studied protestant theology (ThUK) and subsequently did her PhD in Islamic Studies/Anthropology (ISIM/UvA). Nowadays she dedicates most of her time to raising her daughter in Germany, travelling to India at least twice a year, and working as a translator in order to make a living.

Chapter 17

Experiencing Islamic education in Indonesia

Ronald Lukens-Bull

Preamble

More Muslims live in Indonesia that in all Arabic-speaking countries combined. Islamic education is an important tool used by Indonesians for negotiating globalization and the modern world. I have been researching Islamic education in Indonesia since 1992 and have two major periods of research: November 1994–November 1995 and August 2008–March 2009. In my first research, I studied Islamic schools called *pesantren*. They are similar to madrasas in other parts of the Islamic world. I have been known to compare them to Hogwarts when needing to explain them to my children. In 2008–9, I was a visiting professor at the State Islamic Institute of North Sumatra and conducted research on Islamic higher education. My experience of fieldwork in this type of setting has changed over the years. I wished to communicate to the student the experience of hardship, sacrifice, and reward as well as the overall experience of welcome when working with Muslims.

Narrative

Before my dissertation fieldwork in 1994 could begin, I needed to go through a number of bureaucratic reporting steps. About five weeks into that process, something happened that was to fundamentally change my understanding of myself as an anthropologist: my wife nearly died. I had learned that anthropologists adapt to the local culture and 'go with the flow', but this approach would prove inadequate when trying to save my wife. I learned that there was a deep core of who I was as an American that I was not willing to change.

My wife has some health issues that make her very susceptible to food poisoning and once ill, subject to pernicious cyclical vomiting. The main danger in these circumstances is dehydration. After trying unsuccessfully to resolve the problem at the home where we were staying, I checked her into a hospital recommended by our host father, who was a doctor. When it became clear that the hospital was unable to stabilize her condition and that she was becoming severely dehydrated, I moved her from a hospital in a major city to a missionary hospital in a small town which had an American doctor. In the end, we needed to medevac her to Singapore. Throughout this experience, I was confronted by core ethnocentrisms that I had to accept. First was the idea that everyone who came in contact with my wife, nurses, doctors, ambulance drivers, the person coordinating the medevac, should be deeply concerned about her survival, well-being, and comfort. This was simply not the case: she was allowed to sit in an ambulance with no air-conditioning while trying to sort the paperwork that would put her on a commercial flight out of Indonesia, IVs were allowed to run dry, she was allowed to become so dehydrated that her hands and face tingled; a condition, we were later told, which signaled that her body was beginning to shut down. I heard people comment that if the worst were to happen that I would be OK and would be able to find another wife. I could then, as well as now, understand aspects of Indonesian culture that made all these occur. I could very carefully point out why, in Indonesian society, these responses made sense and in no way made the people malicious, cold-hearted, or wrong. And yet, I could not accept them. I had little patience with them. I wanted what I wanted. I wanted her well, and I wanted everyone working on her case to want that as their first priority. I did my best negotiating the circumstances, which were not my proudest moments as an 'adapter to other cultures', and got her to Singapore where I found competent and caring medical professionals. When I tell this story to my Indonesian friends, they remind me not to compare their doctors to American doctors. I tell them that after 20 years of traveling in Southeast Asia, I do not have to and that I can compare them to the doctors in their neighboring countries, some of which, like Thailand, are at a similar level of economic development. I learned that cultural relativism was not about accepting whatever another culture did, but understanding them on their own terms. However, such an understanding did not mean that I could not look for a better way to meet my needs.

My first experience of welcoming, concern, and friendship came in the aftermath of this episode. My host mother's English tutor, a young Muslim man named Basuki decided that I needed a friend when I returned to Indonesia without my wife (she went home to Arizona) around the 10th of December. He was also deeply concerned that I was going to be all alone at Christmas. Obviously this was not a holiday he celebrated, but Indonesian Muslims had a holiday where everyone went home to celebrate, if at all possible. For them, it was at the end of the Ramadan celebration. He understood that being alone on such a holiday, especially after a traumatic experience would be very difficult. I followed his advice and tried to see if I would be welcome back with the missionaries who had helped my wife and me with the non-medical side of our problems (arranging for us to leave on our research visa and come back), but that option was unable to work out. Basuki did not give up and eventually found an American family working as English teachers that would share the holiday with me. This family, the Rays, ended up being long-term friends. I did not spend a lot of time with the Rays during my fieldwork, about once a month I would come over for dinner. Usually I would call when I needed their perspective. The traumatic experience at the beginning of my fieldwork and the long absence from my wife often meant that I confessed to my Indonesian friends that I missed her. Their response, which made perfectly good sense in the Indonesian Islamic context, was to get a second wife, and by the way, they would add that they have a cousin, niece, and so on, who would be just perfect. Although I could understand why they responded that way and even appreciated the love and trust behind such offers, it was not what my American sensibilities wanted to hear. I wanted to hear that such separations were difficult but survivable and to hear strategies about how to make it more manageable. This was long before email or Skype or any of the technologies which I came to depend upon since that time. The Rays were the people I called when I needed to hear an American response to an American problem. But I only knew the Rays because Basuki, an unmarried Muslim man, saw my need for such friends.

The problem of prayer

On my very first Friday at a pesantren, I was dressed up in appropriate prayer garb and 'paraded' to the mosque. In a way, I may have been made a fool. It would not be the last time, but I have found that being willing to be vulnerable is an elemental part of fieldwork; if the fieldworker is too good, too smart, too sophisticated to be treated in this way, people will never talk to them. And that is the heart of participation observation research – the researcher shows respect for the people he or she is working with by doing what they do, especially when asked to join them. This meant that I lived in and around the pesantren and as much as possible, lived like they lived: I ate the simple meals, kept the standards of attire and modesty, adopted the body postures which showed the required deference to the leadership, engaged in late night gossip, and participated in ritual life.

I just could not see how one could get a sense of Islamic life without praying, fasting, and participating in the various dimensions that mark an Islamic life. My willingness to participate often marked me as simply being open minded and decidedly non-Christian, but sometimes it marked me as Muslim. People assumed that if I prayed, I was a Muslim. After a few awkward attempts, I gave up trying to correct that assumption.

The 'problem with prayer' was largely my problem. In the context of my own religious subjectivity, I felt uncomfortable presuming that I could and should participate in the prayers and usually waited until I was invited. However, I was frequently invited to join. In each place that I prayed, I asked permission of the leadership – imam, *alim*, *kyai*. I explained how I was not a Christian and that I was seeking the truth about the God of Abraham (this was an accurate description of my own spiritual search at the time). I also explained that I was a researcher collecting data for a doctoral dissertation. However, they were mostly concerned about whether or not I was a Christian, since I was not, I could participate in the prayers without invalidating them, that I was like a child who does not fully understand. Their hope was that Allah might reveal himself to me, that I might receive *hidayat* (a calling). If the leadership did not allow it, I did not participate – or at least this was my principle – my participation was always encouraged. In most locales, people were happy that I prayed with them. Some assumed that I was a Muslim.

At certain points of my research, the assumption that I was a Muslim opened doors. For example, once while attending a regional Nadhlatul Ulama conference with NU officials, the hosting *kyai* (a religious leader) walked away from me because I was 'European'. The officials with whom I was traveling exclaimed that it was OK for him to talk to me because I was a Muslim, an assumption on their part based on my participant observation practice; an assumption that I had not corrected. The *kyai* came back and welcomed me with open arms to his school (pesantren) and into his home and for the next two days, I was his honored guest. Although an extraordinary example, this event was illustrative of a major theme of my fieldwork: I participated in Muslim rituals and Muslim life and was assumed to be Muslim, which garnered me invitations, interviews, and generally enabled my research.

Shortly after entering the field, I had the great fortune to meet with a well-known Dutch ethnographer who had worked on the topic of Islamic education. I had read his works in preparation for my research on the same topic and I was most interested in knowing his thoughts on how I should represent myself in the field. Over two large beers in the privacy of my hotel room, he advised me to present myself unequivocally as a Muslim, but as a *Mu'allaf*, a beginner, so that any mistakes that I would undoubtedly make could easily be forgiven. He himself had made such a self-representation in the field (in the 1970s and later) with great success. Since his training was in Islamology, he, however, had a greater command of Arabic than I did, or in fact than many of the people with whom he interacted. As a Catholic, he explained, he also thought the claim that he was a Muslim (a submitter to God) was truthful. I confessed that I was not sure that this was the best path and he was perplexed at my difficulty. The setting of our conversation was also significant in thinking about subject position. Here I was with a man who represented himself as Muslim, who advocated that I do the same, and we were drinking alcohol which is against sharia law. However, instead of drinking in the hotel restaurant, we chose privacy in part because of how our drinking would be perceived. In this way, we maintained the public fiction of his being an observant Muslim.

At the start of my research, I elected to participate in rituals and tried to avoid the issue of my subjective religious beliefs as best as possible. In Indonesia, asking someone to what religion they subscribe is commonly part of a first conversation, particularly if their faith is not clear from knowing their name. Further, during the time of my research, Indonesian law required everyone to declare one of five religions: Catholicism, Christianity, Buddhism, Hinduism, and Islam. Even the forms I filled out to conduct my research legally required that I declare a religion.

It was known that I was a student working on a final paper, but because there were few doctoral programs in Indonesia at that time, it was more common for people to associate my work with the BA level thesis that Indonesian universities require than with the kind of project that would yield a book. In terms of my religious identity, two things seemed to be important: my relationship to Christianity and my relationship to Islam. For the most part, my relationship to Islam was defined by my knowledge of it and my respect for Muslims and their rituals and practices. However, it was sometimes defined in terms of the distance I had to Islamic orthopraxy.

A strange visitor

About midway through my research, I shifted gears. Prior to that point I had spent almost all of my time in one pesantren, Al-Fulan. This had allowed me to get a very intimate sense of the daily life of these institutions. But at that point I felt that it was time to get a sense of the larger community. On a short return visit, I met a man in his mid-forties who said he was a new student. A student of his age was odd at Al-Fulan because it offered regular schooling, and hence most of the students were under the age of 25. He approached me and said that he wanted to talk. He told me in a whispered tone that he used to be a minister in the Pentecostal church and that he had converted to Islam and that he felt that he was wrong in leaving Jesus, and wanted my help in figuring out the right thing to do.

I was absolutely confused. I listened in part because scientific interest demanded that I found out a little about the dynamics of conversion and the politics of interfaith relations. However, I felt sort of bad, that this guy was reaching out to someone he thought was a Christian but was not. I told him that I would try to call some friends that might be able to help him. I told him that he would have to talk to the *kyai* to get the Islamic view, but that I might be able to introduce him to people who could help him with the Christian view. I don't know why I felt that I needed to get involved, except that this person reached out to me and I felt some obligation to put him in contact with someone who could help.

We left the school together and as we walked he tried very hard to convince me that he was a Christian, singing hymns and uttering slogans (all in English). I finally told him that I was a scientist and that I did not care what his religion was, but only that I somehow felt obligated to help because he said that he was con-fused. However, he now seemed convinced about what the truth was (from his hymns and slogans) and all that remained was for him to carry it out. He still wanted me to put him in contact with someone, but I refused. I never saw this man again. Non-Muslim friends suggested that he might have been an army agent checking up on me, to see if I was not a missionary in sheep's clothing. At the very least, the person was probably a con artist as he told me that he was planning on conning the headmaster (*kyai*) out of some money.

The real significance of this incident is the perception by locals that the government might be checking up on me. Around this time, Robert Hefner, a well-known anthropologist from Boston University, was arrested for speaking to a group of democracy advocates without a permit. Although I followed intensely the media coverage of this event, it wasn't until years later, that I heard from Bob the full details of what had happened and that it was a tactic to chill the pro-democracy movement. The government did not have intentions toward him per se, or researchers in general. Still, it was a tense time to do research. I feared that a misstep would bring my research to a sudden stop.

Strange bona fides

At about the time I decided to focus my research on the pesantren community beyond Al-Fulan, it had also come to my attention that not everyone in the community around Al-Fulan really respected the school. Since this was contrary to what the literature said about the universal trust and respect of *kyai* and pesantren, I felt the need to investigate. I discuss that data elsewhere (Lukens-Bull 2005: 96–106). But before I could get that data, I needed to reestablish my bona fides. By staying in the *pondok*, I had clearly allied myself with the *kyai* and none of the villagers would talk to me about sensitive issues for fear that I was a spy. I had a friend who lived and worked in the market. He needed to move and so we rented a shop/house together. We set aside one room for me to use when I returned to that particular village.

As a private house-warming, and as a way to convince the other villagers that I was not a spy for the pesantren leaders, my friend Slamet initiated me in what can only be called the other side of village life for Javanese Muslims. We went to the herbal apothecary and ordered a bottle of red rice whiskey which was complete with a label for its medicinal uses. I was a bit puzzled when we left without the bottle. We then procured some ice and some Coca-Cola. Shortly after we had finished our shopping, the apothecary's young son knocked on the door with a paper bag containing our 'medicine'. We drew the shades, because drinking was not generally acceptable and because specifically the house was across the street from the village mosque and hence within the 100 meter 'no drinking' zone established by Indonesian law. Alone by ourselves, Slamet and I got pretty drunk and I woke late the next day. However, when next I went out, I found that the villagers who had previously been hesitant to speak with me, were now open. Very clearly, my willingness to engage in a very different sort of participant observation had bought me a different sort of legitimacy.

To place this drinking bout in a wider context of religious identity, it is important to observe that Slamet spent three years studying at a pesantren in another town. Although Slamet drank, gambled, and rarely prayed, when he engaged in ritual, it was pesantren-style ritual. He rejected the Javanist practices of many of his neighbors including making offerings to local tree spirits (*sesajen*). He observed the Eid holidays after the fashion he learned in his pesantren studies. And although his daughters were being educated in the government school (Sekolah Negeri), out of his meager income, he hired a tutor to teach them *ngaji* – the basic skills of reading and incanting the Qur'an. Slamet's social identity was formed by both his laxity in observing correct Islamic practices and correct observance when he chose to engage in religious or spiritual activity.

Life as a 'rock star'

If my dissertation fieldwork was typified by hardship, confusion, and obscurity, I had the opposite experience when I returned to Indonesia on a Fulbright Senior Scholar grant in 2008. I was no longer an unknown graduate student. My dissertation had been translated into Indonesian, I had published a few articles in Indonesian journals, and my work was known. I had already been an invited speaker at two major conferences and so my work and my perspective was well known especially in the Sate Islamic Higher Education system. My doctoral students at IAIN (Institut Agama Islam Negeri) North Sumatra, who are members of the faculty themselves, would not leave the classroom before I did. They would often compete for who would give me rides to and from

Figure 17.1 Lukens-Bull at a girls' *pondok*

class. Since our class met for four hours on Saturday morning, we often went for lunch after class and not once would they allow me to pay for my meals. I was invited to other universities to speak and given gifts ranging from token memorabilia to substantial gifts. It was easy to arrange interviews on multiple campuses. I would simply tell my students where I wanted to go and they would find connections who would arrange everything for my visit including interview appointments. It was everything my 1994–5 research was not.

An 'orientalist' teaches at IAIN

In 2008–9, I taught at IAIN Medan. Before I came, there had been eight other Westerners to come to IAIN North Sumatra in a five-year period. When Fadhil Lubis started inviting Westerners to the campus, there were protests. Later Westerners were accepted as long as they stuck to teaching English. A watershed was the third scholar, a female sociologist, who worked hard to adapt, wearing long skirts and a *slendang* head cover. After her, the next four were all English teachers. When asked if they wanted me to teach at IAIN SU, the rector had said that, more than want, they needed me, especially as I was fluent in Indonesian, as few previous Westerners on that campus had been. They need the exposure to social scientific approaches in the study of religion.

Figure 17.2 Lukens–Bull dining with friends

It is interesting that I taught in the graduate program in Islamic Thought but the original plans to have me teach undergraduates did not come to pass. The given reason was to give me more time for research. Although it is possible to interpret this to mean that they did not want the students exposed to me, I think the reverse is more likely. They did not want to suffer the embarrassment of having undergrads respond negatively to me. There was sufficient embarrassment about the doctoral student who started out in a very antagonistic mode. Outside of the classroom, though, undergraduates were by and large pleased to see me and even eager to talk to me and help me in various matters. IAIN SU had also previously had visiting scholars from Saudi Arabia and Egypt, but most of them only taught Arabic. Only one or two taught religious subjects. Among students that I interviewed they said that Western people were more communicative than the Middle Easterners.

My teaching assignment was in the Islamic Thought track of the Islamic Studies doctoral program. Originally, I was asked to teach a course called Teologi Agama-Agama (Comparative Theology), it was a required core course for third semester students. Comparative Theology is far beyond my expertise and training and so I negotiated with the graduate dean to teach instead Teori Agama-Agama (Theories of Religion). Because of the rarity of international scholars to this campus, the graduate dean doubled the class size by having the first semester students take that core course a year early. The majority of the students were faculty members teaching in undergraduate programs at IAIN SU. Others taught at other universities in town, and still others were employed in the local offices of the Ministry of Religious Affairs.

In addition to teaching this class, I was asked to conduct a faculty seminar for mid-level faculty members. These are faculty members who have earned a master's degree (many from Western universities) who are not currently enrolled in a doctoral program. The focus on this faculty seminar was on research methods and the question of how to apply anthropological theory and method to the study of Islam.

Aside from the one student already mentioned who expressed concerns about my trying to Christianize them through reading about atheist Jews (Durkheim, Marx, Freud), my reception was extremely warm. It should be noted that the critical student warmed up to me eventually but could at least say that he did not sit sweetly (*duduk manis*) beneath an Orientalist if anyone were to challenge him. For him this may have been important because he also was a *khatib*, giving Friday sermons in various mosques. For the most part, I was treated as an honored guest or even a rock star.

Discussion

Islamic education used to be the only kind of education in what became Indonesia. Pesantren are nearly as old as Islam in Indonesia itself, although essentially the same type of school is/was found in Thailand and Malaysia.

Traditional religious education in pesantren was self-directed and self-paced. It involved both individual and group study. Individual study may be used at the beginning of a student's time for remedial training in basic skills, such as reading and writing Arabic script. Advanced students work directly with the *kyai* on individual areas of specialization. One form of group lesson focuses on creating the basic study tools needed for the rest of a student's career as a religious scholar. These tools are called *kitab kuning*, or 'yellow books' referring to the cheap paper upon which they are printed. They cover all manner of Islamic knowledge.

Briefly, the moral values that are emphasized in pesantren include *Ahkwuya Islamiya* (Islamic brotherhood), *keikhlasan* (sincerity, unselfishness), *kesederhanan* (simple living), and *kemandirian* (self-sufficiency). Beyond these, pesantren aim to instill personal piety and a commitment to the Five Pillars (confession of faith, almsgiving, five daily prayers, fasting, and pilgrimage to Mecca). Pesantren teachers stress that while a day school can teach students about religion and morality, they cannot teach the students to be moral. Moral education in terms of moral behavior, takes experience. Hence, pesantren strive to create an environment in which the morals of religion can be practiced as well as studied.

Starting in the 1970s, newer, non-religious, curricula became an important part of the pesantren community's strategy for negotiating modernity. Pesantren added government recognized curricula to schools, the vast majority of which were madrasa, which have always had a high percentage of religion classes, although it has declined over time. Madrasas also existed outside the pesantren. A few pesantren opened madrasas following a national curriculum. Pesantren educate both boys and girls, although this education is rarely conducted in mixed gender settings. As private institutions, pesantren and madrasas receive some government aid, but most of their funding comes from donations and tuition. Traditionally, pesantren did not charge tuition; students simply worked for their keep in the headmaster's fields or businesses. With a double curriculum, there is not enough time for most students to earn their keep, so tuition is charged. Even so, pesantren are sometimes the least expensive educational opportunities available. For the very poor, the old model of work for education is sometimes still used.

In the 1970s, IAIN were created, in part, to be tertiary education for pesantren and madrasa graduates with the central goals of training Islamic teachers for government curricula schools and government functionaries in the Ministry of Religious Affairs (MORA).

IAIN and UIN are organs of the Ministry of Religious Affairs; however, non-religious coursework must be reviewed and approved by the Ministry of Education. During the time of my Fulbright grant, the Minister of Religious Affairs was M. Maftuh Basyuni (2004–9). Rectors at each campus report directly to the Directorate of Islamic Higher Education which, in addition to overseeing 35 IAINs, monitors and regulates approximately 500 private institutions. The IAIN system is regulated by the Directorate of Higher Education in the Ministry of Religious Affairs. However, this oversight is more of an accreditation process rather than the sort of top-down direct government design of curriculum and teaching methods found in Saudi Arabia and Malaysia. Each campus and each instructor still has a degree of autonomy in the teaching and learning processes.

Starting in the late 1990s and early 2000s, six IAIN transformed from institutes to universities by adding at least two non-religious faculties. Opinions about these changes are mixed both on and off campus. On campuses that have made the change, there is some concern about what will happen to the original religiously oriented faculties; that the new, 'secular' faculties will provide too much competition and will eventually drive their faculty out of existence. On campuses that have not made the change, there has been a call for a wider mandate. That is, they are adding programs like psychology, nursing, management, and public health under the existing faculties. IAIN SU received the specific recommendation to create a public health program in their faculty of *Ushuluddin* (theology and comparative religion) despite not having the staff to do so. Off-campus, some are concerned about the quality of the non-religious programs and conclude that at least for the time being these are not the best places to pursue non-religious topics. The addition of non-religious faculties has introduced some debate about the supervision of IAIN, with the Ministry of Education claiming oversight over the new programs.

Figure 17.3 Lukens-Bull discussing a book

Readings

The literature of Islam in Indonesia is broad, although the literature on Islamic education in Indonesia, at least in English is not nearly as wide. No education about Islam in Indonesia would be complete without reading the seminal works of Clifford Geertz, especially *Religion of Java* (New York: The Free Press, 1960) and *Islam Observed* (Chicago, IL: University of Chicago Press, 1971). Geertz's understanding of Islam in Indonesia was paradigmatic until the publication of Mark Woodward's *Islam in Java* (Tucson: University of Arizona Press, 1989). John Bowen's *Muslims Through Discourse* (Princeton, NJ: Princeton University Press, 1993) also challenged Geertz's depiction of Islam in Indonesia. Book length treatments, in English, on Islamic education in Indonesia are limited. The first was Zamaksyari Dhofier's *The Pesantren Tradition* (Tempe: Arizona State University, 1999) which was based on fieldwork conducted in the 1970s. Next was Anna Gade's *Perfection Makes Practice* (Honolulu: University of Hawaii Press, 2004) and Ronald Lukens-Bull's *A Peaceful Jihad* (New York: Palgrave McMillan, 2005), and his forthcoming *Islamic Higher Education in Indonesia: Continuity and Conflict* (New York: Palgrave McMillan, forthcoming). More recent is Florian Pohl's *Islamic Education and the Public Sphere: Today's Pesantren in Indonesia* (Münster, Germany: Waxmann, 2009). *Making Modern Muslims: The Politics of Islamic Education in Southeast Asia* is also an important collection of essays edited by Robert W. Hefner (Honolulu: University of Hawaii Press, 2008).

Author

Ronald Lukens-Bull is an Associate Professor of Anthropology and Religious Studies at the University of North Florida. He was Fulbright Senior Scholar in Islamic Studies at Walailak University, Nakhon Sri Thammarat, Thailand in 2005. He was Visiting Fulbright Professor at the State Islamic Institute of North Sumatra in 2008–9. He has written two books on Islamic education: *A Peaceful Jihad* (New York: Palgrave McMillan, 2005) and *Islamic Higher Education in Indonesia: Continuity and Conflict* (New York: Palgrave McMillan, forthcoming).

Index

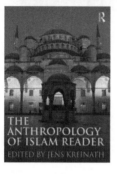

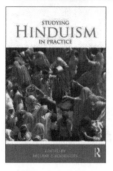

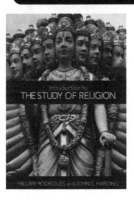

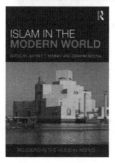